# SOCIOLOGY, ENVIRONMENTALISM, GLOBALIZATION

# SOCIOLOGY, ENVIRONMENTALISM, GLOBALIZATION

## Reinventing the Globe

*Steven Yearley*

SAGE Publications
London • Thousand Oaks • New Delhi

SAGE Publications Ltd
6 Bonhill Street
London EC2A 4PU

SAGE Publications Inc
2455 Teller Road
Thousand Oaks, California 91320

SAGE Publications India Pvt Ltd
32, M-Block Market
Greater Kailash – I
New Delhi 110 048

**British Library Cataloguing in Publication data**

A catalogue record for this book is
available from the British Library

ISBN 0 8039 7516–3
ISBN 0 8039 7517–1 (pbk)

**Library of Congress catalog record available**

Typeset by Mayhew Typesetting, Rhayader, Powys
Printed in Great Britain by The Cromwell Press Ltd,
Broughton Gifford, Melksham, Wiltshire

# Contents

# Preface

It is customary for books to begin with a learned quotation which anticipates or sums up the author's argument. My illustrative text derives from a different source: the top of a yoghurt container. This wholesome product, designated by its manufacturers as 'udderly natural', carries an announcement proclaiming that 'We give 10 per cent of our profits to the planet'. What I find interesting about this claim is not primarily the corporate generosity which it signals. Nor is it even the significant fact that such a statement is taken as good for business, so that instead of dedicating the space on the container to praising the quality of the yoghurt, it is given over to boasting of the firm's environmental sensitivities. Rather, what fascinates me is the idea that 'the planet' can be so effortlessly invoked and its implications so readily understood. The striking thing is that, in Anglo-American culture, we can talk of giving money to the planet and that passes as a clear and, for all practical purposes, unambiguous undertaking.

At least to me, the slogan initially makes perfect sense. It seems to imply that the company has a strong environmental conscience. But, the longer one thinks about it, the more questions appear. For example, 'the planet' does not have a savings account which would allow us to give it money. If the slogan was 'We give 10 per cent of our profits to the New York Yankees' then at least the recipient would be clear. In this case, however, we have to ask, who decides what is meant by 'the planet'? Is the money, for instance, distributed equally by country, or according to the number of citizens? Maybe it is directed to needy countries or regions, but then who determines which areas count as needy? But, even leaving the distributional aspects aside, there is the question of what sorts of needs are met by this planetary generosity. Does the planet include the people on the planet, or does it refer to the 'natural' planetary ecosystems only? Drawing on my own familiarity with, so to speak, the yoghurt culture, I assume that saving the tiger or the panda, or planting forests qualifies immediately as the kind of project fitting the description of giving to the planet. But does this mean that only the non-human inhabitants of the planet count? I suspect that giving money to environmental campaign organizations is likely to be covered as well, even if these groups focus primarily on the improvement of the human environment. Donations to development assistance organizations are likely to be a marginal case, even though many environmental activists and commentators wish to argue that the fate of endangered species, of threatened habitats and even of polluted regions hangs on the development prospects of the underdeveloped world. Giving to the planet has a different connotation to helping the victims of disaster or poverty.

From this example we can see that 'the planet' (as well as various other terms including 'the Earth') is not just a descriptive label for our world as an astronomical object. Rather, it has come to crystallize and embody a certain way of looking at the globe, as an entity in need of environmental protection. To borrow theoreticians' terms, we might say that to talk of 'the planet' in this way assumes the acceptance of an environmentalist 'discourse', and to look at the earth in this way is to employ an environmentalist 'gaze'.

This yoghurt-top slogan therefore offers a very suitable text for this book since it unquestioningly asserts, and accordingly invites us to investigate, the links between environmental issues and cultural representations of the planet or the globe. This book pursues this investigation from, as it were, both ends – both by examining the environmental problems facing contemporary societies and asking if they are global, and (from the other end) by analysing sociologists' attempts to understand the process of 'globalization'.

In relation to the first of these, images of an imperilled global environment are repeatedly brought to our attention in the logos of environmental groups, in media coverage of environmental issues, in official publications from governments and the United Nations, and in advertising campaigns. People give money and campaign for the conservation of rainforests or wild animals thousands of kilometres away, across the other side of the world. With good reason, one would nominate environmental questions as among the most conspicuously global of contemporary cultural issues. Equally, many environmental organizations have sought to cultivate a world-wide membership, and environmental treaties have been drawn up with over 150 signatory nations. These are global-level political phenomena. The labels given to some environmental problems, such as 'global warming', even carry the idea of 'global-ness' into their very names.

In relation to the second point, the last years of the century have seen social scientists increasingly turn their attention to global phenomena. They have pointed to the huge rise in international communications, to the power of global financiers and to apparent increases in the cultural homogeneity of the world as movies, musicians and sports stars are enjoyed and celebrated world-wide. Though these authors have mostly paid little attention to environmental issues as an aspect of globalization, they have sought to describe the emerging patterns of global social relations and to chart the rise of new global actors. Sociologists have also endeavoured to create analytical frameworks for getting to grips with these phenomena.

This book aims to bring together these two areas of debate. It takes environmental issues (surely candidates for global status) and asks how well they can be accommodated by the analyses of sociologists of globalization. At the same time, it asks what substantive advances in the understanding of the world's environmental problems can be made from a reading of the globalization literature. The result is a critical reflection on the globality of socioeconomic and political interests in the environment.

An initial justification for looking critically at this topic can be found in the writings of Claus Offe, a leading German analyst of modern political movements. He has noted that the intended support base for the most recent social movements does not refer to the old left/right split but 'is rather coded in categories taken from the movements' issues, such as gender, age, locality etc., or, *in the case of environmental and pacifist movements, the human race as a whole*' (1985: 831; my italics). In this quote, Offe spells out and, to all appearances, accepts without much criticism the global aspirations of the environmental movement. Any movement or ideology which purports to represent the interests of the human race as a whole demands critical scrutiny. Since environmentalists appeal to putative global interests, there is a ready invitation to study environmentalism and globalization together.

The book's structure follows directly from this rationale. Chapter 1 offers an introduction to sociological thinking about globalization. It outlines the evidence for the emergence of global-level phenomena and consciousness, and examines the principal sociological responses. It also introduces sociological and philosophical writing about so-called universal concepts (such as truth, justice or rationality) – concepts which, because of their universal reach, have frequently been called on to describe and analyse global phenomena.

Chapter 2 turns to the examination of environmental issues, and investigates whether and in what ways they can be thought of as global. The chapter examines pollution, various kinds of resources (including water supplies), population and biological diversity, arguing in each instance that a case can be made out for interpreting these environmental issues as having global dimensions.

Chapter 3 returns to the yoghurt-carton theme, examining in greater detail how it is that world-wide environmental problems come to be 'global'. It analyses both the global distribution of environmental problems and the efforts by various organizations to talk up the global status of environmental problems. Chapter 4 takes this analysis further by using a case-study approach to examine various 'universalizing' approaches to the understanding of the global environment and its problems. The history of international agreements on combating ozone depletion is used, for example, to consider the precise practical value of scientific discourse as a universal language for depicting the needs of the planet. Similarly, the universalistic ambitions of microeconomics and of the discourse of sustainable development are critically reviewed.

The book concludes in Chapter 5 with a broader inspection of the lessons learned about the sociology of globalization and about the issue of the supposedly human-species-wide interests (or 'global-human' interests as Robertson puts it (1992: 133)) behind political movements. The relevance for other political movements of this critical reflection on the globality of environmental interests is considered, as well as the likely future role for universalistic discourses in policy formation. In sum, by examining this complex of issues, the book is able to investigate globalization in a leading major policy arena at the close of the twentieth century and to take a critical look at how the 'globality' of global issues is constructed, negotiated and, therefore, open to creative reworking.

# 1

# The Sociology of Globalization

## Identifying with the Global

To put it at its simplest, sociologists have concerned themselves with two aspects of globalization, one 'subjective', one 'objective'. The aspect which is taken to be objective relates to the rise to prominence of more and more global processes such as global marketing and world-wide financial markets. The subjective aspect refers to the idea that people are increasingly viewing themselves as participants in a globalized world. This may be because, in the words of the slogan, they 'think global and act local'. Or it could be because they are aware of the ways in which the world is – in Robertson's terms – becoming compressed. On the strength of these two processes, the terms 'global' and 'globalization' occur with ever greater frequency in popular and academic writing. In the general culture there seems to be an idea that contemporary society spans the globe, an idea reinforced by advertising and brand names centred on global images, whether cosmetics from the globe, rainforest flavour ice-cream, or the planet-conscious yoghurt mentioned in the Preface. Social scientists too are increasingly producing books and responding to funding programmes with the word 'global' in the title.

In reviewing social scientific thinking about globalization we need to ask what justification there is for talking of global culture, processes of globalization or global problems. Let us start with the subjective aspect, that is with the sense of global 'oneness', what Robertson calls the 'consciousness of the world as a single place' (1992: 183). The key idea here is that increasingly people are aware of themselves and of humanity as inhabitants of the one globe. Along with this growing 'consciousness' of global citizenship, goes the idea that sociology should also assess society on a global scale. In one sense it is patently true that the discipline of sociology has to deal with the global society. Aside from cosmonauts circling in space stations, all human life is on the globe. Still, it might be objected that this realization can hardly be put down as a recent discovery. Dating from way before the 'voyages of discovery' which culminated in the circumnavigation of the globe in the early sixteenth century, many people had formed the idea that the Earth was a sphere and that human society was restricted to the globe. After the initial voyages of exploration in the Atlantic and Indian Oceans, and following the charting of the Pacific in the eighteenth century, the exhaustive mapping of the coastlines, and adventures in the polar regions, the modern notion of the globe became fixed. This, one might say, marked the important acceptance that that was all there was.

For sure, that conviction did not imply that there was nowhere left for Western people to investigate or explore or settle/colonize. Though the shape and extent of the world were very thoroughly understood by the early nineteenth century, the interiors of Africa, South America, Asia and North America were well known only to the indigenous peoples. As various works of European fiction indicated, it was perhaps still possible that under the oceans, deep in the forest, or just possibly beneath the earth itself there might be other peoples. Just over a century-and-a-half later, it is now commonly accepted that the world has been exhaustively visited, mapped and recorded. There can hardly be any places left where a Landrover or Toyota has not been, and where portable radios, and probably CNN, have not brought news and representations of the external world.

The decisive point here, however, is not just that the world has been catalogued, that all the remaining points have been ticked off the cartographer's list, but that what once seemed vast and mysterious now appears limited and familiar. Whereas the rest of the globe was once outside 'our' society and beyond our experience, now it feels as though it is all inside. The globe, the way we now know it, seems to us truly the limit of human society.

In island Britain, possibly in Japan or on Crete too, it was all along possible to have the sense that a society was naturally delimited by its boundaries. Civilization, good manners or adequate sanitation stopped at these limits, at least in the minds of the islanders. But there was always the certainty that there was human life beyond. There was trade and there might be invaders. The feeling of global insularity is qualitatively different. There are no extraterrestrial exports and – interplanetary crop circle artists aside – no expectation of visitors.

One important consequence of this realization is that some geographers and social scientists have suggested that the global is the only natural and adequate level of analysis. For example, if one thinks of economics, there is room for doubt whether national economies should be thought of as adequate as analytic units. Politicians and commentators blithely talk of the 'British economy' and so on, even though many firms operating in Britain are not British and many British firms make their profits overseas. One has to use conventions of national accounting to work out what to count as British and so on. But at the global level, this is not a problem. The globe is a natural entity. In politics too, the so-called 'new World Order' which followed from the breakdown of the Soviet Bloc, invites us to think of the world as a unity, possibly one to be managed in a benign way by the United States.

In these ways, the sense that the globe is all there is – which as I say is not itself new – has lately been intensified. These feelings, that we now know the limits of human experience and that we are for some significant purposes all in the same boat, account in part for the recent journalistic, popular and academic interest in humanity's global identity, the 'subjective' aspect of globalization. But, according to most writers, this stimulus to global identification is complemented by the objective processes of globalization, namely by the globalizing of various fundamental aspects of contemporary culture and economics.

## Global Processes

The candidate examples here are very numerous. There is first of all finance. As was shown by the international speculation which split the European Exchange Rate Mechanism (ERM) in 1992 and nearly undermined the remaining framework a year later, currency markets are no longer national or even regional. The ERM, in the name of promoting unity in Europe, offered to fix exchange rates between European currencies. It effectively promised that the national banks in Germany, France, Denmark and the Benelux countries would go on selling marks or guilders or whatever in return for lira, pesetas or sterling at a fixed rate indefinitely. Potentially, this was good news for manufacture and commerce in all these countries as it allowed people to agree contracts with confidence. A British firm could settle a lira price for selling its goods in Italy and know how many pounds the deal would be worth in the months ahead when the merchandise was delivered. But people who manage money (companies which look after pension funds, the deposits in banks, the holdings of savings groups, as well as some fantastically rich individuals) took a different view. Their experience was that sterling, lira and the peseta had a history of devaluing while the mark did not. They used the suspect currencies to buy the 'firm' ones at the agreed price. By their very actions they made pounds and lira less desirable, the mark more desirable, and the fixed rate deal less and less sensible from the viewpoint of the German central bank. Sensing which way the trend was going, small business people in Italy and elsewhere took their own currency and bought marks at the agreed rate. In the end the situation became unstable because the markets demanded marks more than pounds and so on, even though in theory the relationship between them was fixed. But the more demand there was for the mark, the more valuable it became to hold it in practice – even if that extra 'value' could not be recognized by a greater value on the currency-exchange markets. When the ERM came apart, the pound, lira and peseta fell by around 20 per cent on average, giving a corresponding windfall to all those traders who had sold the weak currencies to central banks, and fat profits to the Italians, Spanish and British people who had sold their own currencies and bought marks. People who timed their move correctly made approximately 20 per cent gains overnight.

The key point in this drama was that it was the disproportion between – on the one hand – the amount of money held by banks and finance companies and – on the other – the available government funds, which ensured that the governments were out-manoeuvred. Governments in small European countries such as the Irish Republic and Portugal (which also devalued in the end) were overwhelmed by the scale of the money-changing operations. Even bigger countries, such as Italy and the United Kingdom, could not commit endless billions of dollars to combating speculative buying in the market. By contrast, the currency market was open to banks, dealing companies and fund-holding agencies all over the globe.

In short, in this case the avowed political objectives of the European Union[1] – including four of the world's leading economies and at the time representing in total the largest and most economically powerful trading bloc in the world – were thwarted by the play of state-less money in global financial centres.

A similar drama was enacted at the end of 1994 and early 1995 when the Mexican peso fell against the dollar and other international currencies. Editorializing, *The Economist* worried that global investors might be 'stampeding' out of Latin American investments (notably in Argentina and Brazil) for no good reason. The paper's view was that:

> As the capital market has become increasingly world-spanning, the prices of financial instruments with identical risks ought in principle to converge across markets. This helps to produce a more efficient allocation of capital. The drawback, from the point of view of governments, is that it also makes the market far more sensitive to individual risks. The more efficient the global market, the more likely it is to reward sound economic policy, and the swifter to take fright at mistakes. . . . [Sadly] Sometimes investors merely panic, and gallop like a herd for the exit. Some of that may be happening in Latin America. (14 January 1995: 18)

As capital markets become global, the fate of whole countries' economies can fall prey to the fears and imaginings of investors in the international money markets.

The 'success' (at least in the dealers' eyes) of these financial operations was based on a second aspect of globalization, the spread of international communications. The growth of commerce and the expansion of empires always depended on a communications infrastructure. All the time that secure transfer of information depended on messengers, news could only travel as fast as the courier could. This was changed by telegraphy and the growing ability to send information down a wire. Still, the spread in the 1980s of information and communication technologies (ICTs) marked an increase in the speed, amount and the range of things which could be transmitted. Not only spoken or written information, but designs and images could now be reliably and cheaply sent between people hundreds of kilometres apart. Together with an increase in the number of communications satellites, these changes meant that geographical closeness was no longer necessarily an aid to communication and ensured that communication within a geographical unit, such as a country, was no longer especially advantaged. Corporations could manage their activities in a concerted way without having to have their plants located close together.

Contracts could be put out to a range of international bidders and orders could instantly be placed where prices were most favourable. Pundits began talking about 'telecommuting', the idea that one could work from home or from a remote centre, without needing to go near the office or factory. By 1995 the Swedish culture minister was running her government department mostly through telecommuting from her home town, deep in the forest (*The Economist*, 25 February 1995: 56). By this means, journalists could write their stories at the site of the accident, interview or crime, and file the report electronically. Designers could work wherever in the world they chose, submitting illustrations or drawings by phone or satellite. Computing businesses in the West could draw on the skills of Indian software writers who could send in their work without ever having to come near Europe or the USA. And US insurance companies could get their claims handled overnight, while North America slept, by computer staff working days in the Irish Republic, who could send back completed records in time for US employees arriving on the companies' morning shift.

The chief point to which sociologists have drawn attention here is that customary links between proximity, in terms of physical distance and therefore travel time, and social closeness have been broken down by new ICTs. Distant people are no harder to contact, and no harder to do many kinds of business with, than those who are close. Of course, one cannot fully build a ship or grow vegetables with colleagues across the globe. But, for a whole range of activities, distance no longer matters. One can buy and sell, write and compose, advise or sue, report and even record with partners thousands of kilometres away almost as easily as with one's immediate neighbours. In that sense, the globe becomes a single, unified place, where in principle everybody can be 'reached' and where notions of closeness and convenience are separated from connotations of physical proximity; instead they become questions of electronic connection.

Though this globalization of communication has so far largely affected the corporate and scientific worlds, recent enthusiasm for the growth of the Internet, the system of computer communication chiefly between private individuals, indicates how it might work for ordinary citizens as well. By allowing relatively cheap, interactive connections between individual computer owners, the Internet offers to put people with shared interests in touch almost regardless of physical location. Early ventures in this area tended to grow around groups of users who had shared interests in computing. But the Internet is being increasingly seen as a way of swapping information, whether that be news for film fans, the supposed language of Klingons, computer encoded pictures of military equipment, or horoscopes. When, in November 1994, a computer hacker allegedly broke into files containing the most top secret telephone numbers in the UK (including royalty and secret defence establishments), there was much alarm over the potential for this information to be sent to 35 million people world-wide on the 'Net' (*The Independent*, 24 November 1994: 1). The vision held up by many is of 'virtual' communities of people who share an interest and who can form links, friendships and undertake activities with others who just happen to have the same enthusiasms. Such groupings are referred to as virtual because they have no physical existence as communities. The people might all be in Birmingham, but they could as easily be scattered across the world. Advocates of the Internet present this as a strong democratic and liberalizing influence.

Reference to films and the celebrated aliens from *Star Trek* leads into the third aspect of globalization, the growth of a common culture. The argument is made that the culture industry and the marketing departments of giant organizations have been largely successful in promoting a world market for popular music, film, fashion, entertainment media including soap operas and even news. The central claim here is that, while cultures used to be associated with a locality or nation, they are increasingly supranational. In part this is a story about the marketing, merchandising and popularity of certain stars. Established celebrities such as Madonna and Pink Floyd sell their works and are broadcast throughout the world. They perform in concerts on every continent and their lyrics, and images from their videos, are known all over the planet. But it is also a story about the way in which culture is broadcast. With the rise of satellite channels, the same music and news programmes are available in hotels, clubs, bars and the homes of the relatively affluent throughout the world. Even if the raw appeal of these artists is not sufficient to attract everyone, the ubiquity of the broadcasts is likely to make everyone familiar with them. Similarly, 'world' sporting events are the subject of news and sports reports – as well as the vehicle for advertising and cultivating a brand image – throughout the globe. To some extent these cultures are supplanting indigenous traditions and enthusiasm, but even where they are not they are adding a level of global familiarity. Madonna and Maradona are a safe bet as topics of conversation more or less wherever one travels. The global spread of local cultures is also encouraged by migrations, as well as the journeys of 'guest workers' and tourists (see Appadurai, 1990: 297).

Of course culture is not only about identity and enjoyment, but also about selling goods. You need a radio, a tape machine or a CD-player to listen to the latest in popular music. Sports events are sponsored by 'global' companies keen to promote product recognition all over the globe. And this issue leads into the fourth aspect of globalization, the globalizing of business. The relative cheapness of transport and the efficiency of modern shipment systems have combined to ensure that some similar goods are available the world over. Some products have been taken as particularly symbolizing this creeping takeover of the planet by consumer culture. Thus Coca Cola, Pepsi and the 'Golden Arches' of McDonald's are brands and brand images which command literally world-wide recognition. Ford suggestively named its most recent saloon model, among the first of its models to be retailed throughout most of the world, the 'Mondeo', the word evoking the idea of the world in Latin languages.

Compared with the other phenomena discussed here, particularly the growth in satellite and computer technology, this world spread of manu-facture and sales cannot be viewed as all that modern. Commentators have long been charting the growth of giant corporations with bases in many countries. Such corporations practise an international division of labour with, for example, certain car parts made in the Far East, some in Australia and others in Europe or the USA. The assembled car is not the product of any one country. Two things however are making the global-ization of such companies more pronounced. One factor is the growing 'state-less' character of the companies. In part, old anxieties about trans-national companies derived precisely from the fact that they were seen as fundamentally German, British or whatever. It was feared that any plant they set up, whether in neighbouring states or in developing countries, would actually be subservient to the interests of the home base. Though this depiction of the company as having a home headquarters or main commitment to the nation in which it originated is still accurate in many cases (Japanese and French corporations particularly come to mind here), there is now a trend towards global companies which have no particular partiality for any 'home' territory. According to Grant:

> A recent development is the emergence of the 'stateless' company. The ownership of the company in terms of shareholdings is internationalized, a development reflected in the composition of the board of directors, and of the senior manage-ment. The company no longer sees itself as being based in one country, but as operating globally. The headquarters operation is very small, and could be located anywhere. There is no longer loyalty to a particular country which is seen as the 'home' country, but rather to the firm which orients itself to the global economy. (1993: 61)

He goes on to quote from an interview with the chief executive of the Swedish-Swiss engineering and technology firm ABB (Asea Brown Boveri) in which the executive claims, 'we change relations *between* countries. We function as a lubricant for worldwide economic integration.'

Grant is careful to limit his claims. Companies may achieve most of their sales outside their 'home' and even have the majority of their assets 'overseas' but still maintain share ownership highly concentrated at home. But Grant's principal claim is that while companies are increasingly global, national governments remain wedded to an older outlook. Governments accordingly run an increasing risk of being 'out flanked' by companies which have no loyalties but to themselves and their internationally dispersed shareholders.

The second aspect of the globalization of companies arises from the fact that competition between these large concerns means that they have to be careful to produce and to promote products for the greatest possible variety of markets. While a few products will work in a small 'niche' market (items based on a local custom for example or the much-publicized Japanese market for retro-look cars), the majority have to be aimed as widely as possible, giving manufacturers a reason to appreciate the global spread of cultural artefacts, trends and icons. Precisely because large sales and large turnovers provide 'economies of scale', companies have to compete on the largest scale they can. The drive towards global marketing is in that sense the logical consequence of commercial competitiveness. No large company can any longer afford to be without a global strategy. In this way, companies are only too well aware that the world is 'all there is'. There is a fixed realm to sell into; the only questions concern retention of market share and the achievement of greater 'penetration'. Companies know full well that there is one, bounded global economy.

The final strand in the diagnosis of globalization deals with the political level. While there are occasional calls for what Porter and Brown (1991: 152) describe as institutions for 'global environmental governance' there are no prospects for global governmental organizations even in the restricted fields of environmental or security policy. There are, however, important international agreements (sometimes backed up by enforcement agencies) which bind governments to deal with each other in stipulated ways. There is, for example, the undertaking to honour 200 mile economic exclusion zones around nations' coasts, as well as the series of agreements (said to be aimed at guaranteeing world-wide free trade) which comprise the GATT (General Agreement on Tariffs and Trade) treaty, negotiated through the first half of the 1990s and culminating in the formation – in January 1995 – of the World Trade Organization (WTO). The WTO is joined by other global institutions such as the International Monetary Fund and the World Bank which, like the WTO, carries its claims to world-wide influence in its very name. Moreover, there are developing 'blocs', most notably the European Union and NAFTA (the North American Free Trade Agreement). While these blocs are definitely limited to certain territories (they are not global in that sense), their rationale is implicitly global, since their existence acknowledges the fact that single countries cannot withstand the competition in the global market. For example, one of the functions which the European Commission is keen should be increasingly performed at the European level is the funding of research to promote European industry, for example in the anticipated growth areas of high-definition television and various aspects of biotechnology. This is implicitly to recognize that there is a global contest in which European countries cannot realistically compete with the American and Japanese economies unless they cooperate among themselves.

Aside from the strategies of states, other kinds of political activity are also increasingly oriented to transnational and global audiences. As many Western governments have discovered, criminal and terrorist organizations are alert to globalizing trends. For example, targets for highjacks or bombings – as with the explosions at the World Trade Center in New York in 1993 – may be selected for their international symbolic value and for the world-wide news coverage they will generate rather than for any close connection between the target and the particular political issue at stake.

Just as governments and official bodies undertake politics at a world-wide level, so too do campaign organizations and pressure groups. As will be seen later on, in Chapters 3–5, campaigning organizations focusing on women's issues, workers' interests, environmental problems, disarmament and social development have all adopted a transnational outlook. The Red Cross, Amnesty International and Greenpeace International are among the most well known and indicative examples of bodies taking a world-wide profile.

### Obstacles to Making Sociological Sense of Globalization

To summarize so far, we can see evidence for globalization both in the sense that various processes are coming to be organized on a global level *and* in the sense that there is an awareness of the interrelations among people on the globe and a recognition of the globe as finite and limited. It is (respectively) these objective and subjective processes that he is referring to when Robertson claims that, 'Globalization as a concept refers both to the compression of the world and the intensification of consciousness of the world as a whole' (1992: 8). Thus, the world is being compressed through the electronic overcoming of distance and through the cultural similarities advanced by the global entertainment industry. At the same time, people are becoming more self-consciously aware that the world is full of intricate connections and that 'our' world is all that there is. These two processes clearly feed each other: the more that products and popular culture become the same wherever people go, the stronger the grounds for people perceiving themselves as members of a global society. The more people see themselves as members of a global community, the more likely they appear to be to support Amnesty International or Greenpeace International (on growing support for 'global' voluntary organizations, see McCormick, 1991: 153–4).

Under the influence of Robertson and other writers, a sociological literature on globalization has recently begun to appear. Before considering sociologists' attempts to interpret and make sense of globalization, however, it will be helpful to examine two specific obstacles which have discouraged sociology from thinking at the global level.

### *Obstacle 1: Sociology, 'Society' and the Nation*

The first obstacle is quite simply the tight connection between the discipline of sociology and the nation-state (see Turner, 1990: 343). While claiming to be the scientific study of 'society' as an abstract entity, sociology has in practice long acted as though society was only found in the form of nation-states. From sociology texts one learns to focus on the class structure, on social mobility, the educational system, ethnic and gender divisions and the sociology of political parties. All these occur in terms of nations. The far-reaching consequences of this are attested to by the experience of teachers of sociology in smaller English-speaking countries, such as the Irish Republic, New Zealand or Scotland. Teachers and students in these countries buy books on 'society' only to find out that the texts are generally accounts of British or US society. The occupational structure of the student's country, its political institutions, its educational systems may be very different from that depicted in the book. But these significant differences have often been overlooked because of an assumption that sociology is the systematic study of society whereas – in fact – it has been the study of nations.

Clearly, to treat nations and society as the same thing is incorrect. Even if we take the short lifetime of the discipline of sociology itself, we can see that at the end of the nineteenth century the world was not organized into nations to any significant extent. Admittedly, with the unifications of Germany and of Italy in the 1870s, the map of Europe took on a super-ficially familiar form. But the countries of Europe were not so much nations as we now understand the term as centres of Empire. Africa was almost wholly divided into territories ruled by imperial authorities, terri-tories which often bore in their names the indication of their subject status: the Belgian Congo, French West Africa, British East Africa and German South West Africa. South and East Asia were extensively under the influence or direct control of European powers. Only in the Americas were there numerous new nations, from the recently peaceful United States of America to the dozen or so self-consciously independent nations of Central and South America. In part, it was this extreme European influence which allowed the war of 1914–18 (in effect a European civil war) to come to be known as a *World* War.

Only in the years after the 1939–45 war (which was this time much more literally a world-wide war, though again driven primarily by European conflicts) was there a great growth in the number of nations, with around three nations a year being granted independence between 1945 and 1975. After a comparatively quiet period in the 1980s, there was a renewed rush of nation-forming in the aftermath of the disintegration of the USSR and of the political structures in the Eastern Bloc, giving rise to the emergence or reappearance of Georgia, Estonia, the Ukraine, Slovenia and so on.

One might have thought that, as the number of nation-states has grown (to around 180, depending exactly on how they are counted) and as the former imperial powers – Germany, France, Britain, Italy and so on – have become 'mere' nations, sociology's disciplinary emphasis on nations would be becoming increasingly justified and descriptively accurate. Ironically, however, this is not the case because many of the new nations are small, economically weak and – in some cases – politically fragile. They do not have the characteristics which sociologists have assumed to be the identifying marks of nationhood and therefore 'society-hood'. For example, their economies may be extremely dependent on loans from international agencies or from private corporations based overseas; their industrial development may be tied to investments by large foreign companies, on whose boards there is no citizen of that country nor any role for formal representations by the government; the most popular and influential broadcast media may not be produced by that country itself. In other words, the very issues which sociologists took for granted as making up the meat of a sociological study of the nation actually turn out not to characterize a sizeable minority of the world's nations. The working assumption (and it was generally nothing more than an assumption) that sociology consists of a nation-by-nation study of the world turns out to be a rather poor basis for analysis.

As well as taking the nation for granted as a unit of analysis, sociologists have often lacked curiosity about the nation itself. More recently, political scientists and sociologists have begun to examine more deeply the status of nationhood and to analyse the processes that contribute to nations' viability. Along with the work of Gellner (1983), the most celebrated analysis has been carried out by Anderson (1991). In his well-known terminology, nations are 'imagined communities', imaginary both in the sense that the members do not meet each other in the way that happens in traditional communities, and in the sense that nations are imaginative (maybe 'conceptual' makes the point better) constructs. Geographical divisions could be (and have been) drawn in quite different ways for quite different purposes, and people's sense of location and identity could be couched in very different terms.

Anderson makes the point that nations differ from other kinds of territorial units (possibly regions, or empires) by exercising limited sovereignty. To be a nation is, by definition, to claim complete sovereignty over your territories but to accept your neighbours' rights to comparable sovereignty for themselves. Of course, in practice, states may disagree about where the 'proper' borders lie. But, once their boundaries are secured, nations – unlike, say, empires – do not make claims over wider areas or for additional peoples. As Anderson expresses it:

> The nation is imagined as *limited* because even the largest of them, encompassing perhaps a billion living human beings, has finite, if elastic, boundaries, beyond which lie other nations. No nation imagines itself coterminous with mankind. The most messianic nationalists do not dream of a day when all the members of the human race will join their nation in the way that it was possible, in certain epochs, for, say, Christians to dream of a wholly Christian planet. (1991: 7)

For this reason, one can sensibly have a 'United Nations' organization in which nations are able to 'unite' because their claims are, by definition, non-conflicting. They unite to offer political support for the rights of nations. In the ideal situation there would be no conflict between nations since they claim exhaustive sovereignty over their lands and peoples. No land, no people are left out and there should be no cases of 'double-booking'. Although these imagined communities have, in historical terms, only comparatively recently been formed, the idea has found extremely widespread acceptance, so much so that it now seems to many a 'natural' condition.

Matching this insight about the meaning of national status have been observations about the mechanisms by which nationhood has been developed. These points have been usefully summarized by Giddens (1985: 116–21, 172–97); he describes the nation-states as 'a collectivity existing within a clearly demarcated territory, which is . . . subject to a unitary administration, reflexively monitored both by the internal state apparatus and those of other states' (1985: 11). By 'reflexive monitoring', Giddens means that certain territories are constituted as nations by the attention of administrative supervision. Accordingly, the existence of nations requires that boundaries are mapped, that time-keeping is systematized, that internal order is maintained by the state's appointed forces, that communication is institutionalized and, commonly, that broadcasting is harmonized. Each of these factors then works iteratively with the cultural assumptions of nationhood to further ingrain the sense of nation. In the archetypal modern nation, there are national newspapers, national advertising campaigns, national car number plate conventions, ways of painting road markings and of displaying signposts. Telephone kiosks have a characteristic design, as do post-boxes, the vans of the mail service, often the trains. The nation's officials wear common uniforms. These are the things which one notices as different when one travels abroad. They are the signs which allow you to recognize you are 'home' after an overnight train journey or long-distance drive. It is not just the customs officials and border signs which demarcate the extent of a nation, it is the cultural practices. Of course, many nations also correspond more or less to language communities so that Norwegians know pretty well when they are 'home', though Austrians and Germans may not. But the more general point is that the signs which denote national identity are so pervasive and so much part of the backcloth of social life that they become almost invisible, except to the stranger.

In summary, the idea of a nation with territorially limited but legally exclusive authority is a relatively recent creation, though actors often seek to legitimate the concept by presenting it as natural. In practice, an iterative process binds the nation together. The system of laws and administration gives people common experiences, producing a solidarity which is attributed to being co-nationals. Sociologists have often been blind both to the extent to which nations are imagined (or constructed) and to the inappropriateness of the term 'national identity' when it is applied to many of the nations which now make up the globe. Before considering sociologists' attempts to move beyond national-level analysis, it is time to look at one other issue ignored in sociological writings.

*Obstacle 2: Society, Sociology and Geography*

If the first point was about the limited self-awareness of sociologists when dealing with the nation and 'society', the second is that the discipline has given predominance to the *social* characteristics of nations' identities. Stereotypically, a sociological account tells one about the social institutions of nations, their political parties, industrial strategies, class patterns and educational systems. As remarked above, these do vary in interesting ways from one country to another: some industrial societies have retained their monarchies, most others have not; women's rights are viewed differently in different modern democracies, and so on. Since these differences are cultural (and therefore, one might say, more or less imaginary in Anderson's sense), it is easy to assume that they can be erased as institutions are copied from one society to another. The trends towards the globalization of culture and media would imply that these differences are likely to diminish. Such an exclusive focus on the malleable, social characteristics of nations draws attention away from the fact that countries also differ significantly in their geographies.

There is a tendency for every discipline to relegate the variables of other disciplines to the role of mere exogenous factors. Economists, for example, scrutinize the prices of goods but tend to leave aside the sociological and psychological elements which drive goods in and out of fashion. Sociology has been no different. To give a crude, though not unrealistic example, sociologists dealing with tropical countries tend to use the standard images of a national society, adding on the additional consideration that the climate is very warm. But if one is realistically aiming to give a sociological account of the global organization of society in the present day then geography cannot be omitted. In particular, if one is interested in the sociology of international environmental problems one cannot overlook the differential consequences which, in part, follow from a society having a high or a low rainfall, having alkaline or acidic soils, or being a region of high or low biological diversity. Accordingly, sociology's view of society as made up of a series of nations needs to be complemented with an explicitly geographical view of what countries' characteristics are. The globe is geographically differentiated in a way that is simply not recognized by the assumption that all societies come 'packaged' as nations.

Any adequate sociological interpretation of global processes and phenomena will need to move beyond sociology's fixation with the nation and will have to make room for an analysis of geographical differentiation (on this issue of complementarity see also Benton, 1991, 1994). In the next section I will examine attempts to elaborate an adequate theoretical basis for global-level analysis.

## World Systems Theory and the Sociology of Globalization

There is one area of sociological interest which has proved to be a notable exception to my claims about treating countries singly: the sociology of development. Particularly within the broadly neo-Marxist tradition, the leading idea has been that there is a relationship of exploitation between the developed and the underdeveloped world. As is well known, the central argument here is that the 'Third World'[2] is not in its present lowly economic condition because it lacks development. Rather, the idea is that this impoverished condition has resulted from what the industrialized world has done to it. Through colonial exploitation and neo-colonial control over trading and finance, the countries of the Third World have been actively underdeveloped. Correct or not (and the idea of dependency is clearly to some extent *descriptively* justified if nothing else, see Berger, 1987: 129–30), what is of present interest about this idea is the way it links the fate of one set of nations (the underdeveloped Third World) to the actions of agencies and companies in others. Pointing to phenomena such as the slave trade, the establishment of plantations to provide raw materials for the colonial centres, and to interventions in overseas economies to guarantee markets for the Western countries' products, writers on underdevelopment have explicitly made the point that the world's economies have evolved in an interdependent way.

The school of thought most intimately associated with this idea is based around the work of Wallerstein. He gives a clear signal of his recognition of this supranational emphasis in the name of his theoretical programme, 'world systems theory'. He argues that one can only understand the development of the various individual societies in terms of the broader world-historical context. Thus, he claims to have always doubted the significance of nations and of explanations which focus on the national level: 'The transition from feudalism to capitalism involves first of all (first logically and first temporally) the creation of a world-economy. Such commodity chains were already there in the sixteenth century and pre-dated anything that could meaningfully be called "national economies"' (1990a: 165). For Wallerstein, the unit of analysis should always have been the world system, not the histories of particular nations.

As is well known, Wallerstein's theoretical analysis depends on dividing the world into three essentially economic categories: the core, the periphery and the semi-periphery. In his view, there has been a discernible world system since around 1600 when the 'core' zones of north-west Europe began to be clearly established. The key point is that subsequent socio-economic development is shaped by trends in the world economy, by trade cycles and long 'waves' of growth and retrenchment. While the overall fortunes of the world system are limited in this way, Wallerstein is careful not to regard the fate of particular regions or countries as determined. They can seize their opportunity (or fail to seize it) to move from the periphery to the semi-periphery and so on. Overall however, it 'has been the world-system then and not the separate "societies" that has been "developing"' (1990a: 165).

On the face of it Wallerstein provides exactly the kind of analysis which appears to be required. As noted by Giddens (1981: 197), he insists 'upon the methodological necessity of studying inter-societal systems . . . [and recognizes that] the capitalist state . . . exists in an external environment in which economic mechanisms hold sway'. But though his analysis explicitly deals with global-level phenomena, it is not adequate for the purpose in hand. In asserting this I am not intending to focus attention on criticisms commonly made of the theory – for example that the criteria for classifying countries into the three categories are unclear, or that the account of how the core 'exploits' the periphery is contentious. Rather, the problem lies with the interpretation of 'global' offered by the theory. If the economy has been operating in terms of a world system for four centuries, if the history of development really has been the story of the development of the world system, then this theory has little to say about the distinctively recent experience of global identity. Had people understood correctly, they would have been thinking in terms of global processes all along.

A second author who has explicitly tried to get questions of globalization taken on to the agenda of sociology is Sklair (1991, 1994). His work starts out from a recognition of the huge reach and global power of transnational companies. In addition to transnational businesses, Sklair also believes it is important to recognize a 'transnational capitalist class' and the 'culture-ideology of consumerism' (1991: 38, 42). In other words, throughout the world there are 'members of economically dominant groups' who align themselves politically with the perceived interests of the 'global capitalist system', that is of transnational businesses (1994: 206). The political power and business successes of these corporations and this class are commonly challenged by political movements, by strikes, by protest campaigns and so on. However, their position is to some extent protected by the 'culture-ideology' of consumerism. The consumerist culture places a premium on new goods and on innovative styles and ideas. This culture offers some protection to the dominant system by allowing critical ideas to be coopted and by providing for oppositional cultural movements to become absorbed into the 'establishment'. Thus, youth cultures become part of the style industry, rap music comes to be used in advertisements, and even anniversaries of challenges to the dominant ideology become opportunities for consumption: 'the celebrations of the twentieth anniversary of the revolts of 1968 became a media event in Europe . . . and were relentlessly commercialized. . . . We shall have to wait for the year 2017 to see what the culture-ideology of consumerism makes of the Bolshevik revolution!' (1991: 42).

In these works Sklair identifies important issues about the world-wide organization of modern societies. Unlike Wallerstein, he does emphasize the newness of globalization. But it is important to appreciate the status of his leading concepts (the 'transnational practices' as he calls them), namely the transnational corporation, transnational capitalist class and culture-ideology of consumerism. Speaking of the ideological role of culture, for example, he notes that

> This is not an empirical assertion, for if it was it would no doubt sometimes be false and usually impossible to prove one way or the other. The idea of cultural-ideological transnational practices and, in particular the idea of the culture-ideology of consumerism in the global system, are conceptual tools in the theory of the global system. (1991: 42)

What this appears to mean is that Sklair is using these terms in a hypo-
thetical sense, believing that they are likely to be analytically beneficial but
unable to demonstrate it in detail. Convinced that society is becoming
globalized, Sklair has developed a terminology to 'capture' or reflect that
globalization, but it is simultaneously a terminology which assumes the
correctness of his original convictions. Where Wallerstein rendered it
difficult to talk about globalization in the contemporary world by making
the whole history of capitalism global, Sklair makes it difficult by assuming
from the outset that production and trade, politics and culture are already
almost comprehensively globalized. He leaves little space for the possibility
that some processes are less globalized than others, and appears to take a
mono-causal view of globalization, namely that it is driven by transnational
capital. Both these authors' ideas are stimulating but they are unsatis-
factory. Both, additionally, reveal how difficult it is to devise an appropriate theoretical perspective for analysing the sociology of global society.

It has become clearer from this review of recent attempts to articulate a
sociology of global phenomena what it is that one should demand of an
analysis of globalization. For one thing, a suitable analysis has to make
sense of the newness of global compression and of people's consciousness of
that compression. Second, the question arises: why is it that a variety
of processes of globalization (cultural, technological, political) all appear to
be taking place around the same time (see the essays in Featherstone,
1990)?

Giddens attempts to address this second issue by considering processes
of globalization in what he identifies as the four 'institutional dimensions of
modernity': capital accumulation, surveillance, military power and industrialism (1990: 59; see also Yearley, 1994a: 154). As McGrew summarizes
it, Giddens' argument is that:

> Each of these dimensions embodies a distinctive globalizing imperative, nurtured
> by quite different institutional forces and constituencies. . . . Globalization is
> therefore understood as . . . a complex, discontinuous and contingent process,
> which is driven by a number of distinct but intersecting logics. (1992: 72)

Though such an approach breaks away from the rather mono-causal
stance of Wallerstein and Sklair, it is not without its own difficulties. For
one thing, the theory is so 'complex' and 'discontinuous' (to use McGrew's
terms) that it is difficult to derive precise implications from it. Its very
flexibility actually turns it, in practice, into a descriptive, nominalistic
approach to global-level phenomena – as is revealed by Giddens' own
definition of globalization as 'the intensification of world-wide social relations which link distant localities in such a way that local happenings are
shaped by events occurring many miles away and vice versa' (1990: 64).
Moreover, as Robertson points out, Giddens appears committed to the
'thesis that globalization is a *consequence of modernity*' (1992: 144; my
italics – that being the title of Giddens' book). In other words, since
(according to Giddens, 1990: 63) 'modernity is inherently globalizing', he

ultimately views globalization as the mere outcome of modernization or of the 'project' of modernity. By contrast, in his work on globalization, Robertson emphasizes the independence of the cultural sphere. He and Lechner assert that there are '*independent* dynamics of global culture' (1985: 103; my italics) – though elsewhere he describes the process as only 'relatively autonomous' (1992: 60). In place of a single theory about the cause(s) of globalization, Robertson's emphasis on the heterogeneous elements promoting globality leads him to develop an historical model of stages of globalization (1992: 58–60). Even this is not the last word, however, since after elaborating this model, he still calls for 'much more' empirical and theoretical work (1992: 60).

Both Robertson and Giddens come closer to offering a more workable sociological approach to globalization but, even so, it is clear that neither offers a fully worked out theory which can simply be 'applied' to such empirical topics as environmentalism.

**Working Down to the Global**

Up to this point we have mostly considered ways of moving up to the global from national-level phenomena. But there is another way to approach the global, namely from the level of phenomena which are taken to be universal, to apply literally everywhere. After all, from the viewpoint of the universal, the global looks rather small-scale. If we know things which are universal, then surely these must be of global validity too.

Systematic analysis of the 'universal' can easily be traced back to the philosophers of classical Greece. Without at all addressing the intricacies of the different views they held, it is safe to say that Plato and Aristotle were both impressed by the realization that while our bodies are restricted in time and place, our ideas seem to give us access to realms of timeless insight freed from the limitations of space and location. One can point to numerous examples. Geometry makes a good place to start. Since Pythagoras outlined his geometrical arguments – to the popular imagination he literally outlined them, in the sand – people have been struck by the idea that conclusions derived from one imperfectly drawn right-angled triangle apply to all such triangles, of whatever size, whatever the other angles, wherever they are. It is easy to suppose that Pythagoras taught us something not just about his particular triangle, not just about all the triangles he and his followers ever drew, but about the idea of 'triangularness'. And this is the key to the argument about universals: somehow through ideas, humans appear to have access to universal truths, truths which apply regardless of time and place. In some ways the intuitively obvious response to this realization was, and is, to think that our ideas must therefore in some manner provide us with access to a 'parallel universe', a universe of essences where truths are timeless and universal, a universe which could hardly be more different from everyday experience.[3]

More fabulous still, this parallel universe provides us with a handle on the everyday one; Pythagorean ideas about triangles allow us to calculate the lengths of actual inclines, to calibrate right angles and so on. As Russell put it: 'Mathematical knowledge appeared [to Pythagoras] to be certain, exact, and applicable to the real world; moreover it was obtained by mere thinking, without the need of observation' (1945: 34).

Once this kind of insight into the universal is recognized and accepted, there is no reason to halt at geometry. Arithmetic follows fairly readily. Mathematicians can do intellectual work on mere numbers, devise theorems and so on, which actually allow us to gain understanding about numbers of things. Purely abstract sums can be done which turn out to be applicable to peas in the pod, starlings in the flock and grains of sand on the beach. But it does not stop there either. There is logic, supposedly allowing us to establish the quality of a deductive argument, regardless of what the argument is about. And there then are questions of right and beauty.

The excitement about geometry, mathematics and logic stemmed from the fact that here were manipulations of pure ideas which somehow have an applicability to empirical objects. But in expressly evaluative matters too, it was argued, that there was a world of universals which informed our everyday meanings. Among the clearest instances here concerns the idea of what is morally right. It has been a standard concern of moral and ethical philosophy to work out what the right thing to do is: whether capital punishment is morally justified or not, whether adultery is wrong and so on. As people have argued over the wrongs and rights of particular issues, they have also had cause to think about the so-called meta-ethical questions, questions about what it actually means to say that something is right or wrong. One time-honoured approach here is simply to submit to the rulings of God. On this view, with superhuman wisdom the divinity has stipulated what is right or wrong and it is our duty to obey those rules; such rules are commonly backed up with some powerful sanction such as that those who do not conform will spend eternity smouldering on the devil's barbecue.

Still, even among religious thinkers, it is common to find an additional idea, namely that people are imbued with a capacity for telling right from wrong, and for taking pleasure from right conduct. Here the prospect arises once again that human reflection can lead to the uncovering of universal truths, though in this instance they are not truths about how the world *is*, but about how it rightly *should be*. For the many philosophers who have dispensed with God as a long-stop in ethical matters, there are few places other than reason to turn for an account of what we mean by 'good'. Admittedly, there are some 'subjectivists' who have given up on the idea of intersubjective standards altogether. For them, 'good' is just what appears correct to individuals, or to communities, or to some other local reference point. Others (utilitarians) have attempted a different approach, suggesting that the real measure of goodness is the greatest happiness of the greatest number. But the two recently-dominant approaches to meta-ethical questions both regard it as necessary that there is something other-worldly (or, at least, not-quite-this-worldly) to ethical standards.

One approach, currently most associated with the legal philosopher Rawls, ties our sense of what is right to reason and to an imaginary contract. To put it crudely, Rawls (1972) argues that the rules determining good conduct are those that would be agreed upon by a group of reasonable people called on to discuss this matter, but who were 'blindfolded' to the extent that they did not know what their own attributes and interests would be. For instance, they would know that some people might be poor and others rich, some unwell others wonderfully fit and athletic, but they would not be aware which category they themselves were in. On the chance that they were among the poor or poorly, we might expect this blindfolded group to favour standards of justice independent of rank and fortune, systematic provision for the poor and so on – in short, to come up with a set of ethical standards similar to modern liberal values. I termed this procedure other-worldly because no such group ever could exist, nor – even if it could – is there any likelihood that other people alive then or subsequently would treat that particular group as the arbitrators of correctness. It offers an ideal against which actual rule-making can be judged.

The second approach is even more directly analogous to the cases of geometry and arithmetic. Here the idea is that, in Russell's terms, by 'mere thinking' (or, at least, by strenuous reasoning) people can arrive at knowledge of what is good. By analysing about what makes a good citizen, a good deed or a good law, we can reason about the meaning of goodness. This exercise has taken various forms in the centuries since the Classical writers but has largely been based on the same general assumptions (as explored by MacIntyre, 1981). Though philosophers may disagree about the particular rights and wrongs, there persists a view that since people can more or less agree about what is good, there must be some independent meaning or standard for that term, just as with Pythagoras' triangles.

Of course, it is conceivable that there might not be any external standard at all. What we regard as 'good' could just be a convention, an arbitrary agreement accepted in our society and therefore only in some loose sense 'correct', such as the habit of driving on the right or on the left. But most philosophers have considered that the 'good', 'justice' and so on have to mean more than this. And, since the good is supposed to transcend (as well as somehow inform) particular judgements, it is assumed to be universal, in the same way that geometrical theorems about triangles and logical conclusions about the structure of arguments are. In broad terms, therefore, the argument appears to come down to this: either what we mean by 'right' is just a convention (in which case there is no enduring reason to pursue it) or it is something more than convention. If it is the latter, it is somehow external to particular human societies and must – presumably – occupy the same sort of realm or parallel universe as do 'triangularness' and perfect deductions. Furthermore, from these views about the right and the good, it is a short step to applying these arguments to questions of beauty and aesthetic value too. Continuing debates over the meaning of 'quality' in art and literature point to the persistent vitality of this issue too.

Whichever basis for validity one chooses for deciding about the good and about people's rights, it is important to recognize that the upshot is the same: these rights are supposedly universal. The same principles are held to be applicable to systems of justice everywhere, to each citizen regardless of rank, or to all human beings. This is the spirit of the idea most famously enshrined in the US constitution where the 'Rights of Man' are 'held to be self-evident'. While Western societies have sometimes been rather more successful in spelling out and codifying these rights than in implementing them, it is fair to say that the ideals of universal rights and universal principles have been very powerful and usually progressive ideas. And, such ideas are plainly connected to the analysis of global problems precisely because of their supposed universality. Any human right worth its salt is – ideally – going to be a right all over the globe. If it were agreed that free speech is a fundamental human right, then one could safely assume it ought to be a right the world over.

Lately, however, some of these universal principles have come under attack, not from conservatives who might regard them as excessively favourable to the undeserving, but from radical critics. Among the most celebrated of such critics is the US legal analyst MacKinnon. Stated briefly, her argument has been that what liberals have come to regard as universalistic principles are, in significant ways, male-orientated principles. The claim to universality is only superficial, a superficiality which in fact is injurious to women's position. A typical argument advanced here turns on the idea that 'free-speech' excuses verbal and graphical violence against women, most notably pornography. MacKinnon expresses her argument as follows:

> In liberalism, speech must never be sacrificed for other social goals. But liberalism has never understood this reality of pornography: the free so-called speech of men silences the free speech of women. . . . First, women do not simply have freedom of speech on a social level. The most basic assumption underlying First Amendment adjudication is that, socially, speech is free. The First Amendment itself says, 'Congress shall make no law . . . abridging the freedom of speech.' Free speech exists. The problem for government is to avoid constraining that which, if unconstrained by government, is free. This tends to presuppose that whole segments of the population are not systematically silenced socially, prior to government action. Second, the law of the First Amendment comprehends that freedom of expression, in the abstract, is a system but fails to comprehend that sexism (and racism), in the concrete, are also systems. As a result, it cannot grasp that the speech of some silences the speech of others in a way that is not simply a matter of competition for airtime. That pornography chills women's expression is difficult to demonstrate empirically because silence is not eloquent. Yet on no more of the same kind of evidence, the argument that suppressing pornography might chill legitimate speech has supported its protection. (1989: 205–6; see also 1987)

In recent years, a similar argument has come to prominence in the United Kingdom over the courts' acceptance of claims that certain crimes are carried out in an unplanned way, on the spur of the moment as the perpetrator lost control. This argument too, it is suggested, is tilted in favour of men. Women may face similar levels of provocation but be too scared to act, the male often being stronger and more accustomed to carrying out acts of violence. Out of desperation women may subsequently produce a violent response, but as this shows signs of pre-planning, they lack the defence of spontaneous action available to men. Such arguments have met with a mixed response. Some commentators have accepted that universal standards may include unexamined assumptions and may not therefore be as truly universal as proposed. Others have suggested that once one starts trying to match principles to specific groups or specific individuals, the power of the principle itself evaporates. In other words, if it is accepted that the 'rights of man' are indeed men's rights – if, in other words, women's rights are allowed to differ (even if only slightly) from men's – this opens the possibility of weak men's rights differing from those of the strong, and so on. Similarly, it becomes possible to argue that women of different races have different rights. Once fractured, universality can begin to split in any number of ways. This issue of the universality of rights and other ethical principles will reappear in Chapters 4 and 5.

There is one further sort of knowledge which briefly needs to be considered before finishing this section: namely, science or systematic empirical knowledge. Up until the last two or three hundred years, philosophers were keen to honour logic and geometry above natural science. As outlined above, logic and geometry appear to be very special sorts of knowledge and they were regarded as superior to science in a number of respects. First, where science may turn out to be wrong and is, at least in principle, constantly open to disproof, logic and geometry are certain. Scientific knowledge depends on manipulation of the world, whereas logical truths can be known by the 'nobler' business of reflection alone. Lastly, logic and geometry are thought to apply for all time and everywhere; science gives knowledge of actual matter which is limited in time and often perishable.

These arguments about the relative standing of science on the one side and logic and geometry on the other, have been actively pursued since the seventeenth century. Over time the tables have rather come to be reversed. For one thing, as the scientific enterprise has grown and the fundamental world-view of science has won wider and wider acceptance, the suggested inferiority of science has come to ring a little hollow. Science now claims to tell us about the origin of the universe, about the evolution of life, the make-up of the human genetic structure and the fundamental constituents of matter. It is hard to sustain the idea that such knowledge is inferior. Second, the advance of science has contributed to the undoing of the apparent certainty of logic, arithmetic and geometry. For example, twentieth-century physics tells us that the universe is not a simple three-dimensional place, and Pythagoras' theorem does not therefore apply through all time and space. Accordingly, the universe itself defies our geometrical intuitions and aspects of our sense of logic. The geometry to which we seem to have intuitive access turns out, according to science, not to be the fundamental geometry of the universe after all. Scientists have found it profitable to invent 'alternative' geometries to chart the universe, and alternative logics and mathematics to interpret it.

On the one hand, therefore, science has made the 'universals' of philosophers look significantly less universal. But that still leaves a question on the other hand: what kind of confidence can we invest in knowledge like science which is 'merely' empirical? The emerging problem of how empirically-based science could 'outgun' logic has been resolved for some philosophers by the suggestion that science follows a rigorous method. This move switches the burden of responsibility on to the method employed in science and away from the substance of the empirical claims which scientists make at any particular stage in the history of science. This argument allows for the fact that scientific theories are sometimes overthrown and rejected. Thus, some eminent nineteenth-century biologists, for example, thought that what we regard as 'genetic material' was carried in the blood. Later, views concentrated on the role of special reproductive cells. Since scientists effectively change their minds about how the world works (in a way that geometricians and logicians never seemed to change theirs), one cannot expect particular scientific beliefs to be universally valid. Current scientific beliefs are all likely to be overturned or subject to adjustment and correction at some future date (see Newton-Smith, 1981: 183–5). Philosophers of science have emphasized instead the method of science; it is the disciplined way in which beliefs are subject to change that is held to account for the special character of scientific beliefs.[4]

In this way, it becomes possible to argue that science too can aim at universal validity in making claims to knowledge. Though no particular scientific claim can count on universal validity, the scientific method offers a universally valid approach to developing knowledge about the natural world. The universe-wide credibility of the scientific approach can be backed up by pointing to the success of science in dealing with the remote and inaccessible worlds of astronomy, prehistory and subatomic particles. Since the 'scientific revolution' of the seventeenth century, philosophical faith in science and in the power of the scientific method to deliver in-practice universal knowledge has grown and grown.

To summarize this section, intellectual history reveals a continuing interest in aspects of knowledge which somehow exceed experience but which none the less allow us to grasp and interpret actual experiences. Kant was so impressed by these forms of knowledge that he invented a special category just for them (he referred to them as the 'synthetic *a priori*'). Such geometrical and logical knowledge is complemented by evaluative and normative forms of understanding which are also believed to possess universal validity. These forms of knowledge have been elaborated in ways – such as in written geometrical theorems and logical proofs – which have come to be seen as 'self-evident'. Recent doubts over the adequacy of some of these 'universal' principles, such as those voiced by MacKinnon, indicate provisional grounds for caution here. Lastly, there is scientific knowledge. Science boasts of its empirical status and is therefore avowedly not the product of reflection alone. Scientific knowledge depends on careful observation and contrived experiment; it is most definitely not self-evident. None the less, the view has arisen that scientific method allows science to enjoy in practice the kinds of universalistic benefits of the other kinds of knowledge: scientific knowledge aims to identify the consistent and generalizable properties of matter and of natural systems.

Armed with these three sources of knowledge which boast of their applicability through time and space, the task of interpreting global trends seems much more easily undertaken. The irony is that, except in the case of science, we are using thousand-year old tools to study a supposedly modern problem.

## Summary: Globalization and the Social Scientific Study of the Environment

So far in this chapter we have established that there are good grounds for taking the idea of globalization seriously. Across a wide range of phenomena, from international markets to telecommunications, from popular culture to mass production, it appears that the world is becoming compressed. That is not to say that people's experiences are necessarily becoming more similar. Even if one looks only at internal differentiation within wealthy industrial countries – the USA and Britain for example – the past fifteen years have witnessed a growing distance between the wealthy and the poor. A global world is not a uniform world. But it is one in which key processes – manufacture, food production, cultural transmission – are increasingly being organized at a transnational level. At the same time, in many ways people are becoming more aware of cross-national and world-wide connections and are being invited to subscribe to supranational identities, whether by Amnesty International, by their TNC employer or by the publicity machinery of the European Union and pro-European political parties.

While it is easy enough for sociologists to document a number of these global processes and to point to agencies and organizations which are proposing global identification, sociology has specific weaknesses when faced with global levels of analysis. Though barely having acknowledged it, sociology has not so much been the systematic study of society (the common textbook definition of the discipline) as the study of a handful of national societies. Furthermore, its emphasis on the social characteristics of these nations tended to draw attention away from geographical and other features which are likely to be of significance in relation to a systematic analysis at the level of the globe (especially in relation to environmental issues). Certain sociological approaches have been developed in response to a perceived need for global analyses but these have sometimes been simply descriptive or, on the other hand, inaccurately theoretical. World systems theory, for example, offers an appropriate level of analysis but proposes that the world has always been global, in which case the distinctiveness of modern globalization is hard to understand. Sklair's theory stresses the novelty of globalization in an attractive way but tends to be restrictive and mono-causal in its approach. Robertson's and Giddens' more nuanced approaches have their difficulties too. Ironically, the academic traditions with – in many respects – the best claims to a concern with humanistic concepts of a world-wide validity have been ethical and epistemological theory.

Though many authors such as Offe (cited in the Preface) and Archer (1991: 144) have noticed that some activists and politicians, spurred on by the fear of threats to the global environment, are trying to assemble a global identity around environmental issues, little attention has been paid to environmentalism or to ecological problems in the bulk of recent globaliz-ation writing (though Sklair, 1994 is an exception; see also Yearley, 1995b). Yet the case of the environment offers itself as a central example of many of the phenomena discussed in this chapter. Environmentalists have been at the forefront in attempting to identify the image of the globe with their political project, and they have succeeded to the extent that talk of 'the planet' or 'the globe' is now commonly heard as 'green talk' (as the yoghurt-pot example in the Preface implied). On the other hand, when globalization authors do mention the environment, they commonly high-light the well known 'global environmental problems' of global warming and ozone depletion; ecological problems are frequently invoked in a rather undiscriminating way as potential catastrophes or 'species-threatening phenomena' (Robertson, 1992: 133). Accordingly, in the rest of this book I shall use a review of global environmental problems and modern environ-mental movements and politics to make a critical examination of globalization in an area where the objective conditions and the subjective awareness appear to be favourable. In Chapter 2 I will begin by reviewing the environmental issues which are commonly taken as making up the principal hazards facing the global environment.

## Notes

1 The European Union was known, before the Maastricht Treaty, as the European Community. To avoid confusion I have used European Union (EU) throughout, even if it is sometimes not strictly correct.

2 Many people now regard the 'Third World' as an inappropriate term, both because the 'Second World' of Soviet socialism has disintegrated and out of an ethical concern that underdeveloped countries should not be given a lower 'ranking' than the 'First'. In any case, it is also pointed out that the Third World is very internally differentiated with, for instance, countries such as South Korea enjoying rapid economic development while others, such as Niger, continue to face colossal economic difficulties. While I accept that there is much to all these arguments, I am choosing to use the term since it is used by many Third-World authors themselves and since it is relatively neutral as regards the reasons why this 'world' exists. To

avoid endless repetition of the term I will, however, also use 'South' and 'North' to indicate the Third and First Worlds respectively, and will sometimes employ 'Western' to refer to European and North American culture.

3 Some advocates of universals do opt to locate them in the actual world rather than in some parallel realm (see for example Kripke, 1980: 113ff.). My thanks to Dave Archard for instructive advice on this section of the argument; remaining weaknesses are solely down to me.

4 Although I present this argument here, I am sceptical about arguments which rely heavily on a supposed 'scientific method' (see Yearley, 1988, 1994b). Rather than argue at an abstract level in this chapter, I have reserved my comments for the discussion of the practical ability of science to make universal claims in Chapter 4.

# 2

# Environmental Issues and the Compression of the Globe

**Introduction**

As was pointed out in the Preface and in Chapter 1, there are reasons for thinking that environmental threats and environmental awareness ought to display the logic of globalization. After all, we commonly hear that environmental problems threaten the globe. Such a threat to the planet, even more than world-wide cultural homogeneity, should perhaps lead us to shift our thinking, analysis and policy-making onto a global level. Some ecological problems, such as global warming, actually carry claims to globality in the very names by which they are known, while other problems, such as acid rain, lend themselves to depiction in terms of threats to the well-being of the planet. At the same time, many environmental organizations make much of their global character, claiming as noted earlier to be Friends of the *Earth* (FoE), *Earth*First! or the *World Wide* Fund for Nature. The aim of this chapter is to review leading contemporary environmental issues in order to assess the extent to which they can be said to give evidence of globalization or to demonstrate the compression of the globe. To get this review underway, let us begin with two illustrative examples.

*Eating Away the World's Ozone Layer*

In the late 1980s unprecedented anxiety was displayed by members of the public in several European countries about the ozone-depleting chemicals (chlorofluorocarbons or CFCs) which were to be found in the majority of aerosol spray cans. Through the awareness-raising activities of groups such as Friends of the Earth (FoE, 1989) and through the response of the media, some manufacturers and a number of retail outlets, the public came to accept that whenever they squirted deodorant sprays or many polishes and spray foams, polluting chemical gases escaped into the atmosphere. These gases are dangerous because they encourage the breakdown of the earth's protective ozone-layer – a stratum of the atmosphere in which naturally occurring molecules of the gas ozone, a gas which filters out harmful ultraviolet radiation, are particularly numerous.

The striking thing about this form of pollution threat was that the geographical connection between the release of the pollutant and the damage it caused was extremely remote. CFCs sprayed in Edinburgh were not likely to affect the ozone layer over the city, nor indeed over London or even Great Britain. The CFCs were carried by winds and only gradually worked their way into the upper atmosphere. The most extreme loss of ozone in fact occurs at the two poles, where presumably there is less call for deodorant. So, pollution emitted in Britain, or Japan, or Brazil could end up causing a problem across the other side of the globe.

People had long got used to the idea that private citizens or companies could pollute their local environment, with loud noise, smelly industry or whatever. But here was a startling example that showed that modern substances and modern technology (CFCs were developed around 1930 but their use grew rapidly in the boom decades after mid-century, rising by 13 per cent annually in the 1960s (Benedick, 1991: 26)) could cause pollution on a global scale. Such pollution compresses the world radically, allowing us to despoil the environment of our 'neighbours', thousands of kilometres away on the planet.

This case is also striking because the danger is insidious and sinister. Before the scare, the authorities (at least in most of Europe and in the majority of industrializing countries) and the few citizens who had heard of CFCs were complacent since CFCs themselves are not directly harmful to human beings and animals, and because none of us ever sees the ozone layer. Yet the ultraviolet radiation which enters through the 'holes' in that layer can promote skin cancers, one of the dread diseases in the industrialized countries. CFCs changed from being harmless, beneficial molecules into an invisible cancer-provoking menace.

## Dumping out of Sight

Kassa Island lies just off the coast of Guinea, a former French colony in the west of Africa, a little north of the Equator. In 1988, the thirtieth anniversary of the country's independence, it was discovered that a large quantity (the Guinean authorities estimated around 15,000 tonnes) of incinerator ash from Philadelphia had been dumped on the island. According to the US Environmental Protection Agency, the ash from such incinerators includes dangerous materials such as heavy metals (the general term for various toxic metals, for example, cadmium) and poisonous organic compounds known as dioxins. The people of North America are increasingly aware of the potential dangers from such materials and do not wish to have them disposed of in their own locality. Hence they were shipped over five thousand kilometres to Guinea and, just to make sure that local people did not object too much, they were redescribed as 'building materials' (*The Independent* 17 June 1988: 8). Of course this ash could be used in the construction business but it is safe to assume that it would not be a popular building material. To add to the international flavour of the incident, the material was transported on a Norwegian-owned ship. Following the discovery of the nature of the ash, the Guinean authorities arrested the Norwegian consul. Norway subsequently undertook to remove the waste.

In this second case too it is clear that people are capable of polluting the other side of the globe. But in this instance it is international trade rather than the transnational dispersion of molecules which links the world. From these two examples we can see that (a) certain modern pollutants can contaminate the global environment while (b) the transnational nature of modern trade allows the waste from industrialized regions and countries to pollute every region of the world.

In this chapter I shall examine the way that pollution and other environmental problems simultaneously *illustrate* and *are brought about by* the compression of the world. I shall review the principal environmental problems, in each case concentrating on and assessing the global nature and globalizing character of the issue.

### How Environmental Problems Can Compress the World

The cases of ozone-depleting pollution and the international voyages undertaken by American incinerator rubbish symbolize in a striking way the theme of this chapter, that the world's growing environmental problems are connecting the lives of people in very different societies. And while individuals can try to minimize the impact on their own lives, it is ultimately impossible to hide oneself away from these phenomena altogether. No humans and virtually no plants or animals are exempted from these problems. That is not to say that all forms of pollution and environmental hazard are now global in scale. They are not. A good deal of pollution, for example, is still local or restricted to a region. Moreover, the impact of any given pollutant is liable to be modified by the details of the local geology and geography. But as we shall see, most forms of pollution and other environmental problems have increased markedly in the last third of the twentieth century and continue to grow. Also, more and more of that pollution has an international spread so that in the closing years of the twentieth century no one is immune from all of it.

But while the experience of *suffering* from pollution and certain kinds of environmental degradation are nowadays almost universal, the rest of the story displays far greater inequalities. Some of the world's people make far more of a contribution to causing pollution and loss of environmental value than do others – and of course wild animals and plants which suffer from pollution cannot really be said to create any. Of the people causing pollution, some derive more personal benefit from each unit of pollution caused than do others. For example, Europeans typically create more pollution than Africans because more of them can afford cars, washing machines, goods with masses of packaging and so on. In other words, the wealthier society tends also to be the more polluting society. But, for every kilometre they drive, car owners in the former Soviet Union and Eastern Europe are likely to cause more pollution than their Western European counterparts because their cars are dirtier and less efficient. The same is true of power stations in the former state socialist countries: on average, for every useful unit of electrical power they generate, they cause more pollution. So, though wealth and pollution-generation are usually connected, they are not completely bound to each other.

Finally, as we shall see in this chapter and the next (and as we saw with Kassa Island), some people cause ecological problems deliberately; they dump substances into the environment because it saves them money or trouble. Others despoil the environment, but with little practical choice about what they do, while there are some people who have pollution dumped on them, without even getting the benefit of the processes which caused it in the first place.

Overall, then, while pollution and environmental despoliation are very widespread experiences, their origins are far less uniformly distributed, and sometimes those who cause such problems and benefit from them are rich and powerful enough to try to limit the impact on themselves by imposing it on others. We can therefore anticipate that there will be many dimensions to the globalization of environmental problems, depending on how and why environmental harm is spread.

The experience of pollution and the growing concern with environmental issues more generally have lent themselves to presentation in terms of globalization. Environmental writers and campaigners have put a great deal of effort into getting people, as the saying goes, to 'think global'. As will be seen in the next chapter, the image of a global identity has been built up through the use of terms such as 'spaceship earth', through the much-used pictures of the globe suspended in space and through a string of conferences and seminars focusing on 'global' themes. Environmental issues sound even more significant if they are described as *global* environmental issues.

As we have seen with the issue of ozone depletion, some pollution problems can plausibly be presented as global by their very nature. At least on the face of it, it is in virtually everyone's interest to oppose such forms of pollution. And this is the message that some environmentalists try to draw from the fact that we are all 'space crew' on our global spaceship. A sense of global identity is supposed to promote the idea that we face environmental hazards *together*. Yet many other 'global' forms of pollution and environmental harm get to have global effects because they are dispersed through trade and the spread of industrialization, not because they are inherently global. It would be wrong therefore to assume that responses to pollution problems are globally harmonious. There may be some common threats, but other environmental hazards result from people in one part of the globe displacing their problems on to other parts. Furthermore, certain kinds of pollution and ecological damage are diminishing in the North (because of tighter regulations or because of technological advances) even while they are on the increase in the underdeveloped world, because of the growth of industrialization. Different parts of the globe may thus be experiencing markedly different environmental-quality trends.

To assess the global significance of environmental problems we need to examine the kinds of pollution and other hazards which are important today and to look at how they are distributed internationally. Those issues are covered in most of the rest of this chapter. There is also the related question about how exactly 'pollution' and environmental problems are to be defined. For the time being I shall work with an implicit notion of pollution, returning to the question of definitions later on, in the section after next.

## The Globe's Environmental Problems: Pollution

To get a sense of how significant a phenomenon international pollution is and to be able to assess whether and why it is increasing, we need to have a way of classifying types of pollution. The commonest method of classification focuses on the medium in which the pollution ends up, whether that is the air, water or land.

### Land Pollution

Beginning with the last of these, we can take a brief look at each medium in turn. Land tends to be polluted either because humans have buried things in it or carried out messy operations on it. For example, it is increasingly being found that current and former industrial sites are heavily polluted. In the United States and Britain, for instance, the places where chemical factories or town-gas production works have been located, especially when they have been there for decades, are typically heavily contaminated. This issue was highlighted in the United Kingdom in the early 1990s because environmental campaigners wanted the British government to publish a register of contaminated sites (Watson, 1993; see also Friends of the Earth, 1992a). The authorities resisted this demand, arguing that only very few sites were actually dangerous to human health and that public disclosure of information about the other 'contaminated' sites would cause unnecessary anxiety and lead property-owners to see the value of their land and buildings decline dramatically. Even buildings on converted farmland can be contaminated, because of the residues from agricultural chemicals, as the US Environmental Protection Agency found to its embarrassment at one of its own regional offices in New York state (*New York Times*, 6 March 1995: B6).

Of itself, one would perhaps not expect contaminated land to constitute much more than a local problem. However, it can be of much wider significance. For example, as was indicated by the example of Kassa Island and as we shall see again later on, one country's land may be contaminated by the actions of other countries. In that way, land contamination can easily be an international issue. Furthermore, while increased regulation in recent years has meant that some forms of land contamination in the North are declining, the world-wide growth of manufacturing and chemical plants dictates that overall the problem is on the increase. It is in danger of becoming a fully world-wide problem because of the spread of polluting industrial activity.

Land is also polluted when waste is dumped in quarries, gravel pits, drained lakes or specially-dug holes. Landfill, as this waste disposal method is known, is still the commonest disposal technique in Britain and in most States in the USA (although incineration is also common); the refuse varies from packaging from shops and builders' rubble, through mixed domestic waste (typically a mix of paper, metals, glass, plastics and other rubbish) to industrial wastes, which may include highly toxic and corrosive material. Until recently, dangerous wastes were deliberately 'diluted' with ordinary refuse, a practice which was made to sound more scientific by being labelled 'co-disposal'. As world industrial production continues to rise and as trade brings manufactured and packaged goods to more and more people, these waste disposal practices are spreading throughout the globe. Pollution from landfill is already causing environmental problems in the so-called 'newly industrializing countries' (NICs) such as Taiwan, Mexico and Brazil. In the countries of the North, the dumping of material is now supposedly regulated, though the presence in the market of suspect private operators and periodic arrests for illegal dumping still give cause for alarm.

Of course, regulation – however effective – does not address the root of the problem, the generation of waste. Since the industrialized countries continue to experience economic growth – if not every year, at least on average – the amount of waste tends to grow correspondingly. In response, some attempts are being made to take material out of the 'waste stream' so that it does not need to be disposed of; this can be achieved through reducing packaging and cutting down on wastage, and by reusing and recycling materials. While very significant changes in the amount of waste produced can be envisaged, at least in principle, companies' marketing divisions are generally reluctant to reduce their use of packaging. For example, beer companies commonly differentiate their products with distinctive bottles. Except in cases where there are huge sales of a particular brand, there are practical difficulties in organizing the reuse of bottles. It may not even make a lot of environmental sense to try, for instance, to send back from the Netherlands the distinctive bottle of a Mexican beer. Standard bottles would make the issue simpler but this is resisted by companies who do not want to surrender what they perceive as a unique feature which assists sales of their product. Both economic growth and global trade accordingly tend to increase the need for waste disposal.

But even if regulators the world over were to control tightly the substances entering dumps and to impose mandatory targets for recycling, there would still be considerable problems since rainwater seeping into these sites can wash out chemicals which can then be transported into water supplies, especially if the linings of the dump-sites tear or degrade. Natural decay in the dumps also gives rise to methane gas which can ignite or cause explosions.

These problems, of methane gas production and of water leaking, indicate that pollution incidents in the three media (land, water and air) are not really distinct. These connections are acknowledged in recent British, European and US legislation which promotes the idea of integrated pollution control; in other words it aims to stop people overcoming their solid waste problems by – for example – burning their refuse, only to give rise to air pollution.

*Water Pollution*

Turning to the second medium, water pollution also has many causes. Rivers have long been used to transport filth away from towns and sadly this process has intensified in the last century. Rivers have been contaminated in three main ways. First, human sewage has been expelled into rivers; this problem is magnified around towns and large cities because of the sheer density of human populations. In underdeveloped countries, city populations have recently grown at extremely high rates adding vastly to water pollution and often overwhelming sewage treatment facilities. Poor countries can afford little expenditure on such infrastructural items – a situation which has tended to worsen in the last decade for reasons which are considered in the next chapter. But urban populations have not been the only culprits. There has been repeated river pollution from farms, both effluent from animal husbandry (slurry from animal wastes and the highly polluting effluent from silage making) and the accumulated contamination from chemicals spread on the fields. Fertilizers, for instance, get dissolved by rainwater and enter watercourses; there they fertilize the growth of microscopic plants (algae and the like), reducing water quality.

These problems too have increased at a global level as more land has been brought into intensive cultivation either to trade or to feed growing populations and as the spread of agribusiness has meant that fertilizer and pesticide use in the underdeveloped world has accelerated. The recently negotiated GATT settlement, which is designed to promote unrestricted international trade, will tend to encourage intensive cultivation in underdeveloped countries and will thus add to the pressures for world-wide agrochemical use.

Finally, industrial wastes have also been dumped into rivers. In Northern countries, industry frequently took advantage of the nineteenth-century sewerage systems to dispose of waste from factories; consequently a good deal of industrial waste can be disposed of free or very cheaply through the sewers. Factories also experience spills, when materials inadvertently (or so it is said) overflow into watercourses. When these episodes are put down to accidents, companies are rarely punished very severely. Environmental campaigners are convinced that spills by one company are frequently used by neighbouring firms as an opportunity to dump their wastes too (see Rose, 1990: 56–63).

The story with sea pollution is essentially similar though the extent of deliberate dumping of hazardous wastes has possibly been even greater:

> Many coastal towns around the UK simply discharge untreated sewage down pipes into the sea while, in other cases, the waste is treated but the resulting sludge is taken out by boats (colloquially known as 'bovril boats') and dumped offshore. Some waste is incinerated at sea before being dumped. Nuclear waste used to be sealed in metal or concrete containers and dropped into deep areas of the sea. (Yearley, 1992a: 34–5)

There are, however, recent signs of progress. The sea dumping of nuclear waste has already been halted (though not renounced entirely) and according to the international agreement known as the 'London Dumping Convention', all industrial waste dumping at sea was to be stopped by 1995 (Susskind, 1994: 161). Further, in line with an agreement among European Union member states, other marine pollution (for example from sewage sludge) will be greatly reduced by 1998. However, the London Dumping Convention has only 66 signatories and the European agreement applies only to EU states; surreptitious sea dumping is extremely difficult to monitor in any case. Elsewhere in the world, growing cities and expanding industry mean that marine pollution is on the increase. The threat of nuclear pollution of the seas may also have been renewed recently with the end of the Cold War. Nuclear submarines are costly to maintain and there is a possibility that obsolete vessels may sink and not be recovered, or even be deliberately jettisoned at sea (see *The Guardian*, 3 June 1995: 11).

The seas are also subject to pollution when boats, especially oil tankers, are wrecked. The general issue of marine oil pollution has been a concern since the 1920s, especially in the UK and the USA, countries with relatively lengthy coastlines (see Mitchell, 1993: 195). In the past thirty years this issue has been highlighted time and again through a series of huge and distressing oil spills, including the Exxon Valdez in Alaska in 1989 and the Braer wreck on Shetland in 1993.

> Yet, surprisingly enough, oil spills from wrecked ships are not the major cause of oil pollution at sea. The United Nations Environment Programme . . . reckons that 500,000 tonnes of the 1.6 million annually discharged into the sea by shipping is released accidentally; the remainder is non-accidental in origin and results from regular discharge by ships of contaminated ballast water and water used for flushing out tanks. [Yet according to] the US National Academy of Sciences . . . [m]ore oil enters the oceans from automobile exhausts, and from oil-changes in city garages that are then dumped down the drain, than from any other source. (Elsworth, 1990: 240)

More recent figures supplied by Mitchell (1993: 185) suggest that this pattern may be changing, with both a net diminution in overall marine oil pollution and greater than average reductions in non-accidental discharges at sea. Accidental discharges may now make up a significantly higher percentage than Elsworth suggests. All the same, it is evident that while a series of large oil spills has dominated media coverage and popular awareness of marine pollution, most oil pollution derives from myriad small discharges. These are so extensive that the world's oceans are now affected world-wide. Though spilled oil does eventually evaporate or become broken down by bacteria, traces of oil can be found in sea water the world over. And since the seas are linked throughout the world they unfortunately serve as a means for spreading pollution internationally.

*Air Pollution*

The third medium into which effluents and contamination can be discharged is the air. In the industrialized world people have been familiar with air pollution for many years and the chronically poor air quality in London in the middle years of the twentieth century has become legendary. At present, our air is polluted in a variety of ways but the chief culprits are the burning of fuels for heating or power generation, the exhausts from motor vehicles, and emissions from factory chimneys and incinerators. Given that we all have to breathe the air and that it cannot be filtered before use, air pollution is probably the most pervasive environmental problem – although some entrepreneurs have tried to come up with a privatized solution, so that for example Japanese commuters have been offered the chance to buy 'gulps' of clean air on the way to the office.

Some dangerous and polluting gases are formed in very large quantities. For instance, the acidic gas sulphur dioxide (known by its chemical symbol $SO_2$) is formed from the inevitable impurities in fuels when coal or oil is burnt in power stations or in people's homes, in fires and boilers. It is bad for people because, in the long term, it can attack the lungs and because it aggravates asthma as well as bronchial and other respiratory problems. It is also bad for the environment in general because its acidity encourages the destruction of many building stones and because it can attack trees and acidify rivers, spoiling conditions for fish and aquatic life. Other acidic gases – various oxides of nitrogen (collectively referred to as $NO_x$) – are produced from power stations and cars; they too irritate lung tissue and contribute to atmospheric acidity. Both these types of gas are formed by the millions of tonnes each year (in Britain alone the amounts of sulphur from $SO_2$ and of $NO_x$ discharged in 1990 were approximately 1.9 and 2.6 million tonnes respectively while France, with its large nuclear power-generating capacity, still emitted 0.7 and 1.8 million tonnes (*The Economist*, 1992: 202; see also Friends of the Earth, 1990: 2–6)). Being produced by motor traffic and by homes, as well as industry, these gases are highly pervasive. Acid rain is caused when they are transported in the atmosphere and then washed down by rain, snow and so on. Since these gases are released in such large quantities and since they are released from tall stacks as well as by ground-level cars, they can be carried over large distances by prevailing winds. In this way one country's emissions can end up polluting a neighbour's air, as happened with British acid rain blown to Scandinavia and with US acid pollution which ended up in Canada. In 1990, both Sweden and Norway suffered sulphur depositions at least double the size of their sulphur emissions (*The Economist*, 1992: 202).

At present policy measures are being implemented to reduce acid emissions in most Northern and former Soviet-bloc countries, in many cases through the Long-Range Transboundary Air Pollution Convention (LRTAP). Set up in 1979, the LRTAP Convention was accepted by the vast majority of European States, the USSR, and Canada and the USA. In Levy's view (1993: 83–4) 'The vast membership is probably a sign of the convention's perceived role in furthering détente.' The LRTAP Convention has a number of curious features. In the first place, it was initially an agreement simply to coordinate national research programmes and to report on policy measures; only later were actual air pollution reductions negotiated and signatories of the convention did not even have to subscribe to these. Second, Canada and the USA were involved in this convention even though they were unaffected by transboundary acid pollution, the parties' main concern, from the other countries. Their involvement was again linked to diplomatic interests at stake, though it did provide further leverage for the Canadian authorities concerned about acidic emissions from their southern neighbour. Lastly, it was literally concerned with *transboundary* air pollution. For example, Levy (1993: 92) reports that the Soviet Union was willing to sign up to an agreement to reduce trans-boundary $SO_2$ pollution, secure in the knowledge that this could be achieved not by cutting overall emissions but by shifting production to power stations in the east which would primarily cause pollution within the USSR itself. With predominantly westerly winds, Soviet power stations were much likelier to cause domestic acid pollution than transboundary effects. None the less, many countries did sign up to a 1985 protocol to the convention demanding 30 per cent cuts in sulphur emissions. Similarly, twenty-three countries agreed to a further protocol three years later to stabilize or reduce $NO_x$ emissions (Levy, 1993: 97). Subsequently, the countries of the EU formed a joint agreement to cut emissions from power stations and other large plant; in Britain this is largely being achieved by substituting gas for dirtier coal (which would otherwise be very expensive to clean to the new European standards).

Since the LRTAP Convention only applies to northern industrial coun-tries, the production of acid pollution is still increasing elsewhere in the world as industrialization proceeds and the low-cost British 'solution' of using gas clearly cannot be adopted the world over – there is simply not enough natural gas for industry in China, India, Latin America and the former Soviet Union to last many years into the future, as will be seen later in the chapter. In any case, when burned without elaborate emission control devices, coal is a cheaper fuel and is therefore likely to appeal to developing economies.

Other forms of air pollution are less pervasive but can be equally alarming. With $SO_2$ and $NO_x$, we at least know what the culprits are. But in other cases of air pollution it is far harder to establish the exact identities of waste gases. Thus, emissions from various factories, chemical plants and incinerators may contain 'cocktails' of gases, some of which are harmful in themselves and others which may be hazardous in combination. So far this form of air pollution has received less attention than the acid gases because acid rain is a comparatively well understood problem suffered by large numbers of people. The only exception is for pollution by VOCs (volatile organic compounds), a rather loose 'basket' of chemicals including many solvents, used in a wide range of industries. The 1991 Geneva Protocol of the LRTAP Convention commits a small number of northern countries to various levels of regulation of these compounds; however, few countries even have good inventories of these substances and monitoring systems are poorly developed (Levy, 1993: 100; Susskind, 1994: 167). While it has been relatively easy to mount campaigns around the theme of acid rain and to interest politicians and policy-makers, there has been slight interest in myriad other sources of air pollution. There has been little official or public engagement with pollution from hospital incinerators and, until recently, only a little more in the emissions from waste incinerators (Connett and Connett, 1994). To date, circumstances have tended not to promote so much public and political interest in the other types of air pollution.

Finally, there are two very important air pollution problems which are highly general. The first was described at the very start of this chapter, the pollution which is depleting the ozone layer. As Benedick, who led the US delegation in the international negotiations to combat this pollution noted:

> [such] issues exemplif[y] the interconnectedness of life and its natural support systems on Earth. Modern scientific discoveries are revealing that localized activities can have global consequences and that dangers can be slow and perhaps barely perceptible in their development, yet with long-term and virtually irreversible effects. The concept is not obvious: a perfume spray in Paris helps to destroy an invisible gas in the stratosphere and thereby contributes to skin cancer deaths and species extinction half a world away and several generations in the future. (1991: 3)

While CFCs in aerosols are the most well publicized problem here, it is important to realize that CFCs are also used in refrigerators, freezers and similar heat-regulating appliances and as gases for blowing foams (such as the bubble-filled plastics used for lightweight containers and for insulating material). Other chemically-related compounds can exhibit similar 'ozone-eating' characteristics, including the smothering gases in certain kinds of fire extinguishers (halons) and some solvents in common use in such products as dry-cleaning kits and typing-correction fluids.

As Benedick points out, these ozone-destroying chemicals demonstrate the hazards of transnational pollution terrifyingly well since they tend to have their chemical impact thousands of kilometres away from the place they were released (climatic factors concentrate their activity around the poles) and because they allow solar radiation to harm people, animals and plantlife across the other side of the planet. These chemicals exert their effects for decades. They are globally inescapable. But, as we shall see in the next two chapters, the response to this global problem was in fact far from uniform across the globe. While environmental groups were campaigning for the removal of CFCs from aerosols in Britain late in the 1980s, they had been banned from most aerosol products in the USA in 1978, almost ten years earlier. Such a disparity over policy towards an apparently global threat between policy-makers in leading areas of the industrial world must cause us to question any idea that global threats inevitably or automatically give rise to transnationally unified responses.

The final example to be discussed here is equally well known and every bit as qualified to be called global. It is the problem of global warming or the enhanced greenhouse effect. Despite the fluctuations of the seasons and even despite the occasional growth of massive ice sheets covering the northernmost and southernmost lands, the average temperature of the earth has remained very stable for the last million years (Ross, 1991: 85). From the hottest to the coldest periods, the overall average temperature change has been around 5° centigrade (9° Fahrenheit). When one considers that this is less than temperature changes common in one's garden, or even in many houses, just in a day, this long-term stability seems remarkable. The Earth's warmth is largely due to the heat arriving from the Sun. This heats the Earth and the Moon alike. But the Earth is conspicuously warmer than the Moon (by about 33° centigrade on average) and this difference is attributable to the greenhouse properties of the atmosphere (Ross, 1991: 77). In a rough way, we can say that the atmosphere acts like the panes of glass in a greenhouse, letting heat in but slowing down its escape.[1] With no atmosphere, the Moon experiences no greenhouse warming.

Some gases in the atmosphere are better at performing this insulating role than others. For example, nitrogen – the gas which is much the commonest in the atmosphere – is a poor insulator. By contrast, methane and carbon dioxide are effective insulators. The more insulators there are, the warmer the Earth's surface and the immediate surrounding atmosphere would become. The current anxiety is that since the insulating gases are present in the atmosphere in extremely low concentrations, human activities which cause more of these gases (the burning of fuels to produce carbon dioxide, or decay from waste tips and leaks from gas fields leading to increases in methane) could alter the temperature balance. Nitrous oxide, a gas released by agricultural practices, notably those using nitrogen fertilizers, and the various CFCs and halons are also effective greenhouse gases. Relatively small quantities of this atmospheric pollution could raise the global temperature to unprecedented levels, taking it outside of the temperature band within which the Earth has been confined since prehistoric times.

This is an unusual form of pollution since we are not worried about the toxic nature of the gases; indeed both methane and carbon dioxide are natural ingredients of the atmosphere and would not be directly harmful unless their concentrations were multiplied many times over. We are not worried about breathing them in or about immediate health effects. Rather, we are worried about a long-term consequence of the gases' release: the concern is that global warming would be extremely disruptive, possibly catastrophic. For example, a rise in world temperatures would lead to expanding deserts, to probable loss of wildlife as temperature bands on the earth's surface shifted (forests for example cannot easily 'migrate'), a corresponding disruption to agriculture and food supply and, because the overall temperature is rising, a melting of ice sheets and an expansion of the water in the seas. Resulting changes in sea levels would lead to flooding, particularly of low-lying countries without sea defences and of port cities which, by their very nature, are seldom far above current sea level.

This form of pollution stands out not just because of the unusual threat it poses, but also because it is almost thoroughly global. Because of air currents, the $CO_2$ produced in one place can affect the temperature virtually anywhere on the globe. Unlike a waste dump or a chemicals spill, the threat is not localized, but very highly dispersed. Furthermore, the uncertainty about the exact impact of global warming means that no country or group can be sure of the impact on them. A little warming might produce benefits for a few areas, with warmer summers and milder winters in Canada for example. But the difficulties of climate prediction mean that no one knows with any degree of certainty what the impact in their area will be, though flood prone countries such as the Netherlands and Bangladesh must see themselves as in the first line of likely victims.

Finally in this section it should be emphasized that both these major global air pollution problems have intensified in recent years. While, as will be seen in Chapter 4, there is now an international treaty designed to cut ozone-depleting pollution, the amount of pollution already in the atmosphere will continue to destroy ozone for decades to come. World carbon dioxide emissions are virtually bound to rise as industrialization proceeds, so that global totals are likely to increase whatever the countries of the North do and, so far, their progress on limiting greenhouse gas emissions has been meagre (see Susskind, 1994: 174). The situation is similar with regard to methane and nitrous oxide too; human production of these gases tends to grow in line with mounting waste disposal, increases in land committed to agriculture and livestock keeping, and the growth in fertilizer use. Bizarrely, the 'greenhouse' gains resulting from eventual reductions in CFC pollution may be offset by the fact that atmospheric ozone itself tends to promote global warming. Equally ironically, it is suggested that acid pollution in the air may diminish incoming solar radiation, so that $SO_2$ may be acting as an anti-greenhouse agent. Any improvements in acid regulation may thus exacerbate global warming. All the same, no matter how complicated the atmospheric chemistry finally turns out to be, it is clear that these two examples both indicate that international solutions and policies are needed if global pollution problems are to be tackled.

*Radiation and Associated Pollution*

Although an overview of the three media into which pollution can enter would appear to be exhaustive, there are in fact significant types of pollution which fall outside this classification. The first and most notorious of these is radiation, the collective term for particles and energy released by radioactive materials. Since the discovery of radioactivity at the end of the nineteenth century, radioactive substances have been used more and more, predominantly but by no means exclusively in the North. These materials have been employed in nuclear weapons, in nuclear power, in X-raying and other diagnostic techniques, in radiation treatment and in numerous other uses. As is well known, radioactive materials are potentially very harmful. High doses of radiation can kill by attacking the central nervous system or bone marrow; radiation can also promote cancers and genetic defects and cause other more diffuse ill health. The threat from radioactive material is greatly increased if the material is ingested, for example by eating contaminated food or by breathing in minute dust-borne radioactive particles. Working from inside the body, low-energy radiation which would not ordinarily penetrate the skin can harm major body organs.

Pollution of this kind is alarming both because of the invisible yet frightening threat it poses and because the danger is hard to guard against. Gamma radiation can penetrate buildings while alpha radiation-emitting substances can occur in the air we breathe or in food and water. The pollution risk is generally higher around nuclear installations (in the mid-1990s there are reckoned to be some 440 nuclear power stations in operation world-wide (*New York Times*, 14 March 1995: C11)), but it can be much more widely spread. As the explosion at the Chernobyl nuclear power plant in the Ukraine in 1986 showed, the risk of contamination from nuclear accidents extends across nations and continents. Similarly, pollution from nuclear testing has been spread around the atmosphere for decades.

Much of the world's uranium is mined in countries of the South, often from low-grade ores. This means that there is a vast residue of mine 'tailings' left behind, waste material which inevitably has some radioactive contamination. Thus, the production of fuel for French or Swedish or British nuclear power gives rise to radioactive pollutants elsewhere on the globe. Furthermore, after energy has been generated the nuclear industry is left with large quantities of contaminated waste, and as the citizens of Northern countries show themselves increasingly reluctant to have it disposed of near them, there has been the prospect of Northern countries trying to find other geographical outlets for it. Among Northern countries, Britain is currently unusual in offering a 'reprocessing' service for other countries' nuclear waste at THORP (the thermal oxide reprocessing plant), located at Sellafield. The extremely costly plant was opened, despite extensive objections and protests, in the hope that it could provide a commercially profitable way of dealing with waste. Before any reprocessing was undertaken, agreements had been signed with Japanese and German nuclear agencies. Thus, Japanese waste is transported almost half the way round the globe for treatment at THORP, treatment which is bound to cause some pollution to the surrounding area and to the Irish Sea. In this case therefore, the Japanese nuclear industry will release some radiation at plants in Japan (no plants can be run without emitting some radioactive pollution, even if it is believed to be medically harmless). But it will also cause some radioactive contamination at the source of the fuel and some more, affecting Britain and the Irish Sea, during reprocessing. Similar reasoning applies to the case of the reprocessing arrangements between Japan and the French nuclear industry.

The globalizing aspects of the nuclear business are also shown by the fact that, as the industry has fallen out of public favour in the North, new 'promising' locations for nuclear power generation have been found in the South and in the formerly-communist countries of Eastern Europe. The manufacturers of nuclear power stations have been extremely active in promoting their product in South-East Asia, in Hungary and in other Eastern European countries with a heritage of nuclear power. New installations arising from these promotional activities will produce their own waste disposal problems within the next few years.

Lastly, it is often said – and quite correctly – that there is a level of naturally occurring 'background' radiation. Life on earth has evolved to withstand some radiation. But the sheer growth of human interest in radioactive materials in the last hundred years has effectively increased that 'natural' level. By mining and grinding radioactive ores, for example, we add to the background levels. This too can be seen to be part of international, indeed literally global pollution.

*Polluted Foodstuffs and Genetic Pollution*

A second additional pollution hazard comes about through the pollution of foodstuffs. Of course, this may be a consequence of other forms of pollution. Plants which are fed with contaminated water, for instance, may themselves come to be contaminated. But there are specific cases which cannot easily be accommodated within the classification developed earlier on.

A graphic example is provided by the case of the cattle disease bovine spongiform encephalopathy (BSE). Otherwise known as 'mad cow disease', BSE is a disease of the cow's central nervous system which was first identified in 1985; to date it has chiefly affected herds in Britain and Ireland. It is believed to be closely related to the degenerative disease, scrapie, which has been found in sheep for at least two hundred years. The key point is that the cattle disease is believed to have originated when scrapie-infected sheep meat was used to make a high-protein cattle feed. Cattle became contaminated by consuming a food which was far removed from their normal diet – indeed, one could reasonably call it extremely unnatural. The danger which commentators now fear is that the disease, having leaped from one species to another through ingestion, could pass to beef-eating humans. Since the BSE scare first became publicized at the end of the 1980s, measures have been taken to stop cows being fed such material and regulations introduced to stop possibly infected cattle material (their brains and spinal cord essentially) from entering the human food chain; miscellaneous cow-meat pieces were formerly used in meat pies and other convenience foods.

Although this example stands out as particularly alarming, it is not the only example of food pollution. Great public anxiety was stimulated in the USA in 1989 around a chemical known as Alar, a plant growth regulator used on apples and other fruit. Evidence suggested, though there was doubt about how definitive the evidence was, that Alar could cause cancer especially in children. The celebrated actor Meryl Streep was closely associated with publicizing these possible risks. I have already mentioned the possibility that agricultural chemicals can enter the water supply; since insecticides are designed to kill certain animals there is clearly a danger that they will harm broader communities of creatures. Early work on long-lasting pest-control chemicals in fact indicated that they could accumulate biologically through the foodchain. A hawk which ate lots of birds which had eaten lots of contaminated insects could get a lethal dose of such toxins. But the Alar case was different. This was not a roundabout threat caused by pollution of the environment, but the danger of directly ingesting a deadly substance which had been deliberately spread on foodcrops. Since agrochemicals are now manufactured for a world market and extensively traded internationally, food pollution too must now be regarded as a global risk.

There is one final twist to this type of pollution threat. Since the prosperous North imports a lot of exotic fruit (mangoes, passion fruit, even out-of-season strawberries) as well as meat and vegetables from the South, the environmentally aware Northern citizen has to worry about agricultural practices not only at home but in the countries where these crops are grown. One may be able to regulate the chemicals in use on the farms of the North but it is far harder to regulate the South where Northern inspection agencies cannot oversee the actions of growers, whether they are indigenous farmers or plantation managers for Northern transnationals. As we shall see later on, Susan George (1992) speaks of this kind of 'feedback' from practices in the South as the 'boomerang phenomenon' since Northern countries may find that hazardous material exported to the South returns to them on their food.

We are, as the saying has it, what we eat. We build our bodies out of the molecules we put into them as food. Ingestion is thus a very direct way in which people can suffer from pollution and it too is an international issue since agricultural production is itself a highly international business.

A third and increasingly important alternative form of pollution can be referred to as genetic pollution. By that I mean that it is a contamination of natural genetic resources. Three quick examples will illustrate what is at stake here. First, consider the case of ornamental ducks. Down the years people have taken colourful ducks from their native areas and brought them to ponds and gardens from where – inevitably – they escape. In the early 1990s, there was a case where introduced American drakes were arriving early on the Spanish nesting sites of a closely related European duck and striking up relationships with all the females before the natural males had begun to swing into action.[2] The genetic stock is in danger of unnatural, unplanned change. A similar example concerns farmed salmon. Such salmon have not faced natural selection to ensure that they are good survivors; indeed they have in all likelihood been humanly selected for quite different attributes such as rapid weight gain and tolerance of over-crowding. When they escape, which they may do in relatively large numbers through spills and leaks, they interbreed with river salmon causing an upset to natural selection. The qualities of the natural salmon, qualities which have ensured their survival for thousands of years, may thus be lost.

The final example of genetic pollution is the starkest; it deals with genetically engineered organisms. There is currently great commercial pressure for the development of genetic engineering, the technology which allows the molecular building blocks of life to be manipulated and 'customized' (see Goodman and Redclift, 1991: 167–200). For example, it may be possible to take the genetic elements which code for disease resistance in certain plants and introduce those elements into foodcrops, so that the need for pesticides could be reduced. Plants, viruses, bacteria or animals which have been treated in this way are referred to as 'GMOs', genetically modified organisms. The companies producing these GMOs clearly want permission to have them used widely, which implies that they will escape the exhaustive control exercised in laboratory conditions. Engineered viruses will move around with the creatures they occupy. Engineered bacteria cannot easily be both widely used and closely contained. There will inevitably be some risk of genetic pollution and in this case it will be pollution by genetic material unprecedented in nature.

To conclude this whole section on the types of pollution it is worth stressing four general points. First, on a world-wide scale, pollution problems are increasing. As economic growth continues and spreads, more of the planet experiences more pollution, spread more widely. However, and this is the second point, not all forms of pollution are increasing. Several pollutants are being successfully regulated in the West (notably acid gases) – though the West's reductions are usually offset by increases elsewhere – and some (notably marine oil pollution and CFCs) are being tackled internationally. Third, some forms of pollution appear to be inherently global (greenhouse gas pollution for example) while most other 'global' problems are rendered global by the effects of international trade and the world-wide spread of industrialization. Finally, the processes by which pollution is spread are diverse. It can be spread by wind or ocean currents, by deliberate export, through chemicals sprayed on a field, by a decision to relocate a factory or by the release of a bacterium.

### Defining Pollution

At this stage, someone might reasonably argue that I have been a little too easy on myself. Although I have discussed many forms of pollution which arise in the modern world and tried to suggest how they each have a global reach, one might still say that I have not tackled head-on the question of what pollution is. At an everyday level this is not usually a controversial or especially complex issue. Most people would probably share ideas about what substances are polluting. But maybe I have chosen cases of pollution which tend to confirm my general argument. Accordingly, it is worth taking a minor detour to look at the definitional question, which is of interest in its own right and a practical matter for at least the following three reasons.

First, it is often hard to decide exactly which substances should be viewed as pollutants. While it might initially seem tempting to suggest that all pollution must stem from non-natural substances, a definition based on that idea would not stand up. Human and domestic animal sewage is perfectly natural but in many societies it causes a pollution problem. Equally, cattle naturally discharge methane gas. As cow numbers have increased, this has come to make a considerable contribution to the greenhouse effect, so much so that New Zealand scientists have apparently introduced anti-flatulence tablets for the nation's cattle (*The Guardian*, 3 June 1993: 12). And other natural phenomena, notably volcanic eruptions, produce toxic and environmentally damaging gases which, when produced by human processes, are regarded as pollutants. Conversely, some substances which would not occur in nature unless they had been produced by people (such as rare and highly reactive metals) break down or recombine into naturally occurring substances and are thus not necessarily a pollution problem. The complementary argument is also heard, to the effect that other human-made substances, such as some plastics, are so inert that they pose no threat of contamination to the natural world.

In the case of some pollutants it is also extremely difficult to sort out the 'human' from the 'natural' element. We have already encountered this problem in relation to the 'natural' background radiation level. It is problematic to determine what level should be taken as the natural baseline. Similarly, there appears to be a growing world-wide problem caused by blooms of toxic phytoplankton, microscopic marine plants which can poison fish and contaminate shellfish. According to the *New York Times*, huge blooms of these plankton 'have been recorded for centuries, but scientists say they are now increasing rapidly' (6 March 1995: A2). In any particular case, it is impossible to say whether the bloom is natural or humanly-induced; in either case it carries a pollution risk to marine life.

Second, some substances are very subtle pollutants and it is hard to know whether they are hazardous or not. Often, complex scientific investigations are needed to try to determine whether substances are dangerous and these scientific tests may be inconclusive or controversial. The membership of the category 'pollutants' is thus not cut-and-dried. For example, it took many years before scientists realized how CFCs could be a dangerous form of pollution and years more to reach agreement about how serious the threat was. There may be other substances which we treat as perfectly innocuous which will turn out to be environmentally damaging in as-yet unanticipated ways.

Finally, in case this whole question about defining a pollutant seems 'academic', it is important to remember that the difficulties mentioned above will lead to problems with the legal definition of pollutants. And, in turn, this matters in a practical way because polluters and those accused of pollution will often try to use the law to protect themselves from attack and prosecution. Unless societies have procedures for identifying what substances count as pollution, it is impossible to outlaw or regulate them. This was a problem in the West African countries targeted by European and North American waste exporters in the late 1980s (see Yearley, 1992a: 35–7); in many cases the trade was initially legal precisely because the receiving countries – having no experience of certain toxic industrial chemicals – had no laws regulating their disposal.

In his recent study of pollution control policies, Weale has defined pollution as:

> the introduction into the environment of substances or emissions that either damage, or carry the risk of damaging, human health or well-being, the built environment or the natural environment. There is no implication in this definition that the substances involved stem purely from human sources. . . . The assumption is simply that emissions or substances introduced into the environment in quantities or concentrations greater than those that can be coped with by the cleansing and recycling capacity of nature constitute pollution. (1992: 3)

Helpful though such definitions are, it is clear that they do not solve all the practical problems, since elements of the definition such as damage to human 'well-being' are likely to be understood in a wide variety of ways. Even apparently factual components of the definition, such as 'the cleansing and recycling capacity of nature' may be open to conflicting interpretations as will be seen in Chapters 3 and 4. Furthermore, pressure groups, industries and governments spend a lot of energy trying to redraw the precise boundaries around 'pollution' in ways which favour their objectives, so – as with so much in the realm of the social sciences – we cannot assume that the definition is a static thing.

Accordingly, in my review of world-wide pollution issues I have tried to take a broad interpretation of the term. As I shall argue in the next two chapters, the question of defining pollution and other forms of environmental hazard is in fact one key component of processes in the globalization of environmental debates. It is as important to examine how the category of 'pollutant' comes to be constructed as it is to try to offer one's own definition of the problem.

## The Globe's Environmental Problems: Resource Depletion

While the threats from pollution are very widespread and serious they are not our only environmental problems, nor are they the only ones plausibly qualifying for 'global' status. The other major threat identified by environmentalists and planners is that we may run out of resources, particularly energy resources, certain minerals, soil and water. The two issues are linked, however. As resources become scarcer, poorer quality seams have to be mined, less and less accessible sources of energy are exploited and so on. Accordingly, the degree of pollution caused tends to rise. None the less the two issues are, in principle, distinct.

Of the resource issues, the one which generally causes most concern, is energy. This is because, unlike water or metals or building stones, conventional energy resources can only be used once. If steel is used to make a car, the metal (or at least most of it) will still be there when the car is traded-in a few years later. But the fuel which powered the car lasts only until it is burned; the energy is used up and cannot be recovered.

There are two particularly significant points about energy resources. The first is that the energy market is conspicuously global. All states in the contemporary world rely on fossil fuels (petrol, gas and coal) and the trade is world-wide. Frequently, tankers registered with one country collect oil from a second, deliver it for further treatment or for marketing in a third, and it is consumed in a fourth. It is therefore extremely common to talk of energy as a global issue. The second is that, in principle at least, politicians, business leaders and planners have been well aware for over two decades that world oil and gas reserves are limited and are likely to be exhausted in a few decades.

A variety of responses has been tried. One can attempt to get the most out of existing resources; reserves of petroleum can be made to last longer if oil is used more efficiently. Since oil resources are consumed chiefly for transport, for agriculture, and for heating/air conditioning[3] and power in homes and industry, a number of responses has been devised. Cars can be made more fuel-efficient, low speed limits can be imposed, motorists can be encouraged to share vehicles, or there can be incentives to switch to public transport. Similarly, power stations can be redesigned to run more efficiently or 'district heating' systems can be developed to use the surplus heated water from power stations to heat homes or offices (this is known as combined-heat-and-power – CHP). Although these options are well understood, they are little used. For example, Britain has next to no CHP capacity. In the USA, there are pressures for deregulation of the electricity supply market which will favour low-cost generation over energy-efficient but slightly dearer production. Speed limits in the USA, which were lowered in the 1970s to save on fuel, have nearly all been raised again. World car consumption is steadily rising and big traffic jams are now routine in many Third-World cities.

Alternatively, one can hope that new reserves will continue to be found. For the last twenty years or so – when dire predictions of fuel shortages have been common – new finds have repeatedly stretched the anticipated life of fossil fuel reserves. In the 1990s very large oil exploration and extraction programmes are underway off the coast of Vietnam and to the south of China. Further oil and gas is likely to be found in contested waters north of Brunei and around the uninhabited Spratly Islands, some or all of which are currently the subject of ownership claims by China, Taiwan, Vietnam, the Philippines, Malaysia and Brunei (*The Economist*, 29 April 1995: 41). New finds could extend the anticipated life of oil for a few years, maybe a decade or two. There may even be novel, unexploited forms of reserves which could further lengthen the life of petrochemicals. For example, at the American Association for the Advancement of Science conference in 1995 delegates discussed the potential of 'gas hydrate', a curious substance essentially consisting of methane trapped in ice, which can be found under permanently frozen soil and in certain locations under the sea bed. This methane-rich ice will actually burn and might be plentiful enough to meet US natural gas needs for decades (*New York Times*, 21 February 1995: C5). But however successful these alternatives are, they do not extend the life of oil and gas more than a few decades. In any case, with rapid economic growth in areas such as South-East Asia, world demand is likely to rise at least as fast as new finds.

Lastly, one can look at alternatives. For about three decades after the Second World War, the favoured 'alternative' among governments in the West and in the Soviet Bloc consisted of various options associated with nuclear power. Crudely expressed, there are three kinds of basis for generating power from nuclear reactions. There is simple fission, which uses the energy emitted from the radioactive decay of metallic uranium or associated substances (Patterson, 1976: 97–8). This is the principle on which virtually all the reactors in the world operate at the moment and the only basis for reactors producing electricity at anything approaching commercial levels. There is probably only enough uranium left to last another hundred years or less if it is used in simple fission reactors. Given that uranium is currently used to generate only a small minority of the world's electrical power, any large increases in the use of atomic generation facilities would mean that the uranium would run out much sooner.

A way of making the radioactive fuel last longer is to use so-called 'fast-breeder' reactor technology. These reactors take advantage of the fact that radioactive decay produces other substances which are themselves radio-active. Fast breeders effectively allow the nuclear reactions to accelerate, thus releasing more energy from the starting materials than regular fission. Since it recovers more energy for every initial unit of nuclear fuel (by allowing the reaction to continue, rather than arresting it, as in other fission reactors), fast-breeder technology would allow the same fuel reserves to last several times as long. But fast-breeder reactors have proved technically very demanding and extremely expensive. There has also been enormous public disquiet about this technology, not least because plutonium – a prime ingredient for building nuclear weapons – forms part of the fuel material. At present, plutonium is one of the waste products of nuclear reactors and poses formidable disposal problems. Fast breeders offer a route for burning up this plutonium. But many environmentalists and also lobbyists and politicians concerned with nuclear proliferation worry that the adoption of fast-breeder technologies would legitimate increased production of 'refined' plutonium in many countries of the world, giving rise to new risks from the spread of nuclear weapons.

The third kind of nuclear power operates on a significantly different basis. Rather than extracting energy from the breakdown of big atoms (of uranium, plutonium and so on), it aims to derive energy from fusing special atoms of hydrogen together into helium. Although the form of hydrogen required occurs very infrequently, there is so much hydrogen on Earth (the oceans are – of course – composed of hydrogen and oxygen) that fusion power could provide electricity for centuries. At present, nuclear fusion has only been achieved under controlled experimental conditions for extremely short periods. In any case, there is room for doubt that fusion stations would be viewed as significantly safer or prove any more economically viable than fast breeders.

Though nuclear power is an alternative to the use of fossil fuels, when environmentalists talk of 'alternative energy' they usually mean renewable sources of energy. While each unit of energy can only be used once, so that fossil and nuclear fuels must one day become exhausted, there are several ways of 'harvesting' power from renewable sources. In effect, these 'renewables' use the radiated energy of the Sun or the gravitational force of the Moon. The most well known examples are wind-powered generators, hydroelectric power stations, various devices, such as estuary barrages, which harvest tidal energy and 'biomass'. Biomass refers to systems of cultivating fast-growing crops for fuel, for example by coppicing willow. It is also possible to grow oil-bearing crops and even to use alcohol – for example from fermented sugar – as a fuel. In these cases, of course, land which could be used for food production has to be turned over to 'growing fuel'. However, with anything like current population levels (see below) there is no prospect of cultivating enough food at the same time as raising crops to replace even a small percentage of global fossil fuel consumption.

Also in this category are rather more 'hi-tech' alternatives including solar collectors (for example, arrays of mirrors which direct the Sun's rays to heat water to drive a turbine), various devices which exploit the capacity of biological cells to split water molecules forming flammable hydrogen gas, and solar cells which convert sunlight directly into electricity. According to various visionary schemes, future energy demand could be met by gantries of huge off-shore wind turbines, used to provide electricity to super-insulated houses, offices and factories, fitted with extremely energy-efficient equipment. Tropical countries kitted out with various solar collectors could export electricity (though here again the demand for land to site these collectors could conflict with agricultural needs; see Pimentel et al., 1994: 360).

Just as the world contains only a finite store of petroleum, natural gas and coal, there are limits to the amounts of mineral substances – metals, precious stones, building stone, sands and gravel and so on. In some cases, though, the amounts of these materials are so large as to make the problem an academic one. Sand, for example, is not scarce (though that is not to deny that the removal of sand from certain beaches can be a problem for the maintenance of local habitats). In any case, minerals can be recycled. Old ships can be disassembled and reworked into ploughshares or guns. The metals from batteries can be recovered and reused. Even old road surfacing can be recycled into new paths and roads.

Inevitably, there are practical limitations to this idea of recycling. Recycling or reuse is simplest when substances are easily separated and collected. Glass bottles or aluminium containers are good examples. Bottle tops, by contrast, readily get lost or caught up with general waste. No practical situation would ever allow 100 per cent recycling. In any case, recycling itself always consumes energy, even just for gathering, sorting and cleaning the materials. But, in a society that is not short of energy, very high rates of recycling can be anticipated.

In any event, to date the industrial world has proved itself very adept at substituting relatively plentiful substances for scarce ones. The price mechanism obviously lends a hand here by making scarce minerals more expensive and giving people an incentive to come up with substitutes. In a famous public wager between an environmental pessimist (Paul Ehrlich) and an economist (Julian Simon) who was optimistic about the inventiveness of free-market capitalism, the economist bet that no significant shortages would arise during the 1980s. Reflecting the view that shortages would drive up the prices of minerals, the bet actually took the form of a wager that the prices of a 'basket' of minerals would not rise through the 1980s. The economist figured that any shortages would be more than compensated by the discovery of new sources and the adoption of substitutes. The economist won the bet comprehensively (Yearley, 1992b: 129; see also Tierney, 1990).

In coming decades, the search for minerals is likely to spread more and more to the sea floors where biological and geological processes cause some minerals to become concentrated. But, despite these new sources and the potential recyclability of mineral substances, minerals are associated with broader international environmental problems. For one thing, mineral mining often causes destruction to habitats so that, for example, the landscape and habitats of Third-World countries are sacrificed to the need

Table 2.1  *The distribution of the world's water resources*

| Compartment | Volume of water (millions of cubic kilometres) | Percentage of global water |
|---|---|---|
| oceans | 1350 | 97.9 |
| lakes and rivers | 0.2 | 0.01 |
| ice | 29 | 2.1 |
| organic matter | 0.00006 | – |
| atmosphere | 0.013 | – |
| Total (approx.) | 1379 | |

*Source*: derived from Silvertown (1990: 74).

for exports and the manufacturing needs of the West or of rapidly industrializing countries. Such instances cause particular indignation among environmentalists when the minerals are used for apparently 'frivolous' purposes, such as the whiteners in toothpastes or detergents. Additionally, because many of the substances used in manufacture – plastics in particular – are derived from petrochemicals, future shortages of oil are likely to raise demands for mineral substitutes. Furthermore, no matter how good we get at recycling, there are limits on the total quantity of each metal that is available in the world. Once, for example, all the nickel or molybdenum is in use there will be shortages, even with complete recycling (for illustrative figures, see Blunden, 1991a: 74).

A third kind of resource which is seldom thought about but which is of undoubted importance is water. Evidently, the world contains an awful lot of water. And there is a natural cycle: rain falls, runs off and through the land ultimately into the seas and evaporates to fall as fresh rain. Natural processes constantly deliver fresh water to land-bound humans. But, in many places, we have been consuming it faster than it is renewed. Frequently, human settlements draw on water from underground, artesian sources, sources which have accumulated over thousands of years but which are fed only slowly by rain. On average, we are using these up faster than they are being renewed.

As is indicated in Table 2.1, the 'water cycle' is believed to involve nearly 1380 million cubic kilometres of water. But nearly 98 per cent of this water is held at any one time in the oceans. The bulk of the rest is retained in ice. Much, much less than 1 per cent of the water in the ocean evaporates per year and, in any case, the great majority of that falls back into the oceans as rain. Thus, while water is plainly not scarce, the amount 'delivered' on to the land regions of the globe each year is very limited. It also varies greatly from region to region. As consumption, by industry and private citizens continues to grow, water shortages can be expected to intensify even though, at a global level, the earth is a very wet place.

Writing in *The Observer* recently, Lean has captured the significance of diminishing water resources:

All land-bound life has to share one ten-thousandth of the planet's water. Less than three per cent of the world's water is fresh, and more than three-quarters of that is frozen, mainly at the poles. Ninety eight per cent of the rest lies deep underground.

The tiny faction that remains should still, in theory, be more than enough. Every year about 27,000 cubic miles of rain fall on the continents, enough to submerge them under two and a half feet of water. But nearly two-thirds of it evaporates again, and two-thirds of what is left runs off in floods. Even the remaining 3,400 cubic miles of rainfall could still sustain more than double the world's present population – if only it would fall evenly where people live. But while Iceland gets enough rain every year to fill a small reservoir for each of its quarter of a million inhabitants, Kuwait, with seven times as many people, scarcely gets a single drop to share between all of them.

In all, 26 of the world's countries – including many of those in Africa and the Middle East – get less water than they need. Over the next 30 years another 40 nations are expected to join them, as their populations outstrip their rainfall. The number of people affected is expected to grow tenfold from the present 300 million to three billion – one-third of the projected population of the planet.

Money, of course, counts for even more than nature. Phoenix, Arizona, gets the same amount of rain as the dusty town of Lodwar in the far north of Kenya, yet its people use 20 times as much water. Immense sums have been spent on water in the western United States. Not a single drop of the great Colorado River – which carved the world's largest gorge at Arizona's Grand Canyon, and drains a fifth of all the once-wild West – now reaches the sea. It has all been dammed and used for cities and agriculture. (1993: 18)

Though nearly all the rivers in the west of the USA are diverted for human use, American agriculture and industry currently get by only by siphoning off underground supplies. As Lean goes on to note, the west of the United States owes its continued fertility to a 'vast and ancient underground sea', the Ogallala aquifer. This thousand-mile broad aquifer is reckoned to hold as much water as one of the Great Lakes. But, as Lean notes, 'this is fossil water, laid down ages ago, which cannot be quickly replenished'. The water pumped out each year far exceeds the rate of refilling, by 130 to 160 per cent according to Pimentel et al. (1994: 354). At present rates of use, these authors estimate, the water supply may only hold out for another forty years.

Elsewhere in the world, water shortages are made evident by conflicts between nations for access to water for agriculture, for industrial and domestic consumption, and for power-generation purposes. For example, if countries located upstream extract a great deal of water for irrigation, the supplies for nations at the mouth of the river suffer. In the historic fertile region of the Middle East around the Euphrates and Tigris rivers, Iraqis complain that water is extracted before they can feel the benefit. The use of water from the River Jordan is also contested. In Europe before the disintegration of the Eastern Bloc, there were Czechoslovak/Hungarian plans to divert the River Danube into a huge hydroelectric scheme. Hungary has now withdrawn from the scheme and has been at odds with the authorities in Slovakia over the future management of the river. According to Seager (1995: 20–1), nineteen present-day states receive over half their surface water flow from outside the country; examples range from Cambodia and Niger, through Uruguay and Romania to Luxembourg and the Netherlands.

Of course, disputes over river water are not only concerned with quantities. Water quality can also represent an international environmental problem, as was mentioned in the section on pollution earlier in the chapter, because when one nation's industry or agriculture pollutes it, that commonly decreases its value for countries further downstream. The majority of the world's major rivers do mark or cross international boundaries so that river pollution is routinely a multinational matter.

Drawing the threads of this section on resource depletion together, the first significant overall point to note is that in each case, it is common for analysts to talk about *global* amounts of each resource. Thus, we talk about how much water the world contains or how many years' oil and gas remain. Even the world's soil is discussed in these terms: Pimentel et al. assert that 'Soil erosion worldwide is about 30 tonnes per hectare per year. . . . Thus topsoil is being lost 20 to 40 times faster than it is being replaced' (1994: 353). For each of these resources, it has come to seem natural to talk about global reserves and potential global shortages. Yet – and this is the second overall point – though it is sometimes convenient to envisage a global amount of these things, in fact they are very unevenly dispersed around the globe. For example, while the world is currently estimated to have around 300 years' worth of coal at today's consumption rates (Reddish, 1991: 10), the coal is not evenly spread. Latin American countries have relatively meagre supplies while the USA sits on around fourteen times as much coal as all of Latin America combined. Of course, these estimates depend on calculations from 'proven reserves' and will not take into account new discoveries nor the matter of how likely mining operations are: there may be coal under Oxford but it is hard to imagine a policy of mining there. Other resources are also less easy to pin down than coal. Natural gas for example is mobile. If it is extracted from one end of a gas field, more tends to flow to that end. Thus Anglo-Dutch gas fields, for example, are not easily divisible into UK and Dutch components since the gas itself can switch allegiances. In some cases, this gives countries an incentive to extract it as soon as possible to prevent others beating them to it. Lastly, whatever way these various resources happen to be distributed, there are strong grounds for believing that they are limited and that current consumption patterns will take demand for several of these resources close to their limits within a small number of decades. In that sense, it is possible to envisage world-wide resource shortages.

### The Globe's Environmental Problems: 'Over-population'

A third major kind of environmental anxiety concerns the sheer size of the human population itself. For many politicians, particularly those from the

North, 'over-population' in underdeveloped countries is self-evidently a leading environmental problem. However, this topic is treated with considerable delicacy by many Northern non-governmental organizations (NGOs), even the ones who are most strident in denouncing other environmental harms, at least in part because the discussion can so quickly be interpreted in the light of North–South inequalities and, potentially, of racism.

There is wide – though by no means all-embracing – agreement that unless some means is found of limiting the world's human population, the environmental implications will soon be globally severe. In the mid-1990s the population stands at around 6000 million people. At present rates it is projected to double in four decades (Pimentel et al., 1994: 349). This total and the recent increases in world population growth which have produced it are without precedent, and though humans are outnumbered by other kinds of creatures (most notably insects and so on), people are coming to use up more and more of the biological production of the planet (Swanson, 1991: 187).

Were food production geared entirely to providing a minimum nutritious diet for everyone, it is more than likely that everybody could be fed. This abstract way of thinking carries certain flaws with it; for example, it is not clear at what rate we can go on producing even basic foodstuffs such as cereals since at the moment their cultivation depends on fertilizers manufactured from non-renewable chemicals. Future agricultural production may have to decline. But, assuming it did not fall, it is still doubtful that the earth could support double the present population no matter how farming was reorganized and whatever foreseeable agricultural innovations were employed. In any case, the total population logically cannot grow for ever. At some point, there has to be a limit. Once the argument has reached this stage it is common for some commentators, drawing analogies with responses to overcrowding in other mammal species, to claim that 'nature' will enforce the limit to population growth, even if we fail to, through disease and conflict (Pimentel et al., 1994: 364).

What is often omitted from this argument, however, is the acknowledgement that we will never have the chance to find out what that limit is because food and other resources are so unevenly divided. Already, around one-quarter of the world population is reckoned to be malnourished and this is because hundreds of millions of people are too poor to buy the food they need. Hence, where some see an overpopulation problem, others perceive an inequality problem.

Given these contrasting starting points, debates over world population can quickly become bogged down. Self-styled 'realists' from the Northern political communities and 'establishment' environmentalists tend to argue that, since social inequalities are not going to be removed in the near future, we have to behave as though population were a self-contained environmental problem. On this view, the governments of the world need to devise policies for reducing population growth and, ultimately, to stabilize population. Favoured policies include family planning advice and the provision of contraceptives, perhaps assisted by incentives such as tax relief for parents who maintain a small family size.

The contrary argument is that population is not *of itself* an environmental problem. The 'real' environmental harm associated with human populations is related both to their size and the amount they consume. Advocates of this position point out that the (approximately) 25 per cent of the world's people in the industrialized North consume around 80 per cent of energy and other resources, leaving the poorest 75 per cent with only a fifth of environmentally-harmful consumption. By this (admittedly rough) calculation, the average Northern citizen is twelve times as environmentally damaging as the average person from the South. Spokespersons from the Third World thus argue that population reduction programmes are, in effect, a ploy by the North to maintain the prodigal lifestyles of its citizens, required – in turn – by its economies. If, so the argument goes, the North limited its average impact to that of the typical Southern individual, the total world impact would fall by over 70 per cent. Accordingly, if the North was serious about wanting to limit the environmental harm caused by human beings it would move to limit consumption before limiting population since that is where real reductions in pollution and resource depletion can be achieved.

This critical line of reasoning is often complemented by a further argument, namely that families in underdeveloped countries commonly have large numbers of children for good, practical reasons. Among these reasons are the importance of offspring for work on the family farm or in the family business and the need for numerous children to bear the costs of caring for parents, in the absence of welfare, once they become elderly. Seen from this perspective, a focus on family planning and on the provision of contraceptives appears misguided since the policy assumes that families want and would benefit from small families. If, however, they do not, if they actually desire large families, then officially sponsored family planning programmes risk being oppressive.

As well as implying that official programmes may be the wrong way to limit population, this point of view does have a positive policy recommendation. Its view is that population stabilization follows from economic growth. Once parents are more confident about their economic prospects and about their long-term security they will opt for smaller family sizes. This, after all, is what appears to have happened in the West, where family size fell some time after industrialization. If one accepts this line of reasoning, the appropriate policy response to 'over-population' is to devise trade policies and forms of technical and economic assistance which stimulate economic growth in the Third World.

Lastly on this point, it is difficult to disentangle the North's concerns about global population levels from particular Northern countries' worries about immigration. The nations of the European Union have a special interest in population growth in North Africa while the USA famously faces problems over immigrants from Central America. The very idea that countries should take responsibility for their own population levels implies that each country has a fixed population. Taken in a suspicious frame of mind, this looks like arguing that, rather than permit immigration into the prosperous North, the USA and the EU want underdeveloped countries to take care of their own peoples. The obvious delicacy of these questions has meant that many environmentalist and development NGOs in the North have trodden very carefully around the population issue (see Taylor, 1992). While Green Parties have often called for a planned reduction in populations even within Northern countries, NGOs – conscious of arguments about underdevelopment and exploitation, and anxious not to advocate policies which might impede self-development in the Third World – have been rather less vocal (Yearley, 1996).

Before taking these opposing arguments further, it is worth describing several other factors which have influenced the population argument. First, these contested positions have been elaborated in a context which is already morally and religiously charged. Given that many Southern countries are Roman Catholic or have sizeable Roman Catholic populations (in effect Central and Southern America, the Philippines, many former French, Belgian, Spanish and Portguese colonies) and that the Hierarchy opposes 'artificial' birth control, some governments have found it hard to make a formal commitment to family planning using modern contraceptives. Furthermore, by implying that contraceptive abortion is commonly associated with family planning programmes, the Catholic Hierarchy has attempted to broaden the appeal of its argument, for example to Islamic leaders and to the strong anti-abortion lobby in the USA. In this way, leftist critics of population control policies (who want a redistribution of wealth rather than limits on population size) have sometimes found themselves making common cause with right-leaning religious authorities.

As well as the apparently high-minded complications posed by religious authorities, there are more down to earth reasons for governments to oppose family planning, at least for their own countries. In the past fifteen years, as mentioned in Chapter 1, all round the world there have been wars and threats of war over national boundaries – around Belize in Central America, between Peru and Ecuador, around Sierra Leone and Liberia, in the former Yugoslavia, within Iraq, over Israel and Palestine, and within the former Soviet Union. For such wars countries need armies, and for armies they need fit young soldiers. If you have an ethnic enemy, no doubt you feel strongly that their population should be controlled, but you may be inclined to make an exception for your own. This point throws into high relief a more general issue, which is that talk of governments combining to limit world population implies that they may all be willing to play their part. In practice, countries may have rather different policy objectives in mind when thinking about the numbers of their own citizens, than when they are contemplating the abstract issue of the 'right' size for the global population.

Within approximately the past decade a fresh set of arguments about population control and about the supposed wishes of Third-World parents have come to be aired publicly, championed as much by the women's movement as by environmentalists or those concerned with development in general. According to this newly voiced view, the supposed wishes for large families were often principally the wishes of males. Similarly, it has been suggested that conventional family planning programmes and advice were poorly directed towards women, even though it is women who bear most of the physical consequences of large family size and women who 'manage' family contraceptive practices. Where previous discourses about family planning seemed to order Third-World peoples to change their reproductive behaviour for the sake of the globe, this more recent discourse offers to empower women to make their own reproductive choices (see Harrison, 1992). Accordingly, at the 1994 UN population summit in Cairo the assumed interest of women was taken as being closer to that of establishment environmentalists than the radical Third-World critique had tended to be. This brought about the ironic situation in which Jonathon Porritt, former director of Friends of the Earth in London and a major influence on the British Green Party for many years, could write a newspaper article calling on UK environmental NGOs to be less timid about the population issue (Porritt, 1994). At the time of the Cairo conference, he called on them to approach the Conservative minister for Overseas Development (Baroness Chalker), a woman who – he suggested – was open to arguments about the need to work through the empowerment of women in the Third World. He felt NGOs should be more strident in calling for internationally agreed policies to cut the global rate of population growth.

I shall return to the many arguments around population in the following chapters. For the moment the key point is that, just as with estimations of 'global' coal or oil reserves, there are serious difficulties in talking about the global population problem. At the simplest level, many would agree that there are too many humans on the globe and that steps ought to be taken to limit (and probably reverse) future growth trends. In this sense, population is a global issue. But, even assuming that the general policy could be agreed, this leaves unresolved the question of how limits should be globally distributed. It also sidesteps the question of deciding whether population per se or something more like per capita environmental harm ought to be the measure in question.

## The Globe's Environmental Problems: Loss of Biodiversity

For many years, this fourth kind of environmental problem facing the globe was symbolized in Europe and the United States by the panda; it was widely realized in the North that certain high-profile species were in danger of extinction. Once again, it should be recognized that this environmental problem is not fully separable from other kinds of ecological degradation.

Animals and plants are affected by pollution, by the fouling of rivers and seas and by contaminated land. But the majority of species loss, in particular among the high-profile animals (the 'charismatic megafauna' as they are usually termed by environmental commentators), comes from another source. At first these animals suffered through hunting; now the threat comes more often simply from habitat loss; humans chop down the trees or tarmac over the land where the species live. The fact that elephants and rhino are still being killed for their tusks and horns indicates that hunting remains a threat to some species too.

Most animals and plants have evolved to cope with very specific surroundings. Their numbers decline when their source of food is damaged, when their migratory routes are disrupted or their breeding patterns are disturbed. Particularly in the West, where indigenous wildlife has been greatly reduced since the onset of industrialization, global nature conservation activities have proved a popular success. Nature programmes on television have captured huge audiences and fund-raising activities to save the charismatic creatures – the elephant or panda or tiger – have regularly been high earners. All the while, and despite this concern for overseas wildlife, intensive agricultural practices and the spread of suburban dwellings have been having a serious adverse effect on the remaining (relatively unglamorous) indigenous wildlife in the West over the last three decades.

This threat to wildlife can be seen as a candidate global environmental issue in at least two senses. First, the charismatic megafauna have come to stand for humanity's common duty to ensure the survival of other beings, particularly majestic or otherwise impressive creatures. In this case it is clear that many individual species are not of themselves an international issue. Europe, for instance, is not directly affected by threats to the rhino or to sloths since, in the natural state, these are not European creatures. None the less, the argument seems to have been widely accepted – not least at an emotional level – that in some sense the world as a whole would be a poorer place without elephants and lions, without blue whales and pandas. No matter that people in Britain, say, have pretty well eliminated all the large fauna apart from farm animals and selected hunt-quarry species, hundreds of thousands of people will give money and lend weight to pressure groups which try to affect international policies in this area.

The second and more roundabout way in which this issue has become globalized is through the development of a language for talking about the world-wide loss of species. The key term here is biological diversity or 'biodiversity'. By using the term biodiversity we can generalize concerns about the loss of species in many different localities up to a global level. Biodiversity refers to the amount of genetic diversity existing on the planet: how many insects there are, how many types of parrot, how many varieties of maize and so on. Since all life is, at a fundamental level, based on variations on the same genetic materials (DNA), we can talk about species loss as a net reduction in the amount of the world's natural genetic variation. The widespread official recognition of this terminology was reflected in the fact that a Biodiversity Convention was signed by representatives of over a hundred and fifty nations at the Earth Summit in 1992 (see Birnie and Boyle, 1992: 483–6; Susskind, 1994: 172).

Through modern agricultural practices and through the destruction of habitats, humans are rapidly decreasing this biodiversity. Tens of thousands of species (including plants and insects) are reckoned to be lost per year (Pimentel et al., 1994: 355). Over the millennia, natural selection has given rise to a spectacular number of variations in the molecular basis of life. In the second half of the twentieth century humans have done a great deal to reduce this variety. Such actions may well rob humans themselves of the biological riches manifested in these disappearing species – for example, it is often suggested that the loss of rainforest plants may deprive us of as-yet-undiscovered medicines or that vanishing varieties of wheat may contain genes which would benefit agriculture in years to come. Furthermore, we may not only be, so to speak, killing off the genetic geese before they lay their golden eggs, but also endangering the adaptive capacity of large sections of the natural world itself by, for example, drastically reducing the number of types of grass which flourish or by limiting the biological variability in the primates which remain.

When we think about species loss and threats to biodiversity, there is a tendency to focus on birds and terrestrial creatures, with whales and dolphins as the outstanding exception. However, the international fishing industry turns out to be a highly significant area for disputes over global biological resources. Up until the late 1970s the seas beyond a narrow (usually three-nautical-mile) limit from the coasts were regarded as a common resource. No state or international body had particular jurisdiction; consequently the fishing fleets of the world went wherever the pickings were rich. Occasionally catches fell, but the fleets moved off elsewhere and were generally able to find new fish stocks. In principle it was recognized that there was a danger of over-fishing but as long as overall catches were sufficient little attention was paid to this potential problem. This situation was very favourable to countries with distant-water fishing fleets, whether privately owned (as with Japan, Norway and the USA) or state-supported (as with the then Soviet Union and East European countries). Boats roamed the world, fishing the rich grounds off distant coasts. In many cases, as with south-west Africa, the coastal countries were in no position to benefit from this activity at all, having only small-scale fishing equipment and no rights over the fish taken. Gradually, through the 1960s and 1970s the size and sophistication of these fleets – together with some newly-emèrging fleets, for example in Peru and Thailand – rendered the industry global. As Peterson notes, 'With sometimes the Soviets and sometimes the Japanese in the lead, distant-water fleets were pushing into new areas of the Pacific, the Indian Ocean, and the South Atlantic by the mid-1970s' (1993: 259).

Such a global spread meant that it was no longer possible to respond to shortages by moving on; there was nowhere left to move on to. The danger of over-fishing then became acute. There were large, technically advanced fleets working all over the oceans, with new countries eager to bring their boats into the business. In any case, fishing is difficult to supervise. There was a risk that too many adult fish would be taken to allow population sizes to be maintained or even that smaller, younger fish would be caught with the result that there would be many fewer 'recruits' into the pool of adults. Attempts at voluntary restriction usually failed because it was too tempting and too easy to cheat. And if you feared that others were cheating, it became 'rational' for you to cheat as well.

The pressures were moderated to some extent after 1977 when 200-nautical mile Exclusive Economic Zones were introduced (Peterson, 1993: 263–4). These gave countries legal jurisdiction over much, much greater areas of their coastal waters. According to Peterson this effectively allocated nine-tenths of all the fishing for edible species to territorial waters, since these fish by and large live on and above the nutrient-rich continental shelves rather than in the deep ocean. It did not, however, reduce the issue of fishery management to a national level. There were two reasons for this. First, countries allowed other nations' fishing fleets into their waters to fish under licence; the arrangements here were similar to other international commercial deals. Second, even if nine out of ten edible fish were living within the coastal regions, that did not mean that these fish spent all of their lives in the coastal region of one particular nation or that the fish did not spend a fraction of their lives in international waters. In the first case, some fish might be Mexican one day and American the next. Heavy fishing in, say, the United States' waters during the fishes' visit could impact seriously on Mexico's reserves. Similarly, 'Peruvian' fish which swam outside the 200-mile limit and were systematically fished by Japanese boats could diminish Peru's expected reserves. If the fish happen to spend their whole lives in your exclusive economic zone then you may have an economic interest in managing the stocks in a sustainable fashion. If, however, they only visit your waters on occasional 'outings' from other nations' zones, then an interest in far-sighted management is much less clear.

As if these issues were not already complicated enough, the difficulty of gaining authoritative knowledge about fish makes the question harder still. Fish are difficult to observe and the people who have the most ready access to data about them, trawler crews, have vested interests which might incline them to withhold information or present imperfect data. More complex still, though recorded decline in fish numbers may indicate over-fishing and thus the need for long-term reform of the industry, such figures may simply reflect a natural variation in population size, in which case the industry does not need to be scaled down but has only to observe a temporary reduction in the size of catches. Attempts at modelling fish populations were also affected by uncertainty about the effects of interspecies interaction. Fishing for one species might deplete its numbers, releasing more food for a competitor and thus boost the competitor's numbers and so on. It was therefore not easy to draw decisive conclusions about the practical implications of the existing data on fish stocks.

In summary, species loss can be seen as a global matter in several senses. First, some commercially important species – most conspicuously fish – are hunted on a global scale, and poorly-regulated competition has tended to lead to serious declines in their populations. Second, some endangered species – such as the panda and the elephant – have acquired a global significance. They somehow embody the frailty and the wonder of nature and have become the focus for attempts at nature conservation. Finally, through the concept of biodiversity, it has recently become topical to talk of the overall loss of biological richness of the planet as a whole. Though these are different senses in which threats to species have come to be interpreted as problems of the global environment, they can readily be related to other global environmental problems. For example, the climate change which is anticipated from additional greenhouse warming is likely to shift climate bands on the Earth, changing the distribution of habitat-types. It is anticipated that this will cause further losses in biodiversity since vegetation, especially forest, is unlikely to be able to migrate as fast as the climate shifts and because the creatures which live in the trees will lose their habitats too. Finally, since trees constitute one major way in which carbon dioxide is taken out of the atmosphere (all plants are built of carbon 'manufactured' from carbon dioxide gas), the conservation of tropical forests has often been argued for on the grounds that it would help counter greenhouse warming. In effect, tropical countries are being asked to conserve their natural resources for the good of the international community. Negotiation of this issue has proved complicated, as will be seen in the next two chapters.

**Conclusions**

The evidence reviewed in this chapter gives us good grounds for regarding environmental problems as increasingly globalized. Modern pollution is very literally, in Robertson's terms, 'compressing' the world as, for instance, nations are obliged to worry about what their neighbours are doing about air pollution and emission control. The diminution of resources and the loss of species are making people aware that there are global limits to the things and the creatures which they count on. To some extent at least, these considerations are giving citizens, governments and corporations a sense that there are real global ties and, perhaps, in principle at least a global identity for the occupants of spaceship Earth. In this chapter we have reviewed how pollution ties the lifestyles and policies of people in one part of the globe to the quality of life of their global neighbours. We have seen also how trade and investment join with wind and air currents and other natural processes in determining the distribution of pollution and ecological problems across the globe. Such global ties continue to be intensified.

Yet while pollution, resource depletion, species loss and population hazards illustrate global connections and seem to offer the possibility for people to embrace a global identity, these problems also indicate that global relations are characterized by inequality and – often – by double standards. Waste dumping continues, a minority of the world's population continues to cause the majority of many forms of air pollution, and fish stocks are hunted almost to depletion in many parts of the world, primarily by the trawling fleets of the North and the former Soviet Bloc. Claims about over-population are met with counter-claims about the North's over-consumption. Furthermore, some forms of pollution reduction in the North are more than offset by the consequences of industrialization in the South. In all, the image of a fragile globe, with limited resources, on which we all depend has not yet reversed the tendency to pollute and despoil that globe. 'Global' hazards are not necessarily unifying.

As this review has indicated, environmental problems are not all becoming graver. There has been international progress in limiting pollution from ozone-depleting chemicals, and marine oil pollution is declining. But in many cases reductions in environmental harm caused within the North are dwarfed by increasing damage in the South, brought about either by the displacement of the North's problems or by 'development' within the South.

Following from the above conclusions is a further point, the realization that environmental problems can become 'global' in different ways. Far from all environmental problems are inherently global. As mentioned earlier, air pollution from vehicles and land contamination are predominantly local. The dust, noise and loss of visual amenity associated with quarries are regionally concentrated. The effects of discharges from chemical works are usually felt only locally. And even apparently major environmental catastrophes such as large tanker wrecks have their predominant impact in a restricted area.

Of course, whenever such 'local' processes are repeated all over the world they do in a sense become global phenomena. There can meaningfully be international federations of anti-mining campaigners for example. Coastal communities the world over can join in their concerns about marine pollution from oil tankers or about the loss of fish stocks. Such alliances make particular sense when the campaign target is an international firm or industry. Thus Rio Tinto Zinc, a huge transnational mining concern which has been the target of many anti-mining actions, forms a focus for international action at the local level. Local community groups facing the prospect of having waste incinerators built in their region can collaborate internationally, exchanging data and tactical information.

But this should not lead us to assume that the local is always global. In some sense and with enough ingenuity, all environmental problems can be made out to be global but, one might be tempted to say, some are more global than others. Furthermore, as we will see in the next chapter, one has to take into account the fact that it benefits some people to advance claims about 'globality'. Clearly, environmentalists look more important if, instead of complaining about a local grievance, they can lay claims to global concerns. They benefit from upping the stakes. But, more insidiously, a nation or a company which benefits from a particular environmental policy or reform may want to see that policy adopted as broadly as possible, in which case a 'global' label is very handy, as we saw in a preliminary way with the population issue. In other words, certain groups may have an ideological interest in having specific environmental problems treated as though they were global and therefore special. To put it crudely, there may be other reasons than pure environmental concern for wishing to see certain environmental issues handled as matters of international, global priority. It is to this issue of the 'globality' of global environmental problems that we must now turn.

## Notes

1 The example of a glass greenhouse is often used to illustrate this point, though it is equally frequently disputed by atmospheric scientists. A garden greenhouse is effective mostly because it traps warm air. Without the greenhouse roof, the warm air would tend to drift upwards taking the heat with it. With the Earth's atmosphere, of course, there is no 'roof'. The greenhouse effect works because the greenhouse gases slow down the passage of heat. In this sense, they operate more like the insulating jacket around domestic hot water cylinders than panes of glass in a greenhouse. But this analogy also has its weaknesses, most notably the fact that hot water cylinder jackets do not let the sun's radiation heat the water in the cylinders. On balance, the greenhouse analogy is the best we have.

2 I should like to thank Kay Milton for alerting me to the story about the American drakes misbehaving in Spain.

3 Although in northern Europe and the north of the USA it is easy to think of the need for heating, with the increasing numbers of office blocks and the growth of populations in Third-World urban areas, the greatest demand world-wide is soon likely to be for cooling rather than heating.

# 3

# How do the World's Environmental Problems come to be 'Global'?

### Introduction: The Global Environment and Two Complications Facing Global Action

As we saw in the last chapter, carbon dioxide and other 'greenhouse' gases are accumulating in the atmosphere, leading to the possibility of unprecedented atmospheric warming, warming which could disrupt climate systems, upset agricultural production, cause catastrophic flooding and result in significant loss of natural species. Following the United Nations' 'Earth Summit' in Rio de Janeiro in 1992, the vast majority of countries publicly accept, at least in principle, that policies need to be put in place to prevent this problem from becoming disastrously bad. Furthermore, these countries agree that they have to coordinate their responses, since greenhouse gases are highly mobile so that, for example, Russian emissions can affect any other country and any other country's emissions could affect Russia. It makes no sense for countries to look only to their own interests.

But this is no easy matter, such as altering shopping hours or harmonizing a new off-side rule in soccer. The regulation of greenhouse gas emissions goes right to the heart of domestic policies in these countries since it requires alterations to energy, transport and industrial policies. Yet, in the absence of a global authority, countries have to consent to work together. They are sovereign actors who have to bargain until an approach is agreed; then they have to rely on diplomatic pressure to ensure that the others adhere to the agreement. Most countries can be relied on to approach these negotiations selfishly, wanting to secure as advantageous a deal for themselves as possible. The monitoring of agreements can also be costly, and countries are unlikely to want to spend more than the minimum on civil servants and scientists to check that they are sticking to the agreed measures. Obviously, international agreements are not novel; governments have long cooperated over very many areas, for example over trade, defence and navigation. But this is a new area which requires an important degree of surrender of sovereignty over matters central to the business of the modern state. Accordingly, some commentators have claimed that greenhouse warming and similar global environmental problems are giving rise to a new phase in transnational politics, through a new politics of the environment (see Weale, 1992: 23–8).

While we might expect formidable difficulties (arising from conflicts of interest and political antagonisms) to stand in the way of countries coming to negotiate environmental agreements on issues of global significance, two additional factors further complicate this story. For one thing, governments are not the only parties to these world-wide negotiations. There are other types of conventionally political agents besides governments. Most obviously, there are supranational political entities including the United Nations and the European Union. Whereas the constitutional and legal status of nations is pretty clear, the standing of these supranational bodies is much more debatable and in practice open to negotiation. The European Union, for instance, is – in the terms of Jacques Delors' famous quip – an 'unidentified political object', whose powers and competence are still being negotiated. Still, as we shall see, these bodies have played an important role in proposing and brokering agreements on transnational environmental issues.

But supranational bodies are not the only political entities which exert an influence over the negotiations between governments. Perhaps surprisingly, subnational bodies have also played a key role in responses to global warming and other transnational problems. As we shall see later on, some regional authorities and city councils have embraced the opportunity to act on international environmental problems, whether by putting pressure on their national governments or by introducing policy measures of their own.

In addition to these official political bodies, there are at least four other sets of participants. First, there are pressure groups and campaign organizations, some of which such as the World Wide Fund for Nature and Greenpeace draw support from citizens of tens of countries and aim to represent the interests of the environment at a planetary level. Such groups can achieve levels of cross-national agreement and coordination which are often beyond national governments. Generally, such groups campaign for tighter reduction targets and better enforcement, and for the wealthier countries to bear a greater part of the reduction obligations. Second, there are scientists (atmospheric chemists, biologists, economists and so on) working for universities and research institutes, sometimes for governments and even pressure groups, who offer expertise on the targets and on the mechanisms for meeting them. As global warming is a hugely complex technical matter, its analysis depends on a large amount of scientific co-operation. If scientists arrive at an international consensus on an environmental issue, it is often difficult for national governments to adopt a conflicting view without seeming to be guided by suspect motives. Third there are companies and commercial organizations which, as discussed in Chapter 1, have a transnational reach. They form a hugely powerful lobby, directly influencing the policy options favoured by governments. Their international spread also means that, in practice, they restrict the sovereignty of governments since governments will not wish to introduce policies which may encourage companies to relocate their businesses elsewhere. The final category comprises local groups, community associations and small-scale initiatives concerned with some aspect of policy tied to global warming: for example, with local afforestation projects or proposals for small-scale wind power. They can draw on global-level justifications for their local action, thus winning themselves some independence from national authorities.

The second obstacle to arriving straightforwardly at international agreements arises from the fact that very few global environmental problems are global in the direct, physical sense that global warming is (and even its global uniformity can be opened to doubt as we shall see in this and the following chapter). Accordingly, we need to take into account the question of how 'global environmental problems' come to be viewed as global, and by whom.

## Making out a Global Interest in the Environment

Advocates of all political movements tend to claim that their philosophy is in the common interest. Thus, nationalists argue that people are happier and more satisfied if they live with their co-nationals. Socialists have typically argued that public ownership of the chief engines of the economy advances the common good. And many environmentalists have chosen to make this claim for their beliefs too: they assert that environmental degradation is a problem that humankind faces in common and that therefore environmentally beneficial objectives can be expected to be favoured by everybody. In this section I will review the evidence and the kinds of arguments that environmentalists have used to make this claim. Later on I will evaluate how robust their case actually is.

On the face of it, environmentalists seem to have it easier than others when it comes to advancing this kind of argument. Socialists, for example, have to persuade people to view their class identity as an important, common characteristic. And, by and large, they have found people resistant to this identification. All too frequently, people have reverted to racial, ethnic or gender divisions, and class solidarity has been forsaken. Environmentalists tend to think they enjoy an advantageous position when it comes to making this appeal because the common interest they speak of is – in their view – a material and palpable thing. It is not common consciousness they are promoting but a common response to the physical and health-threatening effects of air pollution or to the threat of shortages if the world's resources are all used up. People have good physical grounds (or so it is argued) for viewing things the environmentalists' way.

Furthermore, thanks to industrialization and the spread of Western techniques throughout the globe, the physical threats to the environment are becoming more similar the world over. Air pollution problems are common to virtually all large-scale cities whether in rich or poor countries, irrespective of political systems or geography. Similarly, urban sewage disposal is a world-wide management problem. Accordingly, the idea that the world's population has common environmental interests seems to be becoming more credible.

The case can be made out even more readily in those instances where the environmental threats are themselves transnational. For example, air pollution caused by vehicles is a large problem in most of the world's major cities, but in every case it is locally produced pollution that causes the local hazard. If Sydney or Bangkok could change their ways, they would remedy their own problems. So, though the cities are all in the same boat at the moment, each one could jump ship individually. Other problems do not have this character. As was detailed in the last chapter, some air pollution problems are global in scale. Carbon dioxide emitted in one country is as likely to upset the atmospheric balance in another country as in the area in which it was emitted. The dangers resulting from the destruction of the ozone layer follow the same logic. The world shares one ozone layer and the pollutants each of us emits act cumulatively to deplete it. In the cases of these global forms of pollution the arguments for there being a collective interest in pollution control appear even stronger. No one can meaningfully go it alone, so the only reasonable political responses depend on cooperation. We have a common interest in protecting the global environment and can recognize good grounds for acting concertedly to protect it.

Green political thinkers have tried to take this process one step further. They have sought to suggest that people should see themselves not as citizens of some country, not as members of an ethnic group, not as comrades within a class, but as 'citizens of planet Earth'. Environmentalists have used visual and poetic images of the Earth to promote and engender this process of planetary identification (see Sachs, 1994). As mentioned earlier on, these images have also been incorporated into the names of environmental groups – such as EarthFirst!, the Global Action Project, the World Wide Fund for Nature – and deployed in their logos, most particularly by Friends of the Earth, which from the 1970s to the 1990s used a simple image of the globe as its logo. The photographic portrayal of the globe viewed from an orbiting spacecraft has been used repeatedly to evoke the Earth's isolation in space, its fragility and wonder, and the sense that the beings on it share a restricted living space surrounded by an unwelcoming void. Greens seem to imply that a realization that people are astronauts on spaceship Earth will lead them to take each others' interests to heart and to work cooperatively for the good of the Earth.

Some green political writers have attempted to underwrite these convictions with the support of scientific evidence. According to the analysis of a highly reputable, but maverick scientist – Jim Lovelock – the Earth itself and the life on it should really be seen as a 'superorganism', a superorganism he has christened Gaia (1988: 15–41). He argues that life on Earth has somehow collectively organized itself so as to withstand external shocks and internal malaise. For example, during the history of the planet, the Sun has aged and the heat energy coming from it has increased. Yet the temperature of Earth has not altered correspondingly; it has been maintained at more or less its previous level by the operations of the various forms taken by life on the planet. Lovelock draws the comforting conclusion that, just as ordinary organisms have defence mechanisms to cope with ill health and changing environments, so Gaia has the capacity to withstand changes at the planetary level. Of course, certain species may go extinct (potentially including human beings) but the living planet as a whole is likely to find ways to adapt.

Scientists are conspicuously divided over Lovelock's 'Gaia hypothesis'. For many, it seems to amount to a *Star Trek*-like claim that the Earth is 'life, but not as we know it'! But whatever the eventual verdict of the scientific community on Lovelock's innovative hypothesis, some greens have seized on it as a legitimation for the idea that the planet has a real oneness (Yearley, 1995a: 474–5). On this view, the planet as a whole is a real, coherent entity – a superorganism. This is perhaps the strongest possible basis for the claim that the Earth should properly be considered as a global whole. It offers a scientific and philosophically-realist foundation on which intellectuals and populists of the environmental movement have sought to erect the idea that our ecological problems demand global solutions and global awareness.

In their book, *The Coming of the Greens* Porritt and Winner give expression to the radical green view which, they claim:

> seeks nothing less than a non-violent revolution to overthrow our whole polluting, plundering and materialistic industrial society and, in its place, to create a new economic and social order which *will allow human beings to live in harmony with the planet*. In those terms, the Green Movement lays claim to being the most radical and important political and cultural force since the birth of socialism. (1988: 9; my italics)

It has clearly been in the interest of environmental philosophers and activists to claim that they are working for a global mission and that they represent the interests of the whole of humanity, perhaps the whole of the biosphere. But, as we shall see, some of these claims are open to question. Even apparently global physical problems, such as the depletion of the ozone layer, where arguments about 'oneness' appear to be most secure, actually turn out to be more severe in some areas (the poles) than in others. Claims about humankind's universal interest in solving environmental problems cannot be taken at face value.

Having set the rhetorical and political scene for claims about the global nature of environmental problems, these issues are developed in the next two sections of this chapter. First, in the next four subsections, I shall examine the reasons why environmental problems have come to have a world-wide spread. After that I shall consider whether this world-wide distribution amounts to a 'global' spread in the sense that greens and other commentators propose. Lastly, attention will be turned to the role of the various kinds of actors in negotiating the global (or otherwise) standing of the world's environmental problems.

### How do Environmental Problems get to be World-wide in Scale?

On the face of it, one might expect the answer to this question to be an ecological or physical science one. For example, one might anticipate answers such as that ozone-depleting chemicals constitute a global problem because of their world-wide dispersal by air currents. Without wishing to downplay the significance of this type of consideration, it is important to realize this type of answer is never the whole reason, and sometimes hardly a part of the reason for the world-wide scale of ecological problems at all. Thus, in the last chapter we reviewed the chief types of pollution and the principal threats to resource depletion, but we have not yet asked what determines where and whether pollutants are produced, and in what quantities and combinations resources get used. A simple, yet still quite informative answer to this line of questioning is that the types and extent of pollution and of other forms of environmental harm are influenced by the political economy of present-day production, trade and regulation – in other words by developments in economic activity and by the outcomes of political contests. Thus, it is clear that the vast majority of pollution and environmental despoliation arise from economic activities themselves, from power generation, from the operation of chemical plants, from mining operations, from travelling to and at work, and from agricultural enterprises.

Of course, environmental problems are not limited to modern industrialized societies. It is well documented that certain earlier societies ran down – sometimes disastrously – their natural resource base (see Yearley, 1992b: 118–20), while manufacture and mining have always been able to generate contamination. But three things set the modern economy apart. First, there is its scale. Modern societies are enormously more productive than their predecessors so that overall they place far greater demands on natural resources, including water, and generate far more pollution. These societies also trade and operate internationally to an unprecedented degree, so pollution can get dispersed along with the goods. The world-wide spread of development has tended to eat away at natural habitats and to coincide with biodiversity loss.

The second factor is the nature of modern production. It is only for the last hundred years or so that industries have been producing numerous innovative substances which are not directly derived from naturally occurring organic materials. Only in this century, for example, have people introduced radioactive materials for medical, military and energy-generation purposes. It is only recently that humans have produced vast quantities of plastics and other organic chemicals which are foreign to the natural world. These first two points amount to a restatement of the points indicated by the two examples with which Chapter 2 began: that (a) certain modern pollutants can contaminate the global environment while (b) the transnational nature of modern trade allows the waste from industrialized regions and countries to pollute every region of the world.

The third factor has to do with the way that pricing works in a free-market economy. The free market is supposed to lead to the optimum use of goods and services because prices respond to demand and availability. As things become scarce, demand for each one intensifies and so the price rises, giving customers an incentive to search for an alternative; as we saw in the wager between Ehrlich and Simon, the environmentalist and the economic optimist, described in the last chapter. But certain things escape this price mechanism. Until relatively recently, industries used to use the environment as a cost-free waste disposal facility. Unwanted gases were simply discharged into the atmosphere, while waste fluids were pumped into the sewers, into rivers or the sea. Because use of the environment was free, there was no incentive to try to minimize your firm's effluents or your firm's impact on the environment. Even if a small investment would have allowed you to reduce your waste gases by 90 per cent, there was no financial incentive to do so – rather the opposite. The firm that performed the clean-up would reduce its profits while its competitors saw theirs maintained. Only altruistic 'mugs' would pay their own money for an improvement which benefited the general good but did not help their own business; such mugs could even risk going out of business since their dirtier competitors would be able to undercut the cleaner firm's prices. When a firm's actions result in a load or cost being borne outside the firm itself (in this case they are borne by the environment), economists refer to this as the imposition of 'negative externalities' (Jacobs, 1991: 27).

To make this point about externalities is not to imply that industrial pollution is unique to capitalist, free-market systems. On average, state socialist countries had a worse record of pollution, particularly when one bears in mind the low levels of productivity they achieved. Their emphasis on production targets gave them a different kind of reason for disregarding the pollution they caused. Rather, the point is that the free-market system, which is now the dominant global model, provides a systematic incentive to firms to lower their costs by causing pollution. Firms which operate in a country with lax pollution control legislation will – all other things (such as wage costs and so on) being equal – enjoy higher profits than those operating in a cleaner environment. The 'logic' of the market inclines companies to pollute. Furthermore:

> An important feature of external costs is that they increase in the process of industrial modernization. As population rises, particularly in cities, more people are affected by pollution. There are fewer places where waste can be deposited without harm. Moreover, as pollution and resources use rise, their impact is likely to be cumulatively greater. Each emission or unit of resource extracted adds to previous ones. In this sense external costs can form a vicious spiral, each one worsening the effects of the next. (Jacobs, 1991: 28)

For the reasons Jacobs gives, pollution has come to be seen as the inevitable consequence of economic development, particularly in the under-developed world. It is almost as though environmental degradation is the 'cost' to be paid for growing material wealth. For example, according to an article by Stott in the development journal *Links*:

> Brazilian delegates at the 1972 UN Conference on the Human Environment proclaimed that it was their country's 'turn' to industrialize, and assured multinational corporations that it was alright [sic] to send this pollution down to Brazil so long as they sent the industries and the jobs that went with it. (1984: 28)

Politicians and business people coming from or dealing with the developing world have often been willing to bear (or – at least – allow their employees and the people to bear) the negative consequences of development in return for an increase in wealth. This willingness to tolerate pollution has interacted with the strategy of Northern firms to ensure that the negative externalities of modern industry have been spread around the globe, as we shall see in the next section.

*Where Industries Locate*

There has always been controversy over the location of industry because of the effluent it produces. In the nineteenth century aristocrats and large landowners in Britain complained that emissions from the soap and allied chemicals business were poisoning their livestock (less consideration was given to workers' health). Planning laws have since been tightened to ensure that consideration is given to the consequences of location. But another factor has worked in the contrary direction. Industry has spelt jobs and the prospect of wealth. Accordingly, there has generally been a trade-off between wanting the benefits that industry brings and wishing to avoid the pollution. Many working-class communities have simply had to put up with high levels of pollution in order to keep jobs in the local economy. It was not that the businesses could not be cleaner; it was that rather than pay the costs of cleaning up, they would have located elsewhere.

The trade-off of jobs for pollution can even be self-perpetuating. For example, the concentrated presence of the British nuclear industry in Cumbria around the Sellafield plant has meant that it is easier to locate successive developments in or close to the same site than to get other communities to accept the nuclear industry. Following community opposition at a series of sites elsewhere in Britain being examined for their suitability for disposing of nuclear waste, in 1987 the British government cancelled these investigations (Blowers and Lowry, 1991: 312–21). By the early 1990s the revised plan was to dispose of the waste beneath the Sellafield site. Successive investments come because of the proven acceptance of the nuclear industry, an industry which other communities regard (rightly or wrongly) as unacceptably polluting.

This problem has been internationalized in two ways. First the effluent has itself been dispersed internationally. As the scale of industry has grown, there have been more wastes and these have led, for example, to the pollution of large rivers such as the Rhine and Danube which pass through many countries, bearing Swiss wastes to the Netherlands or Austrian wastes to Hungary and Romania. Similarly, air pollution has been 'handled' by building higher chimneys. For a long while, firms (notably in the smelting industry and in electrical generation) tended to respond to complaints about emissions not by reducing the production of pollutants so much as by trying to spread them more thinly. Thus, in 1972 Inco (the International Nickel Company of New York) responded to pressure to clean up the sulphur dioxide and particulate emissions from its nickel and copper smelting plant in Sudbury, Ontario by constructing a 387-metre 'super-stack' to cut the impact in the immediate vicinity (Blunden, 1991b: 102). Inco was far from alone in adopting this strategy. In all cases, pumping the effluents higher into the air reduced local contamination but meant that they landed over a wider area and further away, leading to pollution of neighbouring territories.

The second path of internationalization has been the decision to locate businesses away from the Northern countries in areas desperate for jobs, investment and economic development. In the most well known examples, from the 1970s US companies started moving away from the pioneering domestic environmental legislation to Southern countries with laxer laws.

There is a push and a pull effect here. The push is the urge to escape tightening regulations which would mean increased costs or limitations on productivity. For example, new laws which demand cleaner emissions to the atmosphere or which impose charges on the dumping of wastes into sewers drive up production costs. Firms also face tougher planning controls on the development of new plant. If these companies can find overseas locations which are keen to get investment and with less demanding laws, they are able to make the same products more cheaply. On the face of it this urge to escape regulation looks morally dubious. If a substance is harmful in the USA or France, then one can only suppose that it is harmful elsewhere too. In other words, by relocating these firms are imposing risks on the host country which are deemed unacceptable in their home state. Firms often seek to rationalize this decision by arguing that the new regulations are unnecessarily tight; they tend to imply that they are the victims of a form of environmental hysteria. In some cases firms relocate not so much to escape regulations as to avoid protest and the delays which accompany public inquiries. For example, whatever the actual facts about the dangers of waste incinerators (and these 'facts' are fiercely disputed at present), no community in the industrialized North is keen to take the risk of having an incinerator cited near them. Firms which want to build such a facility know they will face prolonged protest and legal challenges. It can be this prospect rather than the laws themselves which incline them to look overseas.

The complementary pull comes from the governments and development authorities of countries eager for investment. In the same article as was mentioned earlier, Stott cites the example of a brochure designed to persuade companies to locate in an industrial complex in Trinidad. The text informs companies that '*In the absence* of legislation dealing with the discharge of effluents and other forms of pollution' (1984: 30; my italics) intending investors have to convince the development authorities that the environmental impact of the proposed factory has been properly assessed. What this means is that at the time Trinidad itself had no legislation covering the discharge of likely pollution; the only obligation on incoming firms was to convince the economic development agency that an assessment had been made of the environmental impact of the development. Given that this agency's job was to stimulate investment, one can only assume that they would have been sympathetic to investors' claims about the cleanliness of their operations. This arrangement, where the planning agency is closely associated with the development authority is not confined to Third-World examples. This issue came to a head very publicly over a large-scale fire at Hickson Pharmachem in Ringaskiddy, just outside Cork, in the Irish Republic in August 1993. Overseas chemical companies around Cork had been involved in repeated environmental controversies in the previous two decades (see Peace, 1993). What made this case stand out was that the supposedly-independent Environmental Protection Agency (EPA) had been set up only the previous month. Its first major public act was thus to investigate the fire (see Peace, 1994). According to Peace's analysis, there were two main kinds of difficulty with the EPA's response. First, there were a set of problems around the notion of the agency's 'independence'. These arose from, among other things, the fact that the EPA board members were selected by the Minister (rather than, say, being selected representatives of a variety of interests), and from the reliance of the EPA on external experts who might not share its mission of environmental protection. More direct concerns over political independence were also stimulated because the junior Minister for Environmental Protection arranged that the EPA should not hold a public inquiry on the fire, but only an in-house investigation. Successive governments' partiality towards economic development and the preference shown towards industrial interests by some state agencies was commonly presented by Irish environmental campaigners as evidence that the state could not be entrusted with the care of the environment (see Yearley, 1995d). It appeared now that even the new EPA's independence from 'development' interests was suspect.

Through the 1970s and 1980s more and more attention was focused on these reasons for relocation and on the possibility that dirty industry from the North was spreading pollution around the globe (see the studies in Ives, 1985). Michalowski and Kramer's study noted that as Northern companies exported 'their industrial operations to developing nations, many of the hazards of industrial production and the associated possibilities for corporate crime are relocated from developed to developing countries' (1987: 35). As these authors go on to note, a dispute arose over 'whether pollution control costs actually play a significant role in location decisions'.

In other words, there are many economic factors which incline Northern companies to move to the underdeveloped world, including cheaper labour, fewer legal benefits and rights for employees, more lenient tax laws and direct financial inducements such as subsidies for building factories. Where the avoidance of pollution control costs comes in any hierarchy of benefits is hard to specify. Leonard carried out a comparative study of this issue, published at the end of the 1980s, and he concluded that the story varied greatly from one industrial sector to another. In some businesses environmental protection measures are very costly; in others they are more or less negligible (1988: 86–93).

All the same, and this is Michalowski and Kramer's chief point, even if it is some factor other than the avoidance of pollution control costs which directs TNCs to the Third World, once located there they 'remain legally free to expose the water, air, soil and bodies of workers to hazardous substances at rates higher than those allowed in their home countries' (1987: 37). Even if they did not move to the South in order to pollute, companies may be tempted to pollute once they get there. To install pollution abatement equipment which is not required by law would only cut into one's profits.

### Where Wastes End Up

It is clear that the countries of the South can face environmental damage if dirty industries relocate there. Given the low standards of environmental control which often prevail, local firms are also likely to pollute. But, as the example of Kassa Island vividly shows, the South can sometimes end up with the pollution without even the benefit of hosting the industrial processes which cause it. Some countries are so poor, so in need of earnings of foreign currencies (to pay for necessary imports and so on) and so lacking in resources (a problem often compounded by the over-exploitation of ecological resources such as forests, which exhausts any major natural riches the country may originally have had) that they will consider any trade that is likely to generate an income. In the 1980s, as citizens of Northern countries became more aware of environmental threats, there was a growing problem of hazardous waste disposal. Such wastes were either very expensive to dispose of because the authorities insisted on special treatment, or impossible to dispose of because no community would tolerate having the waste dumped near their town. Local politicians tended to side with the outraged citizens of their constituencies so it became difficult for governments to impose a solution in the face of parliamentary protest. The obvious answer was to export the wastes to countries which were so desperate for income that they would overlook the risks. Such deals were easier when the receiving country had a non-democratic government. They were easier still when the recipients were misled about the nature of the wastes or when local officials were offered bribes.

The double standards in this trade are, however, immediately apparent and disclosures in the late 1980s led to protests in the receiving countries as well as in the North. Through bodies such as the Organization of African Unity, the receiving countries (many of which, like Guinea, were in western Africa) were able to cooperate in pushing up standards and in 1989 the United Nations Environment Programme agreed an international convention regulating the trade in wastes, namely The Basel Convention on the Control of Transboundary Movements of Hazardous Wastes and their Disposal (Susskind,1994: 172–5). However, as Susskind and Ozawa point out (1992: 147), this Treaty allowed the significant loophole of admitting bilateral trade arrangements between individual signatories and non-signatory nations. In other words, one could sign up to the Treaty but still off-load or receive waste from a non-signatory nation which could – in turn – pass one's waste on to another Treaty-member (see Birnie and Boyle, 1992: 332–43).

The European Union subsequently developed more demanding policies for its member nations, measures which – in essence – were adopted by the OECD nations (with the exception of the USA) in 1994 (Seager, 1995: 61). In a complementary move, the great majority of African countries adopted the Bamako Convention in 1991, banning the importation of hazardous wastes (Susskind, 1994: 175). Such measures may have halted the most glaring waste-dumping practices, but they have not stopped it entirely. Countries can still trade hazardous waste and, as with any UN agreement, there are always countries which refuse to be signatories and which, with the assistance of unscrupulous operators, can act as routes for avoiding controls.

Two further factors have led to the perpetuation of this trade. The first – ironically enough – is the continuing rise in environmental standards within Northern countries. For example, Germany has recently introduced demanding regulations on recycling. Picking through waste to sort and recycle the various components is labour intensive work and can only be made economically attractive if it is subsidized or if wage rates are very low. Consequently, an attractive approach to recycling policy is to collect the waste of wealthy people and send it to poor countries with low wage rates. This makes some sort of economic sense, but an 'incidental' benefit of course is that it helps to solve one's waste disposal problems. Better still – at least for those doing the exporting – the North is no longer 'dumping' waste on the South but providing the South with environmentally-sound employment opportunities! (See *The Guardian*, 15 March 1994: 2 for an example.) There is also the additional worry that it may be difficult to define precisely what counts as hazardous waste and what counts as materials for recycling; some commentators fear that 'international recycling' could become a way of bypassing some of the provisions of the Basel Convention (Edwards, 1995: 5).

The second factor is rather more complicated and demands a section to itself.

*International Debt, Monetary Institutions and Transnational Environmental Problems*

Countries seeking to develop industrially usually suffer from a lack of capital. They want modern factories, for example, but before the factories ever generate any profit the countries will need to make a large investment. As we have seen, one way to overcome this problem is to attract foreign investors by making one's country a cheap or convenient place to set up business. An alternative approach is to try to get loans or aid (in the form of grants or 'concessionary', that is reduced-rate, loans) to assist with the initial investment costs. In the 1970s the sources of such loans were revolutionized when Northern commercial banks began to seek new business in the South. Banks are obviously in the business of making loans and living off the profits from the interest. For big Western banks, such as the Midland and Lloyds in the UK and the Bank of America, Chase Manhattan and Citicorp in the USA (George, 1988: 35), lending to Southern countries was appealing for three reasons. First, this was a relatively neglected area so there was initially little competition in the making of loans and less regulation than in home-country lending. Second, certain Southern countries' economies – for example Mexico's and Brazil's – were expected to grow quickly thus yielding a good return on the loan. Third, there was a belief that countries were a special, low-risk sort of borrower; unlike individuals or even companies who might default on loans, countries would always be there – as Lever and Huhne expressed it (1985: 53), people believed that 'Countries simply could not go bankrupt.'

The banks, notably US ones, lent enthusiastically and loans accumulated so that by the 1980s several South American countries had debts around $100 billion and so that the total indebtedness of the Third World came close to $1000 billion. And, effectively, these big debtors did start to go bankrupt. In their eagerness to lend, the banks had backed some very poor investments. They even lent to corrupt states where much of the money simply disappeared. Very little of it generated enough profits to pay the interest on the loans, though the banks still demanded their repayments. In the worst cases, countries were having to use all their export earnings just to service their debts and their populations were therefore not benefiting at all from trade or from the loans.

Through the 1980s this complex and distressing story unfolded. Three consequences are of particular importance to the present discussion. The first and pivotal consequence was the growing importance of two international financial bodies, the World Bank and the International Monetary Fund (IMF). As the commercial banks fretted over the extent of their bad debts and the indebted countries tried to work out a strategy for survival, these two bodies assumed a powerful advisory and brokerage role. Although they are both international agencies they are dominated by Northern representatives (whose governments, they would point out, put up most of the money) and their object is to assist debtor nations within a framework which is committed to safeguarding the international monetary system.

The second and third consequences followed from the strategy advocated by the World Bank and IMF. Their view was that debtor countries should try to meet repayments by increasing their export earnings. They should thus do more to attract investment even if that meant accepting dirty industry or building incinerators to deal with the wastes of the North, and they should be willing to increase the rate of exploitation of their natural resources, even if that entailed poorly-regulated mining and increases in logging. These institutions' advice thus made pollution, resource depletion and biodiversity loss in the underdeveloped world more likely. This focus on increasing earnings was to be coupled with decreases in government spending, a policy which hit expenditure on such government tasks as maintaining sewerage systems, reserve maintenance, pollution monitoring and abatement measures. At the same time as environmental harm was likely to be on the increase, spending on environmental management was reduced.

In February 1992 an internal World Bank memo, written by the Chief Economist Lawrence Summers, in the form of comments on another Bank document, was leaked. The memo was quickly faxed around the world and created what Rich describes as 'a public relations disaster of unique proportions' (1994: 248). Though the World Bank subsequently insisted that it was meant ironically, many took the memo to be acutely revealing. It suggested:

Just between you and me, shouldn't the World Bank be encouraging *more* migration of the dirty industries to the LDCs [least developed countries]? I can think of three reasons:

1 The measurement of the costs of health-impairing pollution depends on the forgone earnings from increased morbidity and mortality. From this point of view a given amount of health-impairing pollution should be done in the country with the lowest cost, which will be the country with the lowest wages. I think the economic logic behind dumping a load of toxic waste in the lowest-wage country is impeccable and we should face up to that.

2 The costs of pollution are likely to be non-linear as the initial increments of pollution probably have very low cost. I've always thought that under-populated countries in Africa are vastly *under*-polluted; their air quality is probably vastly inefficiently low [sic] compared to Los Angeles or Mexico City. Only the lamentable facts that so much pollution is generated by non-tradable industries (transport, electrical generation) and that the unit transport costs of solid waste are so high prevent world-welfare-enhancing trade in air pollution and waste.

3 The demand for a clean environment for aesthetic and health reasons is likely to have very high income-elasticity. The concern over an agent that causes a one-in-a-million change in the odds of prostate cancer is obviously going to be much higher in a country where people survive to get prostate cancer than in a country where under-5 mortality is 200 per 1,000. Also, much of the concern over industrial atmospheric discharge is about visibility-impairing particulates. These discharges may have very little direct health impact. Clearly trade in goods that embody aesthetic pollution concerns could be

welfare-enhancing. While production is mobile the consumption of pretty air is non-tradable.

The problem with the arguments against all of these proposals for more pollution in LDCs (intrinsic rights to certain goods, moral reasons, social concerns, lack of adequate markets, etc.) could be turned around and used more or less effectively against every Bank proposal for liberalization. (*The Guardian*, 14 February 1992: 29; original italics)

Summers' views became very well known and his renown has endured, even if not everyone was scandalized by the memo. Thus, according to a recent article in *The Economist* about competitors for the post of head of the World Bank, it was noted that Summers' chances of winning the appointment were lessened because his 'outspokenness [has] annoyed many . . . especially environmentalists, who were upset by one of his memos which pointed out – *correctly but too frankly* – that pollution had lower social costs in poor countries than in rich ones' (*The Economist*, 11–17 March 1995: 73; my italics).

Whether his memo was meant ironically or not, this passage makes clear why the free-market responses to the problem of debt would tend to encourage international pollution and restrict the ability of governments to regulate environmental problems. Even the World Bank's own special adviser for the environment, Piddington, has noted that the Bank encounters difficulties in relation to the need for strong governmental institutions to regulate for successful environmental management in developing countries owing to 'the deliberate move we have made in the opposite direction, namely to support deregulation as part of the strategy to speed economic reforms in our borrowing countries. The second [problem] is the absence in those countries of the institutional framework and technical skills which are needed' (1992: 222–3).

In her studies of special export-orientated industrial developments in Mexico (known as the 'maquiladora' zone) George has sought to document how the free-market solutions proposed for overcoming the debt aggravate environmental problems. As she observes, 'there are few environmental regulations in this zone . . . and virtually none that Mexico can now afford to enforce . . . [local officials say] that "the red tape and the expense" of American environmental law is a powerful motivation for firms to come to Mexico' (1992: 25). But George goes on to make the additional point that environmental problems arising from countries' responses to debt are not confined to those countries themselves. In the case of the maquiladora zone, the consequences spill over into the United States. For example untreated sewage from the growing cities in northern Mexico has already forced sporadic closures of Californian beaches while 'The maquiladoras themselves generate huge quantities of toxic wastes, many of which end up in California via the New River which flows northward' (1992: 26). In other words, their 'developed' neighbour has to suffer the air pollution from Mexican factories, the waste from industrial areas which is disposed of through the sewerage system, marine pollution from poorly treated human sewage and contaminated foodstuffs from Mexican agriculture. For the USA, the most important source of Third-World lending and the dominant voice in the World Bank, there is certainly an irony: the environmental costs of Mexico's debt are rebounding on US citizens too.

Drawing together this whole section on the numerous and overlapping links between economic activity and environmental problems, it is worth restating three points. First, though it may seem a little obvious, it should be recognized that the overwhelming majority of pollution, resource depletion and habitat loss arises from economic activity. Therefore, the ways in which countries' economies are organized inevitably have a strong influence on the types and amount of pollution and other environmental hazards which are caused.

Second, today's large firms and industries are globally mobile. They think carefully about where to locate themselves, from where to draw their materials and where to dump their wastes. Environmental considerations play a significant part in these deliberations. Though the importance of this factor varies from one type of industry to another, firms can be drawn to set up plants in pollution 'havens' where pollution control is meagre. They also have a strong economic incentive to take advantage of weak pollution control laws in a country or region even if that was not the firm's reason for locating there. Additionally, they have a pressing economic interest in disposing of their wastes as economically as possible. All three of these considerations (concerning location, the exploitation of weak laws, and the search for cheap waste disposal) tend to encourage the world-wide spread of environmental impacts.

Third, the fact that very many underdeveloped countries have been led to become heavily indebted means that they are in urgent need of investment and may be inclined to accept environmentally dubious contracts, whether for resource exploitation, 'dirty' manufacturing operations or for waste disposal. Environmental problems are therefore also trade/debt problems. It may appear that these countries act as a 'sink' for pollution but such is the potential of some forms of pollution to spread internationally that the North's polluting practices can sometimes boomerang back on itself. Shifting pollution to the other side of the globe does not necessarily free you from its effects.

## Just How Global are 'Global' Environmental Problems?

As we have seen there are good physical grounds for regarding some environmental problems as global. Some processes genuinely do have global reach and global impact. If the sea level rises, it will rise everywhere; a radiation cloud from a nuclear accident could travel for thousands of kilometres in any direction. There are also grounds for accepting that the globalization of production and commerce tends to spread even local environmental problems until they are global in scale. Third, there are philosophical and principled reasons for accepting that the green message has a global flavour. All over the globe, humans are threatening the well-being of other species, by disturbing or removing their habitats. Some form of coordinated response will be required if the Earth's other inhabitants are to get a chance to prosper. Equally, it is clear that – one way or another – energy and mineral resources are limited. For the sake of long-term survival, lifestyles which do not recognize these limits need to be altered world-wide. However, we have also observed that many pressure groups and certain companies may benefit from propagating the idea that all environmental problems are truly global. We must accordingly be cautious about accepting claims about 'globality' at face value, and when people make such claims we should examine their arguments carefully. In this section we shall take a critical look at claims about globality.

*Global Heterogeneity*

There are two major issues at stake here. The first point is straightforward, but no less significant for that. Even literally global phenomena have different impacts at different places on the globe depending on geographical and economic differences. Thus, ozone depletion is one of the best candidates for the status as a 'global' problem but physical processes ensure that, in fact, the ozone layer is most depleted at the poles. In many respects, equatorial countries have less to worry about (at least in terms of immediate impacts on personal health) than near-polar ones, a fact reflected in the leadership role in ozone-protection negotiations adopted by the Nordic countries. Global warming demonstrates the same variability. In this case the uncertainty of the consequences of atmospheric warming mean that it is harder to pick winners and losers, but if sea-level rise is a leading anxiety the Swiss clearly have less to worry about than the Dutch. Other geographical variables can exert an influence too. Thus, acid precipitation causes less of a problem where soils and bedrock are slightly alkaline and can therefore neutralize the impact of the acid than in areas, such as large tracts of Scandinavia, where the earth's surface is already neutral or mildly acidic.

But in addition to variations in geography and the earth's physical processes, there are variations due to wealth. Large areas of the Netherlands are already below sea level; clearly the Dutch have learnt to cope with this problem. Further sea-level rises will cause great expense but engineers can envisage ways of managing them. Countries of the Third World which are faced with the same threat cannot feel so sanguine. Bangladesh is already subject to frequent flooding; the Maldive Islands stand only a few metres above sea level at their highest point. Both lack the financial resources and the decades of engineering experience needed to counter the effects of global warming. A supposedly global process will impact very differently even among the low-lying countries of the world.

Given the significance of these differences in geography and, particularly, in wealth, talk of global 'challenges' and calls for united, global responses can be seen as misleading and tendentious. The emphasis on the global nature of current environmental problems tends to imply that there is much more of a common interest in combating them than is, in fact, the case. This false implication mirrors an ideological problem which Dobson identifies at the heart of green politics. He notes that green thinkers have often been rather naïve in calling for a simple change of attitude or consciousness. He refers to a quotation from Arnold Toynbee, cited approvingly by Jonathon Porritt, in which this naïvety is made explicit:

> The present threat to mankind's survival can be removed only by a revolutionary change of heart in individual human beings. This change of heart must be inspired by religion in order to generate the will-power needed for putting arduous new ideals into practice. (cited in Porritt, 1986: 211)

Pleas for such a value change are bolstered by calls for education but Dobson goes on to quote Pepper who observes that 'people will not change their values just through being "taught" different ones. . . . What then is the real way forward, if it is not to be solely or even largely through education? It must be through seeking *reform at the material base of society, concurrent with educational change* (Pepper, 1984: 224–6; original italics). Dobson endorses this diagnosis but wonders how to achieve such reforms. His answer is instructive:

> The answer to this question might just turn on initially sidestepping it and asking instead: *who* is best placed to bring about social change? A central characteristic of Green political theory is that it has never consistently asked that question, principally because the answer is held to be obvious: *everyone*. The general political-ecological position that the environmental crisis will eventually be suffered by everybody on the planet, and that therefore the ideology's appeal is universal, has been perceived as a source of strength for the Green movement. What could be better, from the point of view of advertising an idea, than to be able to claim that failure to embrace it might result in a global catastrophe that would leave no-one untouched? For the present point of view this may be the movement's basic strategic political error because the universality appeal, is properly speaking, Utopian. It is simply untrue to say that, given present conditions, it is in everybody's interest to bring about a sustainable and egalitarian society. A significant and influential proportion of society, for example, has a material interest in prolonging the environmental crisis because there is money to be made from administering it. It is Utopian to consider these people to be a part of the engine for profound social change. (Dobson, 1990: 152; my italics)

As Dobson correctly points out, it is utopian to suppose that there will be consensus on environmentally far-reaching reforms *even within the context of an industrialized nation.* How much more unrealistic then is the assumption that global problems will call forth a unified international response, across all the disparities of wealth, geography, religion and ethnicity of the globe.

*Questioning the Global Interest*

The first major difficulty confronting the idea that globally unified responses will flow from common global problems stems from the disunifying influences of differences in geography and wealth. The second possibility is that the very claims to globality will come to be interpreted as expressions of special interest. It now appears that in many instances 'global' policies have been perceived as attempts by First-World governments to solve their own problems at the expense of the Third-World's development potential. This accusation is made by, for example, Middleton et al. (1993: 5) who argue that at the Earth Summit, by giving priority to 'an environmental agenda [that is, not a poverty or redistribution agenda] the North has once more concentrated on its own interests and has called them "globalism"'. This issue has particularly come to the fore over the management of global warming. As was described in the last chapter, the gas principally responsible for global warming is carbon dioxide ($CO_2$), produced by fossil-fuel burning power stations, furnaces, boilers, vehicles and fires. The most appropriate policy for combating global warming appears to be limiting and then reducing overall $CO_2$ emissions. But limiting emissions is far from easy since the gas is a direct product of such key economic activities as generating power and running factories. If the countries of the Third World are to increase their economic production using roughly the technologies employed in the North, overall world $CO_2$ emissions will rise rapidly. From the perspective of the South, proposals to limit these emissions threaten to impose a brake on their economic development prospects.

Accordingly, when official agencies and campaign groups in the North propose that overall $CO_2$ production must be stabilized and then cut, the key question in the South is, how is that 'cut' to be divided up? Proposals to limit $CO_2$ emissions from the Third World which are not matched by drastic reductions in the First-World's output are seen as merely hypocritical. Voices from the South argue that the industrialized world has enjoyed 200 years of wealth based on carbon emissions. Now, they say, it is the South's turn. Officials in the North are more inclined to favour pollution limits based on current emission levels. But any such proposal tends to reinforce today's economic inequalities by restricting industrialization in the South. This is because it is hard to see how underdeveloped countries could advance their industries and raise living standards without at least coming somewhere near the per capita emission levels of the industrialized world. The starkness of these differences in outlook are revealed in Figures 3.1 to 3.3, which employ data from the late 1980s. In this case, while Brazil is a very large current overall producer of $CO_2$ pollution (from Figure 3.1) and significantly exceeds the output from Canada (by a factor of nearly 3), the cumulative pollution record of Brazilians is far better than that of Canadians; in the preceding twelve-and-a-half decades Brazilians had, on average, generated only about one-eighth the $CO_2$ pollution of Canadians (see Figure 3.3).

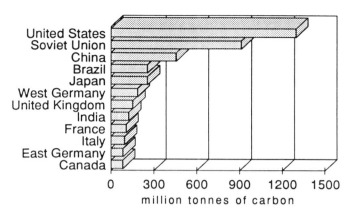

Figure 3.1   *Carbon dioxide emissions from selected countries in the 1980s: annual carbon dioxide release (Friends of the Earth, 1994: 9)*

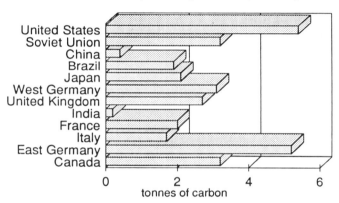

Figure 3.2   *Carbon dioxide emissions from selected countries in the 1980s: annual carbon dioxide release per person (Friends of the Earth, 1994: 9)*

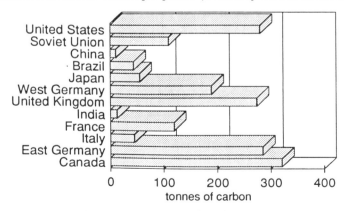

Figure 3.3   *Cumulative historic carbon dioxide emissions from selected countries, per person, 1860–1986 (Friends of the Earth, 1994: 9)*

Table 3.1 *Industrial carbon dioxide emissions from selected countries in the early 1990s*

| Country | Industrial $CO_2$ emissions (million metric tonnes 1991) | Population (millions 1995) | Emissions per head (tonnes $CO_2$ per head) |
|---|---|---|---|
| Brazil | 216 | 161.4 | 1.34 |
| China | 2543 | 1238.3 | 2.05 |
| France | 374 | 57.8 | 6.47 |
| Germany | 970 | 81.3 | 11.93 |
| India | 704 | 931.0 | 0.76 |
| Japan | 1091 | 125.9 | 8.67 |
| UK | 577 | 58.1 | 9.93 |
| USA | 4932 | 263.1 | 18.75 |

*Source*: derived from Seager (1995: 92–9).

More up to date (and slightly differently calculated[1]) figures for several of these countries are provided in Table 3.1. As is clear from this table, Indian per capita emissions are about one-eighth those of the average French person. But if Indian consumption rates were to rise to even half those in France (itself a modest $CO_2$ polluter by Northern standards because of its heavy reliance on nuclear power), overall Indian output would still have to rise more than four-fold, and India would become a larger emitter than Germany, Japan and the United Kingdom combined.

It is significant in this context that the data for per capita emissions in the countries of the former Soviet Bloc (as provided in Figure 3.2) are about the same as those in Western countries, even though Soviet economic productivity was lower. Since, typically, industrializing countries have sought to develop their economies in part through encouraging heavy industry – shipbuilding, heavy engineering, vehicle manufacture and so on – it is likely that they will be relatively large-scale emitters of $CO_2$. Eastern European countries were exceptional in their commitment to heavy – and thus highly-polluting – industry, but there is no reason to believe that today's developing economies will be able to move directly to the highly efficient, low-energy practices now being advocated in the leading Western nations.

Furthermore national policy responses to these international environmental issues may get blocked or grind to a halt in the light of suspicions about the vested interests which may be smuggled in behind appeals to 'global needs'. According to McCully, writing in *The Ecologist*, the way these issues come to be debated *within* countries can actually lead to a situation of stasis:

> Demands for huge amounts of climate aid [that is, aid intended to help offset increases in $CO_2$ emissions] for the Third World give First-World governments an excuse to do nothing except point out to their electorates the huge costs of dealing with the problem and enable them to shift the blame for global warming from the historic and present high emissions from industrial countries onto the

projected future emissions from the Third World. It also gives Third World governments the excuse of not doing anything because they can claim it is too expensive and the First World will not stump up the money. (1991b: 251)

In other words, though the great majority of governments – indeed of politicians of virtually all persuasions – may be prepared to admit in principle that climate change and enhanced global warming amount to a world-wide environmental problem, this recognition of itself does not lead them to act in a globally coherent way. Seeing a threat as a 'global' threat does not necessarily make it more likely that policy-makers will respond. Persistent differences in ideas about who is responsible for causing the 'global' problem may lead to unwillingness to act, thus allowing the problem to intensify.

This complex of issues became more starkly transparent in relation to a new initiative of the World Bank, launched in 1990, the Global Environment Facility (GEF). The idea was for a jointly sponsored funding provision supported by the Bank and the United Nations Development and Environment Programmes (UNDP and UNEP). The remit of the GEF was to 'finance the *incremental cost* of projects in developing countries which generate *global environmental benefits* in four focal areas, but which would not normally be funded from normal development assistance' (Jordan, 1994: 265; original italics). Thus, the fund would not pay for whole projects but would meet the additional costs of undertaking the project in a way that was 'friendlier' to the global environment. The GEF was set up in the 1991 financial year with a budget of $1.3 billion for its pilot phase. In his critical assessment of the environmental performance of the World Bank, Rich takes the GEF to task for a number of reasons. He points to the dominant role played by the Bank, despite the supposed partnership structure, and to the lack of consultation in the decisions over the disbursement of the funds (1994: 176–8). Second he suggests that the GEF may well go towards redressing the environmental damage caused by the sort of development projects the Bank probably would have funded before ecological issues came to the fore. In the case which Rich describes, GEF funds were committed to a 'Congo Natural Resources Management Project' which actually involved opening new areas of forest to logging. The GEF funds were coupled with a (larger) regular development investment, and the role of the GEF component was to make the project less environmentally damaging than it might otherwise have been. As Tickell and Hildyard put it (1992), these loans, rather than preventing ecological damage, seek to compensate for it. Implicitly, the critics argue, this means that the GEF will allow environmentally damaging projects to go ahead which, in the absence of the Facility, might have been opposed.

But the third and more subtle point is that the GEF only directs funds to ecological problems which are construed as 'global'. GEF funds are only available for projects which conserve biodiversity, impact global warming, tend to protect international waters or combat ozone depletion (according to Seager the first two have taken about 40 per cent each of the funding, and international waters the bulk of the remainder (1995: 90)). But, as I have already argued, the globality of environmental problems is not an inherent or obvious quality. In effect, the Bank gets to define what is 'global' and what is not. And the Bank's Southern critics argue that it has been construed to coincide with those environmental problems seen as most pressing in the North, and not those – such as poverty – which groups in the South might prefer to regard as global. According to Jordan (1994: 266), when the increased, second phase GEF funding was agreed in 1994, the management structure was revised to give Third-World countries a greater say, but the problem of the disproportion between the Bank's general development resources and its focused environmental spending persists, as does the broader issue about the restrictive definition of what can count as a 'global' environmental issue.

The question of which environmental problems are 'global' ones is further complicated by the possibility of disagreement about which issues are global *environmental* matters. Even where policy-makers appear to be in agreement about a desire to take action on global environmental problems, difficulties have arisen over the interpretation or definition of the term 'environmental' itself. The first question asked has been, what is to count as an 'environmental' issue in which we all, supposedly, have a common interest. Certain issues, such as air pollution, biodiversity and water pollution have come to occupy the centre ground of the environmental agenda. But other items are more often on the fringes. As was described in Chapter 2, for some officials and campaigners in the North, population is taken as an environmental issue. Others see population per se as a comparatively marginal issue; it is resource use not population itself that matters. Similarly, campaigners in the South have often tried to argue that poverty itself is an environmental problem. Officials in the North have resisted this definition. Since politicians and policy-makers appear unable to agree about what is properly an environmental problem, it seems unrealistic to believe that they will come to find agreement over humanity's supposed common environmental interests.

A second, closely related issue concerns the relationship between environmental topics and other social and economic priorities. All the time – for example – that people demand cars, that companies benefit from selling them, that the motor lobby campaigns on their behalf and national fortunes depend, as Margaret Thatcher said, on the 'great car economy',[2] environmental policies will not be assessed in their own right but in relation to the value people place on cars, and so on. There are few areas of environmental concern which can be considered in relative isolation. Energy policy might be one. If people can light and heat/cool their houses equally well with energy-saving methods, then they are able to adopt them without significantly altering their lives and their values. But most other aspects of environmental policy impact in a broader sense on the way people live their lives, organize their work and conduct their personal relationships. Even if all environmental problems were straightforwardly global (in the way that ozone depletion almost is), people in different regions and countries would still have other priorities which interacted in differential ways with those common environmental problems. The difficulty is that environmental protection measures cut directly across so many political and economic policy areas.

Finally in this section, there is one last issue to be taken into account when asking just what it means for global problems to be 'global'. This goes back directly to the point made at the end of Chapter 1 about the supposedly universal discourses such as logic, geometry and science. The significance of this link stems from the central role that scientific reasoning and expertise play in the diagnosis and management of environmental problems. It is only through science that we can know of the potentially harmful effects of ozone depletion or work out whether global warming is likely to occur. Given the centrality of science to the diagnosis and analysis of these global environmental issues, it is understandable that the discourse of science will affect the way that environmental problems are conceptualized. Typically, science aspires to universal generalizations. Unless there are powerful reasons to the contrary, scientists assume that natural processes are consistent throughout the natural world. The very term 'biodiversity' that was introduced in the last chapter displays this universalism. The notion of biodiversity takes for granted the idea that all living beings are based on related genetic materials and that there can therefore be a measure of genetic variability which is applicable across the globe.

To say that science has a 'universal' orientation is not necessarily to imply that scientists are always internationally minded or that there is good scientific collaboration around the globe (though these things are often true). Rather, the point is that science typically aspires to universally valid truths, truths which apply the world over. Accordingly, spokespersons for science proclaim the unique utility of science for addressing global environmental issues, while policy-makers in search of objective, universalistic methods are attracted to science and to the other universalizing discourses including microeconomics. This orientation has left its stamp on the overall international discourse of environmental management.

However the impartiality and universalistic objectivity of many of these discourses have also been called into question. Suspicions about the way the North interprets 'global' interests have spilled over into misgivings about the use of the (alleged) universalistic discourse of science (including economics) to diagnose the globe's problems. This is an issue we shall return to in detail in the next chapter.

To summarize this whole section, it is increasingly the case that international environmental hazards are being described and treated as 'global environmental problems'. In some cases, their globality arises from the nature of the problem itself (for example, the globe has a protective ozone layer which is suffering depletion). In other cases, environmental problems rise to global significance because – like habitat loss – they are repeated the world over or because one region's problems are distributed or displaced elsewhere. However, the status of 'global' problems is far from straight-forward. Being global, one might suspect that everyone should worry about them equally. But, in fact, global problems turn out to have different impacts and implications, depending on geographical and socioeconomic factors. Even the most inherently global hazards such as 'global warming', turn out to have differential impacts. Because of climate, altitude and other geographical factors, their impacts will be greater in some areas than in others. Furthermore, on average, wealthier societies and the wealthier and more powerful groups within societies will be better placed to withstand their impacts than will other groups.

Accordingly, the label 'global' has itself come to be disputed. Organiz-ations come to refer to a problem as global when they want it to be taken especially seriously and when they want to present its solution as in the 'common interest'. In some cases, spokespersons from underdeveloped countries have argued that the North's identification of 'global' environmental problems is very selective. On this view, the North has tried to give priority to its concerns (for example over the four topics which are the focus of the GEF) by implying that these problems are the most urgent for the *globe as a whole*.

Lastly, scientific analysis has been central to the identification and measurement of global environmental problems, such as ozone depletion and biodiversity loss. However, even the universalistic status of scientific claims has met with suspicion, with critics of the North's policies arguing that putatively universal discourses can conceal partiality, and that the assumptions associated with scientific analysis are not always conducive to the just interpretation of international environmental problems.

## Globalizing Actors

If the question of the 'global' nature of global environmental problems is not cut and dried, then there is clearly scope for various actors to try to affect policy-makers' and the public's perception of environmental issues. The strategies and stances adopted by various collective actors are reviewed in this section.

### NGOs as Advocates for the Globality of Environmental Problems

As mentioned earlier, some environmentalists have gone about this advo-cacy by invoking images of the oneness of the planet and by appeals to humanity's supposed common interest in the environmental well-being of the planet. More concretely, since the early 1970s, environmental campaign organizations in the North have tried to stimulate public awareness and media interest regarding growing evidence about pollution and its possible health effects, about the loss of unspoilt wild areas and about dangers to wildlife. Commonly, they have implied that the changes they propose would be for the planetary good. In the underdeveloped world by contrast a major additional stimulus to environmental protest has been the aware-ness of double standards. Campaigners and activists have built on the resentment, felt by politicians and many citizens in the South, that has arisen from the fact that these countries are being made to bear risks which the North will no longer accept. The international trade in waste was a particularly powerful stimulus to this way of thinking since in these cases the underdeveloped world gets all the risks without any of the benefits of the industrial process which generated the waste in the first place (apart, that is, from a small waste-handling fee).

For their part, leading environmental organizations in the North, such as Friends of the Earth, Greenpeace and the World Wide Fund for Nature (all of which have national bodies as well as international coordinating groups on which Southern countries are represented; for a representative country-by-country listing see Seager, 1995: 88–9), have increasingly joined in with a strong response to these double standards. In essence, this has come about for three reasons. First, they realize that some pollution is inherently transnational. To shift ozone depleting chemicals or marine pollution to the Third World does nothing to reduce the problems about which they have campaigned. Thus, campaigning about policies in the South is an obvious extension of their current work. Second, because of the 'boomerang effects', the countries in which such groups attract most of their support (Germany, the UK, the USA) are not insulated from Third-World problems such as food contamination or air pollution. It makes no sense to protest about these problems within their home countries yet to ignore the problems in their trading partners. Third, environmental organizations have realized that they too are in danger of practising double standards. They can hardly campaign for improvements in environmental conditions in the North if that is only achieved by inflicting environmental damage on poorer countries (for example by protesting about incinerators in Britain but ignoring their construction in Ecuador, the Philippines or Russia). These organizations have faced some internal tension over this question since their supporters want to see progress at home in return for their financial and other donations. But, increasingly, these leading organizations are moving on to an international level of campaigning and, according to McCormick's research, it is precisely groups which concen-trated on international issues that grew most successfully throughout the 1980s (1991: 153–4; see also Bramble and Porter, 1992: 317–18; Seager, 1995: 88). In the USA, the work of these campaign groups has been complemented by influential but small-membership lobbying organizations such as the World Resources Institute and the Environmental Defense Fund (Bramble and Porter, 1992: 318); such groups can easily address world-wide issues without having to take so much into account the benefits which their campaigns deliver to their domestic membership.

Increasingly, global (or, at least, transnational) campaigns are being coordinated in two ways. Groups in the South are joining with Northern NGOs to document and oppose the double standards of commercial companies and the environmentally harmful policies of international monetary organizations, and to draw the public's and politicians' attention to problems such as resource depletion and habitat loss. Northern NGOs play a particular role in lobbying these international bodies and by pressing their home governments to raise standards in their dealings with the Third World (for examples see Bramble and Porter, 1992; Stairs and Taylor, 1992). Second, particularly since the preparations for the Rio Earth Summit in 1992, environmental NGOs are realizing that their agendas overlap with those of development NGOs such as Oxfam and ActionAid (Yearley, 1992a: 182–3). They appreciate that solutions to the world's pollution and conservation problems commonly stand no chance of being implemented unless these solutions simultaneously take into account the requirements of the world's poorest people. The joint expertise and the joint voices of environmentalists and development campaigners are needed to devise widely-credible policies in these areas.

Given that it is relatively easy to point to cross-national aspects of environmental problems, green NGOs have seen far-reaching opportunities for international cooperation, opportunities which they have generally seized with greater alacrity than governments. Cynically expressed, governments have an interest in getting other nations' leaders to do as much about remedying a problem as possible so that they themselves have to undertake a minimum amount of work. Social movement organizations are not subject to this logic. By and large they are free to press for optimal action on environmental reform. Furthermore, they can use the ecological performance of the leading reforming country in any particular area of policy to berate their own governments. In the decade preceding the recent European Union Directive on the fitting of catalytic convertors, US legislation on car exhausts and on freedom of information was repeatedly pointed to by European campaigners with an argument such as, 'If the US government can insist on catalysers and still retain a car industry, surely European governments can do the same.' This line was adopted in the infamous Greenpeace poster campaign in Britain at the end of the 1980s which employed Ford's own slogan ('Ford gives you more') to point out that a British Ford gave you much more toxic pollution than an American Ford.[3]

These pragmatic strengths, coupled with their growing expertise in environmental policy matters, have meant that NGOs have gradually managed to obtain various kinds of participation and representation on international policy-making bodies. For example, in the early years of international discussions over the regulation of ozone-depleting chemicals (see Chapter 4 for more details of these negotiations) NGOs played only a very minor role in the negotiations. If anything, governments tended to listen exclusively to the advice of industry lobbyists. Gradually, during the 1980s, industry's voice diminished in importance on many of the national delegations (Parson, 1993: 50), while the views of NGOs were beginning to be taken into account. By 1991 it was even agreed to admit NGOs to the meetings of the Executive Committee controlling the funds for transfers of 'ozone-friendly' technology from North to South (Parson, 1993: 51). Susskind claims that NGOs played a significant role in the CITES (Convention on International Trade in Endangered Species of Wild Flora and Fauna) treaty negotiations where they also carried out much of the scientific and technical work (1994: 48; Lindborg, 1992: 4), while Levy (1993: 86) observes that NGOs have been admitted to the Long-Range Transboundary Air Pollution Convention meetings, where – he notes – the British branches of Greenpeace and Friends of the Earth have been particularly active. Equally, Piddington – the special adviser on environmental issues to the World Bank mentioned earlier – expresses his respect for 'the individuals in the NGO movement' who criticized the Bank, and acknowledges that:

> They were undoubtedly instrumental in bringing about the changes that were initiated in 1987 [to increase the 'clout' of the Bank's environmental section], and they keep in close touch with Third-World NGOs through their institutional networks, which means that they do offer an important perspective on the impact of Bank-funded projects. (1992: 217)

This increased official recognition, coupled with the fact that different countries' NGOs tend to be more agreed than their respective governments, has actually provided environmental NGOs with the opportunity to exert pressure on the direction of international negotiations at key points. For example, Benedick (1991: 166) notes that at the 1990 London meeting for ozone-protection negotiations the US lobby group, the Natural Resources Defense Council (NRDC), was able to collect information on all the governments' proposals for cuts in the various ozone-depleting pollutants. It then drew up its own proposal based on the most far-reaching reduction for each chemical proposed by any government; this proposal was then used to undermine official negotiators' assertions about the 'impossibility' of various suggested reductions. More strikingly still, Fred Pearce (1991: 283) claims that behind-the-scenes negotiations between leading staff at the World Resources Institute (WRI) and the Environmental Defense Fund, conducted at the 1988 World Conference on the Changing Atmosphere in Toronto, led to the assembled NGOs falling in behind their proposal for a reduction target. The impasse at the parallel official meeting meant that only the NGOs had an agreed proposal for an international policy target; it was the one finally pushed through at the official meeting (see Bramble and Porter, 1992: 338–9).

The role of NGOs was so well established by the time of the Earth Summit in 1992 that elaborate negotiations were conducted beforehand in the so-called 'PrepCom' (preparatory committee) meetings. Lindborg claims that the Earth Summit:

> [broke] new ground with regard to the amount of support and access provided to NGOs by countries, as well as the degree of participation granted to NGOs at national and regional levels, particularly in the North and in certain Southern countries such as Brazil. (1992: 14)

But this increased recognition raises in a particularly acute fashion two further questions. The first was about who exactly should count as an NGO; the second concerns a whole complex of issues around the degree to which NGOs are 'representatives', whom they represent and to what extent they are accountable.

In relation to the first of these questions, as Lindborg notes, in the run-up to the Earth Summit conflicting definitions appeared. In 1990 an umbrella group for already-involved NGOs urged that the official definition should essentially be that:

> NGOs are non-profit, non-party political organizations, including groups such as environment and development, youth, indigenous people, consumer and religious. Organizations of industry, trade unions, parliamentarians, academics and local authorities are not NGOs. (cited in Lindborg, 1992: 2)

But the official body which finally coordinated the UN-sanctioned, parallel conference for NGOs, which ran alongside the intergovernmental Earth Summit in Rio, took a different line, accepting representatives from the 'independent sectors' which they took to include indigenous people, youth, students, scientific organizations, women, trade unions, religious/interfaith groups, the media, grass-root farmers and peasants, human rights/peace organizations, and business and industry, as well as the 'regular' environmental and development NGOs (Lindborg, 1992: 3). This extremely catholic approach was greeted with derision by such commentators as Middleton et al. (1993: 27), who draw attention to the presence of some 'sixty or so' industry-interest groups on the NGO list. The point they overlook, however, is precisely the difficulty of deciding who should count or even of figuring who might be in a position to decide that very question. Middleton et al. appear to harbour few objections about the inclusion of labour interests, though the relationship of organized labour to environmental groups has often been uneasy (see Yearley, 1993b). One could as easily argue (see below) that certain industries actually have a vested interest in higher environmental standards and that their participation would accordingly be beneficial to the environment. A parallel example comes from Benedick who appears at ease with the inclusion of an Australian 'youth' delegation at the London ozone meeting; he takes them as symbolizing or maybe even representing the interests of future generations, though without apparently demanding proof of their qualifications in this regard (1991: 197).

The extent to which this definitional struggle is itself assuming increased importance comes from a recent publication by Greenpeace USA. They have taken the trouble to compile and publish *The Greenpeace Guide to Anti-Environmental Organizations* (Deal, 1993) which attempts to expose such things as industry fronts and think-tanks set up (allegedly) to support anti-environmental objectives; the book lists over fifty such organizations.[4] Given my earlier arguments about the difficulties of defining precisely what 'pollution' or 'the environment' or 'global environmental problems' are, we cannot expect a ready answer to the problem of determining which NGOs to recognize.

In any case, this question of whom to recognize shades over into the problem about representation. Environmental organizations with a mass following clearly have some sort of claim to be voicing 'public concerns'. But apart from political Green Parties (who would, significantly, be excluded under the first definition of NGOs above), environmental organizations have no official political mandate. As right-leaning politicians are fond of saying to environmental pressure groups, 'who elected you?'. The answer, of course, is that no one did. In fact, the great majority of such NGOs are not even explicitly run as democracies. They are managed as companies or as charities, governed by a board and executive officers. Both Greenpeace and Friends of the Earth, for example, have large popular followings, but they are not democracies. Their policies are not governed (even if they are influenced) by the votes of members (see Allen, 1992: 223). US lobby groups such as WRI and the NRDC are even more 'top-down' in their style of organization.

On top of this, the sheer number of NGOs causes a problem for ideas of representativeness. For the Earth Summit, accredited NGOs outnumbered nations by around seven to one. Even among environmentalist groups, the NGOs varied from outfits with over a hundred staff and annual incomes of several million dollars to essentially unfunded groups working entirely with volunteers. And these distinctions tended to have a North–South component to them, so that the wealthier and more influential organizations tended to come from the North and to come from a background in campaigning on global environmental problems. According to Bramble and Porter 'In the North the majority of groups are basically environmental in orientation, whereas in the South many of the groups focus on social justice, or represent grass-roots movements or unions' (1992: 350). Not only would the South's citizens be under-represented in the composition of NGO delegations but the interpretations of global environmental problems might well be typical of that of the North. This is the view adopted by Middleton et al. (1993: 26) and certainly Southern states have, on a number of occasions, objected to the presence of NGO delegations in international treaty meetings (Lindborg, 1992: 12; Susskind, 1994: 47), apparently viewing the NGOs' outlook as too 'Northern'.

In sum, therefore, there are reasons, deriving from NGOs' political ideology, which incline environmental organizations to adopt a global outlook, as the earlier discussion of Dobson indicated. There are also good practical reasons arising from their campaigning strategies. This orientation is further fed by two positive feedbacks. First, as noted at the start of this section, the more globally-orientated organizations are precisely the ones which have experienced the greatest growth in numbers and the largest increases in celebrity. Second, as NGOs have been recognized as effective lobbyists and as one way of increasing the apparent public openness of international negotiations, institutional space has been created for them around such issues as CITES and the ozone-depletion negotiations (Birnie and Boyle, 1992: 76–7). Participation in such transnational frameworks has tended to be most open to NGOs with an established commitment to global issues. At the same time, the very act of participation has brought further legitimacy, recognition, publicity and funds to these groups.

This last issue is partly a matter of organizational sociology. And this aspect of NGOs has further ramifications. For example, a further, organizational factor promoting international cooperation by campaign groups is the fact that it is less susceptible to intra-movement competition than national campaigns since international 'partners' are not often fishing in the same pools for support. If two campaign organizations in Britain cooperate this lessens their distinctiveness and may risk members drifting away to the other organization. This is not a danger in liaisons between, say, Swedish and British groups. Both Rucht (1993) and Bramble and Porter (1992) cite other organizational advantages arising from transnational cooperation. Rucht, talking principally about intra-European cooperation, outlines the virtues of mutual learning, the potential for gathering a broader range of information and the pooling of organizational resources (1993: 77), while Bramble and Porter, focusing mostly on South–North cooperation, highlight the possibilities of political coordination, attacking the same campaign target from many points, the capacity for using the international media and the benefits of resource sharing (1992: 346–53). As Rucht notes:

> With the growing internationalization of economies and capital, new technologies and their spill-over effects, the emergence of transnational mass media, and the partial shift of political decision making to international and supranational bodies, those affected have more reasons than ever before to respond in forms extending beyond national boundaries. (1993: 78)

Of course, some practical features do militate against such internationalism. Environmental campaign organizations develop a deep familiarity with their own countries' laws, politicians, civil servants and media. They are often so busy addressing these issues that the scope for internationalism is limited. And, as Bramble and Porter observe, these differences are exacerbated in North–South relations, where the groups have different styles of dealing with the government, the press and industry. Further, the 'ignorance of many Northerners (particularly US groups) about other countries, and the impact of our government and industry upon their citizens, causes old resentments to rise' (1992: 350–1). Environmental groups are far from transcending national barriers but there are good organizational reasons and strong incentives arising from their ideology and strategy why they have experienced some success and will continue to work in this direction.

*Firms and Local Authorities as 'Unlikely' Globalizers*

I suggested earlier in the chapter that the vast bulk of environmental problems result from economic activity and I briefly examined the market pressures on companies to cut costs by exploiting the environment.

However, once it is clear that environmental regulations are going to come into play, companies' outlooks begin to change. A good number of companies begin to have a commercial interest in harmonizing regulations and some firms may even wish to see environmental standards driven up worldwide. Within the European Union, for example, companies have been very active in pressing for uniform standards so that they can sell straightforwardly into all the member states' markets. Furthermore, high environmental standards effectively reduce the competition from cheaper but less 'green' producers outside the Union; they act as a palatable alternative to trade sanctions. Even within the EU, industry spokespersons in the less economically advanced states have complained that the Commission's preference for high environmental standards tends to favour the 'northern' member states (Germany, Denmark and the Netherlands, and now Austria, Sweden and Finland too) (Aguilar-Fernández, 1994). Similar arguments apply to specific US and Canadian firms within the context of NAFTA; they can preserve their markets from Mexican competition by arguing that high environmental performance standards are in the continent's interests.

Firms can also have a commercial reason for wishing to see the introduction of tougher environmental standards if they are strong performers of research and development. Increasingly, firms commission research to anticipate future regulatory trends and, naturally enough, once the research is completed they are keen to receive the 'pay-off' in market terms. As will be seen in the next chapter, this was conspicuously the case with DuPont, the leading manufacturer of substitutes for ozone-depleting chemicals. The company moved from early opposition to support for regulatory changes. In these ways, through their transnational spread, firms can place strong pressure on governments to shape their environmental and regulatory policies in ways which suit the firms. Depending on the economic and market conditions, firms can exercise pressure for stricter as well as for looser environmental policies. And in this context it is worth recalling that while Greenpeace and Friends of the Earth are known as 'pressure groups', firms and industrial associations are also formidable exercisers of pressure. As we have already seen, they are keen to be present at major international environmental conferences and have created bodies to lobby for shaping the 'global environmental agenda' in ways which suit their various commercial interests. As brief illustrative examples, the gas industry is keen that global warming and acid rain should be taken seriously since gas generally out-performs other fossil fuels in these regards. Equally, the nuclear industry is keen to present nuclear power as 'climate friendly' since (once up and running) fission power stations are non-emitters of carbon dioxide; they thus provide one possible option in the light of limited supplies of fossil fuels.

On the face of it, it might seem unlikely that there should be significant local initiatives in response to transnational environmental problems. One might have thought that nation-states and cross-national lobby groups would be the lowest level at which action could be anticipated. Yet, particularly since the Earth Summit in 1992, there has been a number of locally-based responses addressing both small- and large-scale environmental issues.

One of the chief products of the Earth Summit was the document *Agenda 21* (United Nations, 1992). *Agenda 21* is a long document, listing the activities which governments have agreed should follow from the summit. For each item (for example the conservation of biological diversity) it lists overall objectives, specific recommended activities and a costing estimate. One chapter in particular (Chapter 28) is devoted to 'Local authorities' initiatives in support of Agenda 21'.

While the response across the globe has been far from overwhelming, local authorities in a number of countries have taken up the opportunity offered in *Agenda 21*. For example, local environmentalists and city planners have pioneered a scheme in Brisbane to reduce its contribution to global warming through recycling (reducing emissions from manufacturing and methane emissions from waste dumps) and energy efficiency schemes. Related city programmes have appeared in Austria, Germany and the Netherlands. In the UK in 1994 Friends of the Earth launched its 'Climate Resolution Scheme'. This called on local authorities to sign up to a pledge to cut carbon dioxide emissions from their area by 30 per cent by 2005. The organization had been careful to sign up three authorities (Cardiff, Leicester and Newcastle upon Tyne) for the launch in February 1994. Friends of the Earth published a detailed guide showing authorities what they could achieve by using, for example, energy audits, combined heat and power schemes, a switch to diesel for certain vehicles and so on (1994).

One factor encouraging participation by some local authorities in Great Britain is that they feel they have been stripped of power and influence by successive centralizing Conservative administrations. The Friends of the Earth scheme is calculated to appeal to them by giving them the chance to participate in solving 'global' problems, while also improving local environmental quality *and* yielding the opportunity to be seen to out-perform central government, which has adopted much less ambitious $CO_2$ abatement targets. Additionally, such local authority action is also popular with sections of the European Union which are keen to establish links with regional and city authorities as a means of bypassing recalcitrant national governments.

### *State and Supranational Organizations as Agents of Globalization*

As one commentator drolly put it, the typical responses of governments to environmental policy problems has been to 'think national, act national'.[5] Even so, in certain areas – as with transboundary air pollution and with contaminated waterways – governments have shown some inclination to behave differently. Governments have accepted that certain policies towards the environment need to be coordinated above the national level or, to express it in a less favourable light, governments have learned that they need to worry about their neighbours' policies. As will be seen in the next chapter, this was the case in transnational discussion about the protection of the ozone layer. Similarly, in what is probably the most-cited European example, Scandinavian governments were concerned about damage to their forests attributed to acid rain stemming, to a large extent, from British power stations. The Swedish government could not act to protect its own timber resources because the problem was being brought in from Britain by the prevailing winds. Imported pollution seriously out-weighed domestic production since, as mentioned in Chapter 2, around two and-a-half times as much sulphur is deposited in Sweden as is emitted from Swedish sources. They had to combat the pollution problem through international negotiations since they had no direct legal control over British industry or the principal electricity generating company.

Governments seldom have 'pure' interests in environmental quality. In the Swedish case just mentioned, the state had a direct economic interest in the condition of forestry. The protection of the countryside is commonly related to the tourist business also. States may have concerns about the health consequences for their citizens of neighbouring countries' pollution. However, governments' interests in environmental policy issues stretch even wider than this. For example, governments are aware that industries in countries with lower pollution control standards than their own will typically have lower expenses. Therefore, it is in the industrial interests of the leaders in environmental policy to demand that others raise their standards; otherwise they will risk being undercut. As just noted for the case of large corporations, these considerations have played a large part in the drive for rising and uniform standards in the European Union; in a single market, countries with low environmental standards ought to perform better economically. In other words, some governments favour high environmental standards not so much for the environment's sake but because high standards suit their industries.

In some cases, governments' perceptions that they would benefit from working together has led them to establish bodies delegated with powers to propose and agree common policies. Such acts of intergovernmental cooperation can be illustrated through one of the best-known examples, the Mediterranean Action Plan. Around twenty states border on the Mediterranean, some (such as France and Italy) wealthy and industrialized, others much poorer (Egypt and the Lebanon). Some fish it, nearly all use it for leisure and tourism, most dump human sewage into it and all pollute it to some extent by industrial and agricultural practices. Several of the bordering countries are members of the European Union and therefore can be expected to have more or less harmonized policies. Others, however, are separated from France and Italy by great cultural and economic differences. Yet all – to some extent – have an interest in managing the environmental quality of the Mediterranean. Thus, from its inception in 1975, the Mediterranean Action Plan has grown both in terms of the number of subscribing countries and in the extent of the agreements made (see Haas, 1989, 1990).

Although the Mediterranean Action Plan could have grown up simply as a pact between governments, it was brokered through the United Nations Environment Programme. This fact points to a further, very significant stimulus to supranational action: the involvement of international bodies such as the European Union (EU) and – in particular – the United Nations (UN). They have fastened on to environmental issues as a way in which they can act in the 'common good' and thereby augment their influence. The environment appeals to such bodies because they can argue that it is inherently international, and therefore within their purview, and because it can be presented as a public interest issue. If, for example, the UN is putting forward proposals which supposedly advance the global environmental good it is hard for national politicians to oppose these without seeming to argue out of national self interest and thus to surrender the moral high ground. Additionally this means that environmentalists may therefore find these international bodies afford a 'softer' lobbying target than do national governments. However, it should be noted that the costs and administrative demands of lobbying at this level tend to screen out smaller environmental organizations and thus to favour the larger campaign groups (see Mazey and Richardson, 1992).

The United Nations has played a key role as a forum in which international environmental issues can be aired, a role which was first formally adopted following the 1972 'UN Conference on the Human Environment' held in Stockholm. As Thacher notes:

> it is widely acknowledged that the international *assessment* functions under UNEP's 'Earthwatch' monitoring, research and information-exchange activities have been well discharged by the UN system. . . . But when the time came to take *management* action at the national level . . . the effectiveness of [the UN-brokered] agreements has been curtailed by lack of political will or inadequate resources. (1992: 187–8; original italics)

As well as providing a focus for supplying authoritative documentation of cross-national environmental problems and for trying to advance treaty negotiations (see Birnie and Boyle, 1992: 33–52), United Nations committees have had a key role in introducing the vocabulary and conceptual tools for the development of environmental policy. Thus, the concept of sustainable development – a form of socioeconomic development which can continue indefinitely without exhausting the world's resources or overburdening the ability of natural systems to cope with pollution – was publicized through the Brundtland Report of the World Commission on Environment and Development (1987; see the next chapter for further discussion). And though many authors have reservations about the precision and utility of this concept, it is notable that it has attained considerable practical importance. It provides campaign groups with an officially-sanctioned yardstick by which they can gauge governments' performance and it has been publicly adopted by individual states and by the European Union as the objective of their environmental policies.

In his recent study of the politics of pollution control (1992), Weale has argued that there have been two waves of policy responses to environmental problems. In the first wave in the 1970s, governments established environment departments which had responsibility for protecting the natural environment. Well meaning and far sighted though some of these bodies were, their problem was that they existed alongside other departments whose business often resulted in adding to pollution. Agriculture ministries strove to increase food yields by encouraging the use of chemical fertilizers; transport ministries favoured road construction; and ministries of energy commonly encouraged nuclear power or the development of polluting fossil fuel-powered generating stations. In his view, the second wave – which is still gaining momentum – should see the introduction of environmental considerations into the business of all ministries, including the Treasury or finance ministry. For example, governments may move towards high rates of taxation on polluting substances, thus partially addressing the problem about externalities described earlier on. 'Second wave' policies will also be developed in open acknowledgment of the fact that international collaboration is needed to respond to transnational pollution problems.

By the mid-1990s Weale's interpretation is beginning to look a little mono-directional. In the USA the Endangered Species Act is under attack from landowners and deregulation-minded politicians; many political actors in the newly-revitalized Republican Party regard environmental restrictions on factory location as excessive and there are some anti-environmental pundits who argue that over-regulation causes job loss and stunts economic growth. In the European Union too there are concerns that proposed environmental quality standards may be too high and unnecessarily costly. The recently formed World Trade Organization, committed to removing obstacles to free trade (see Chapter 1), and the general enthusiasm in the world's finance ministries for open markets represent a potential source of coordinated antagonism to further environmental regulation. None the less, as was made clear in Chapter 2, the 1980s and early 1990s have seen a number of successful intergovernmental agreements. European Community members agreed steep reductions in emissions of acidic gases; an agreement was reached on ozone-depleting chemicals and some advances were made in combating marine oil pollution as well as general pollution in the North Sea and the Mediterranean. Furthermore, in principle, thanks to a UN agreement at the Rio Summit, countries are committed to devising plans for moving to sustainable development. Despite undoubted successes, supranational agencies such as the UN have encountered serious problems in getting states to agree far-reaching environmental reforms. In large part this is because environmental issues are intimately tied to questions of economic development and the distribution of wealth, questions over which countries have strongly competing interests.

**Concluding Discussion**

The aim of this chapter has been to examine, so to speak, how global environmental problems have got their globality. At one level I have argued that certain environmental issues can plausibly be seen as inherently global. Others have been rendered global by the transnational expansion of production, trade and communication. Partly in response to this trend (and also partly promoting awareness of it), there have been increased international collaboration and coordinated action on environmental themes. Many policies have had to be formulated cross-nationally; campaign organizations have internationalized; there have been new UN bodies established in the environmental field; and there have been innovations in international science.

However, the globality or universality of global environmental issues is also susceptible to a certain degree of deconstruction. Even the most strongly global problems turn out to have differentiated impacts. The identity of 'global' problems has been contested and even the definition of what is to count as an 'environmental' issue has not proved unproblematic, as the case of 'over-population' clearly shows. Furthermore, the appeal to common interests in global environmental management actually appears rather fragile. The potential for exploitation and injustice keep reappearing through the talk of universal values, even though many officials and some commentators propose that there are common human interests in environmental protection. This idea is even encapsulated in the title of the UN Brundtland Report (World Commission on Environment and Development, 1987): *Our Common Future*.

The unevenness of development and the inequalities of power and wealth associated with globalization indicate how idealistic – how 'Utopian' in Dobson's sense – the notion of a 'common future' is. The majority of transnational environmental problems – most notably the need to abate carbon dioxide emissions – are easier to read as displays of conflicting interests than as instances of people shaping a future in common. In the next chapter I turn to the possibility that certain universalizing discourses may provide objective guidance for finding a route out of this apparent impasse.

**Notes**

1 There are two significant differences between Figures 3.1–3.3 and Table 3.1. First, in the Table the data are given in terms of the mass of $CO_2$ whereas in the Figures the information given relates to the amount of carbon that the gas contains (carbon makes up a little over a quarter of the mass of $CO_2$). The second difference is that the data in the Table refer to industrial sources of $CO_2$ whereas the Figures include other sources, such as the burning of rainforests. Hence Brazil appears to perform 'worse' in the Figures than in the Table. The question of how exactly carbon emissions should be counted is examined in detail in the next chapter.

2 Even in Britain, which has lost all of its home-owned major car-making companies to

overseas concerns, the motor industry is still the largest industrial sector (*Times Higher Education Supplement*, 31 March 1995: 7).

3 Ford objected to being singled out by this campaign since no catalysers were routinely fitted to the majority of cars for the British market at that time; catalytic converters were subsequently made obligatory by EU regulations. The poster is reprinted in Yearley (1995c).

4 This book is published in the 'Real Story' series, other titles of which include investigations into the real story behind the respective assassinations of J.F. Kennedy, Robert Kennedy and Martin Luther King.

5 This was pointed out by Douglas Boucher in an address entitled 'The Earth as seen from Congress: just another special interest' at a conference on 'Environmentalism and the Politics of Nature' at Virginia Polytechnic Institute and State University, 8 April 1995.

# 4

# Universalizing Discourses and Globalization

## Talking of the Global

So far we have reviewed ways in which environmental issues have been a stimulus to transnational, even global, organization and 'consciousness' – by governments and intergovernmental agencies, by firms, by social movement organizations and in terms of the international character of the issues themselves. Chapter 3 finished by noting that, despite the growing trend to analyse and respond to environmental problems on a global level, the recognition of global threats has not brought about a unified response. Though one might think that world-wide environmental problems pose a threat to humanity as a whole and would thus stimulate concerted action, economic and political interests have led to divisions, divisions over the policies to be adopted and even over the nature of the environmental threats themselves. International responses have not been well coordinated. Some countries, particularly those in the South, have alleged that others have used the 'global' label as a cover for self interest. Attempts to talk about 'global problems' or 'global interest' – the attempted use of global discourse – has itself come to be viewed with suspicion.

However, as was described at the end of Chapter 1, there are established analytical resources[1] which are supposed to allow policy-makers and intellectuals to speak universally. The rigour of logical procedures, the exacting language of rights and the scrupulous discourse of science are all designed to transcend the local and to lay claim to universal validity. It is understandable that policy-makers, lobbyists and commentators have frequently appealed to these analytical resources when they have set about trying to interpret the globe's environmental problems. These universalizing discourses have held out the prospect of resolving apparently intractable global problems by providing us with the tools to describe and analyse those problems in objective and authoritative ways. The hope has been that these universalistic discourses would supply insights that transcend national differences and political interests, and thus offer binding interpretations of the environmental problems confronting the globe.

The purpose of this chapter is to examine the recourse to these universalizing discourses and to chart how that move operates in practical terms. The chapter will conclude by considering the amenability of global problems to universalistic solutions. The discourses to be examined include those of natural science, of logic and rational economic choice, and of the newly-minted language of sustainable development.

## Globality and the Discourse of Science

Scientific knowledge is usually said to be of global (indeed universal) validity because it is founded on a unitary scientific method (see for example Mendelssohn, 1976: 8). The archetypical laws of science apply everywhere on the globe. Advocates of the universality of science commonly and quite reasonably point out that the law of gravitation cannot be suspended by governmental action nor is Ohm's Law (concerning resistance and current in an electrical circuit) subject to cultural variation. It is therefore attractive to suppose that a disinterested scientific analysis of the world's environmental problems would be incontestable and binding. If one wishes to have an authoritative analysis of the globe's environmental condition and to know which remedies are needed for current problems, then one obvious place to turn is to scientific expertise.

In one sense there is nothing very surprising about this ambition to employ the cognitive authority of science. Throughout the twentieth century there have been periods of great optimism about the social role of science, and people have entertained the hope that scientific objectivity and precision would allow the control of all manner of social ills, including issues such as disease and crime. In the case of environmental issues, science has a peculiarly central role since it is key to the identification and interpretation of environmental problems (see Yearley, 1992a: 113–19). As Taylor and Buttel express it:

> Since scientists a generation ago detected radioactive strontium in reindeer meat and linked DDT to the non-viability of bird eggs, science has had a central role in shaping what counts as environmental problems. . . . We know we have global environmental problems because, in short, science documents the existing situation and ever tightens its predictions of future changes. Accordingly, science supplies the knowledge needed to stimulate and guide social-political action. (1992: 405)

As was briefly pointed out in Chapter 3, given the centrality of science to the identification and remedying of environmental problems it is only to be expected that the discourse of science will shape the way that environmental issues are approached. Since scientists generally aspire to universal generalizations and to laws of general validity, scientists will tend to assume that natural processes are consistent all over the globe unless there are very strong reasons for not doing so. As mentioned earlier, this point is well illustrated by the term biodiversity. The basis for the use of this term in assessing the loss of species world-wide is that, because all living creatures are patterned on related genetic material, there can be a measurement of genetic variability which is applicable the world over. Scientific analysis offers, so to speak, a common currency in which the loss of biological riches in any part of the world can be assessed. And this common currency is based on an experimentally tested theoretical basis. Assessments of biodiversity loss are not just a conventional scoring system (such as the system of stars applied to hotel accommodation) but are rooted in established scientific theory. Moreover, adequately trained biologists from any national or ethnic background can make these assessments, and the assessments ought to be the same whoever makes them. In other words, the universalizing discourse of science implies several things. There is a common currency; this common currency is not arbitrary but is founded in well established scientific theory; any properly trained scientist can use this common currency to make assessments which will be recognized as objectively valid by other scientists (and therefore policy-makers) the world over.

In recognition of these kinds of arguments, some authors from the international relations tradition have proposed that so called 'epistemic communities' are very influential in proposing, negotiating and implementing international agreements on such issues as international environmental policy (see Haas, 1989 and the studies in Haas et al., 1993). According to Haas:

> An epistemic community is a network of professionals with recognized expertise and competence in a particular domain and an authoritative claim to policy-relevant knowledge within that domain or issue-area . . . what bonds members of an epistemic community is their shared belief or faith in the verity and the applicability of particular forms of knowledge or specific truths. (1992: 3)

The key assertion of epistemic-community authors is that members of such communities can come to agreed analyses of issues or problems with a degree of independence from their political bosses. Among biologists or economists or arms-control experts from different countries there exist 'intersubjective understandings' (1992: 3). Accordingly, these expert communities' control over knowledge and information grants them independent power in shaping and coordinating international agreements.

As noted in the last chapter, this is not to imply that scientists are personally well disposed to cross-national cooperation or that they are necessarily internationally minded. The point made by epistemic-community authors is that scientists and other technical experts have the potential for powerful cooperation. Scientific experts are in this apparently favourable position because science aspires to universally valid truths, truths which apply the world over (see Jasanoff, 1996). This universalizing orientation has left its stamp on the overall international discourse of environmental management.

### Global Discourse and Global Warming

So far we have reviewed reasons why (in principle) scientific knowledge ought to be of special value in diagnosing and offering solutions to the globe's environmental problems. In this section we move on to examine the actual fitness of science for expressing global environmental truths and for formulating policy prescriptions. Though it will later be of key importance to look at the use of science by official agencies, let us begin with an example from a conflict between two respected and influential lobbying groups.

Far from science succeeding in resolving international environmental issues because of 'intersubjective understandings', existing suspicions of the North's interpretation of global interests have in many cases been exacerbated by the use of the (supposedly) universalistic discourse of science to diagnose the globe's problems. There are several detailed issues at stake here and it is better to start with an example and work back to the issues of principle. Thus, in 1990 the World Resources Institute (WRI), a prestigious Washington-based think-tank, sought to produce figures indicating each country's $CO_2$ emissions and thus their contribution to global warming for 1987 (Dowie, 1995: 119). The WRI had shown an early interest in global warming (as noted in Chapter 3) and had been especially influential in publicizing an emissions-reduction target against which governments' policies could be assessed (F. Pearce, 1991: 283–7). Their next task was to provide data on each country's performance, allowing the appropriate amounts of 'blame' to be attached (World Resources Institute, 1990: 345).

This task faced many practical difficulties. For example, the data were hard to come by and countries had good reasons for concealing the extent of their pollution. There are, as noted in Chapter 2, many greenhouse gases, and their effects needed to be integrated. But, in principle, the task seemed straightforward. From the point of view of global warming, one molecule of $CO_2$ is scientifically speaking the same as another and the global warming impact of one methane molecule is the same as that of any other. According to their analysis three of the top six net emitting nations were underdeveloped countries. In descending order the countries were the USA, USSR, Brazil, China, India and Japan. If all the EU member states were counted as one country it was even possible to argue that the remaining four places in the 'top ten' were occupied by the EU, Indonesia, Canada and Mexico. On this (possibly peculiar) view, fully half of the ten leading net emitters were from the non-industrialized world (a view presented for instance in the chart in Pickering and Owen, 1994: 81).

While the WRI authors described their method as straightforward (see Hammond et al., 1991: 12), the study stimulated a fierce attack from Indian researchers (Agarwal and Narain, 1991) based at the Centre for Science and Environment (CSE) in New Delhi, as well as a good deal of subsequent discussion and debate (see Ahuja, 1992; Jasanoff, 1993; McCully, 1991a). The CSE authors offered several arguments in their critique. First off, they suggested that the sources for the figures were defective. For example, Agarwal and Narain present evidence to suggest that the rate of rainforest clearance in Brazil was anomalously high in 1987 and that the felling rate declined considerably in the following year, due to changing financial incentives (1991: 4). Accordingly, the year selected gave Brazil a much higher apparent 'average' figure for $CO_2$ emissions (from burning the forest) then was truly average for the 1980s. Similarly they argue that the figures used to represent the loss of forest in India were based on data from the 1970s when forest clearances were more common.

Though these problems of data gathering tended to cast Third-World countries in an unfavourable light, this was not the main focus for the CSE critique. Their more decisive argument was that the scientific discourse and apparent objectivity of the report listing nations' respective contributions concealed two issues. The first had to do with assumptions implicit in the way 'net emissions' were calculated, while the second concerned the classification of types of emission.

Taking these points in order, like any model the procedures used for the WRI report depended on certain assumptions. A key assumption concerned 'sinks' for the greenhouse gases. When carbon dioxide is released into the atmosphere, not all of it remains in a gaseous form. Some of it is dissolved by rain or directly into the oceans while a large amount is taken up by plants and soils. In fact, the annual natural cycling of carbon through the atmosphere greatly exceeds the amounts added by human activity (Pickering and Owen, 1994: 83). Far from all the additional carbon pushed into the atmosphere each year by human activities remains there; according to WRI and CSE over 56 per cent of humanly produced carbon dioxide is absorbed by environmental sinks. The figure for methane is even higher, around 83 per cent (calculated from Agarwal and Narain, 1991: 10).

The methodology of the WRI study recognized this fact. Loosely speaking, it was taken into account by discounting all emissions by the rate at which they are absorbed. In other words, if 56 per cent of all $CO_2$ emitted each year is reabsorbed, countries are actually only causing a warming in proportion to 44 per cent of the total amount of $CO_2$ they emit. For methane the figure is 17 per cent and so on for other pollutants.

On the face of it this seems perfectly reasonable. However, Agarwal and Narain contended that this was actually unfair because it shared out the natural sinks in proportion to how big a polluter each country was, since one received a 'discount' for every single molecule of pollutant produced. They advocated an alternative approach which treated the sinks as something like the global entitlement of the human race. On this approach, one might wish to add up the absorptive capacity of all the natural sinks and then divide them equally between the global population. One could then allocate 'shares' to the various countries according to the size of their populations; only at this point would each nation's emissions be reduced by the appropriate discount. Although India as a nation is a large greenhouse polluter, according to the WRI figures the average Indian citizen has a greenhouse impact of 0.3, compared with 4.2 for a US citizen and 2.7 for British and German people.[2] Treating the figures in the CSE's fashion allows one to argue that Chinese and Indian people are actually living *within* the limits of the natural cycling capacity of the planet, whereas

North Americans, the Japanese and Europeans are not. In other words, if everyone on the planet only emitted at Indian or Chinese per capita levels, the natural sinks could be expected to cope with all the greenhouse pollution from carbon dioxide. As Agarwal and Narain put it:

> WRI's legerdemain actually lies in the manner that the earth's ability to clean up the two greenhouse gases of carbon dioxide and methane – a global common of extreme importance – has been unfairly allocated to different countries. . . . Global warming is caused by overexceeding [the] cleansing capacity of the earth's ecological systems. The WRI report makes no distinction between those countries which have eaten up this ecological capital by exceeding the world's absorptive capacity and those countries which have emitted gases well within the world's cleansing capacity. (1991: 10)

The CSE authors treat it as relatively unproblematic to assign 'shares' in the global sinks in proportion to various countries' populations, without observing that this approach is not self-evidently correct either. Such a method, though clearly related to principles of equity, has the drawback that it effectively rewards countries for increasing their populations and does so without regard to the allocation of resources (say, between rich and poor or women and men) *within* countries. A possible alternative would be to consider the actual distribution of sinks, so that there would be a systematic incentive for countries to maintain their forests. However, such an approach would quickly run into huge difficulties, not least over the allocation of the oceans which are extremely important carbon sinks. If coastal nations received a 'credit' for their off-shore waters, this would be disadvantageous to land-locked countries, and so on.

None the less, even if matters are not as straightforward as Agarwal and Narain seem to imply, the first key argument in the CSE document is that the apparently factual matter of drawing up greenhouse gas 'budgets', the kind of task to which universalistic scientific principles appear so readily applicable, actually resists straightforward scientific depiction. In particular, the issue of how the benefits of the world's sinks are to be allocated turns out to be contentious. Agarwal and Narain received a sympathetic hearing for their argument that the WRI report traded on an implicit, but extremely debatable, basis for parcelling out entitlements to these sinks.

The second major argument advanced by Agarwal and Narain is considerably more straightforward. It deals with sources of greenhouse gases rather than with sinks. The authors object to the fact that the WRI figures make no distinction between the sources of $CO_2$ or of methane. Gases emitted from the exhausts of people driving a short distance to the grocery store (when they could have cycled or taken public transport) were – scientifically – equated with people breathing out, with families burning fuel for cooking, and with methane produced from small-scale farming activities. As they expressed it:

> Can we really equate the carbon dioxide contributions of gas guzzling automobiles in Europe and North America or, for that matter, anywhere in the Third

World with the methane emissions of draught cattle and rice fields of subsistence farmers in West Bengal or Thailand? . . . no effort has been made in WRI's report to separate out the 'survival emissions' of the poor, from the 'luxury emissions' of the rich. (1991: 5)

In this passage the apparent universality of the scientific rendering of this issue is presented as, in practice, inaccurate and immoral.

While the thrust of this criticism is readily understood, it is extremely difficult to make any rigorous distinction between survival and luxury emissions. The WRI's response to this point was that the recognition of the two categories 'involves essentially political judgments that are beyond the scope of the World Resources Report, which is intended to provide accurate, accessible information on which there is substantial expert or scientific agreement' (cited in Jasanoff, 1993: 35). The WRI sought to distance its factual method from the 'political' approach of the CSE. Other authors offered a different critique of Agarwal and Narain's reasoning. Ahuja suggests that the use of any such distinction may actually make greenhouse-warming reduction more inefficient since it tends to discourage the pursuit of greenhouse gas savings from 'survival' sources (1992: 84). For instance, it may be possible to abate the emissions from farming practices or domestic heating at less cost than from other, less clearly 'survival' uses. For this reason, the exclusion of 'survival emissions' from greenhouse gas reduction policies would be irrational.

But whether or not one wishes to try to reinstate some form of distinction which separates 'unavoidable' from 'optional' greenhouse pollution, the key point is that the protestations by WRI about the 'non-political' nature of their information are very questionable. As noted earlier, their figures deal with 'national accountability' for greenhouse emissions. Any such figures depend on the authors being able to separate out emissions for which countries are 'accountable' from those for which they are not. It seems clear enough that volcanic emissions fall into the latter category and car fumes into the former. But there remain questions about the exact dividing line. As Ahuja notes, 'What about anthropogenic modifications of natural sources, such as draining wetlands, or of natural sinks, such as reduction in terrestrial biomass productivity because of acid precipitation?' (1992: 84). In other words, forests are natural sinks, but if – because of acid pollution – German forests are functioning less effectively than they used to, shouldn't the difference between the forests' actual fixing of carbon and their potential for absorption count as a net contribution by Germany (or by the producers of the acid rain)? This decision depends 'essentially on . . . judgements' (to borrow the WRI's terms) but this time on judgements they seem happy to make.

In sum, without necessarily endorsing Agarwal and Narain's call for a distinction between survival and luxury emissions, it is evident that even the distinctions between natural and humanly-caused emissions are provisional and open to dispute. It is not that CSE's proposed distinction depends on judgement while the WRI's does not. Both do. Accordingly the WRI cannot dismiss Agarwal and Narain's counter-claim simply on the basis that it demands judgements.

Overall therefore, the Indian researchers challenged the suitability of existing scientific comparisons as the base-line method for comparing countries' contributions to pollution. Scientific methods gain much of their power through their appeal to universal standards. But, in this case, it was argued that politically weighted assumptions underlay the putative scientific 'facts'. Agarwal and Narain proposed that explicitly moral and ethical considerations (about equity for example) should have played a part also. Science, perhaps the leading intellectual tool for analysing the globality of environmental problems, was presented as deficient and in major respects unsuitable.

### Scientific Discourse and the Protection of the Ozone Layer

The second illustrative case concerns agreements, largely thrashed out between government delegations, designed to conserve the ozone layer.[3] Benedick, the US negotiator whose work was mentioned in Chapter 2, starts his account of the negotiations leading to international treaties regulating ozone-depletion with a very strong statement about the role of science:

> The Montreal Protocol was the result of research at the frontiers of science combined with a unique collaboration between scientists and policymakers. Unlike any previous diplomatic endeavor, it was based on continually evolving theories, on state-of-the-art computer models, simulating the results of intricate chemical and physical reactions for decades into the future, and on satellite-, land-, and rocket-based monitoring of remote gases measured in parts per trillion. (1991: 9)

A major claim appears to be being made here to the effect that the scientific evidence drove the agreement and that it was thanks to the quality of the evidence that a good agreement was reached. Other commentators appear to share this favourable interpretation: 'the scientific case is beyond any serious question; CFCs really do strip stratospheric ozone and boost incoming harmful radiation – nobody argues otherwise and industry no longer objects' (Thacher, 1992: 198). Thacher implies that the firmness of the scientific evidence led to a correct, common view of the problem. Here, then, is a case where a universal discourse appears to have been effective.

However, the story is actually rather more complex than these accounts imply. As was noted at the start of Chapter 2, there were prominent campaigns around the removal of CFCs from aerosol spray cans in Europe in the late 1980s, almost a decade after those substances had been banned in spray cans in the USA. This indicates that, at the very least, different types or levels of scientific evidence were demanded by policy-makers in two areas of the world with approximately equal standards of technical sophistication and industrialization. This difference in the policy response to scientific evidence leads to some problems for the idea that science commands global assent (see Jasanoff, 1990b).

To begin the detailed analysis of this issue it is necessary to sketch the background to the agreements. The USA, as mentioned earlier, had taken action on non-essential CFC use (that is, in spray cans) in the late 1970s and was quickly followed by Canada, Norway and Sweden, though these last two were only consumers, not producers, of CFCs. With the Nordic countries in the lead (at least in part because of their proneness to the problem of polar ozone loss (Benedick, 1991: 170)) and encouraged by the United Nations Environment Programme, these four countries plus Finland formed a united front on this issue; they received support also from Austria, Switzerland, Denmark and Australia (Parson, 1993: 38). From 1983, this association of countries (which the USA joined a little later on) was known as the Toronto Group (Benedick, 1991: 42); it called for an international ban on non-essential uses. European Union representatives, apparently reflecting the interests of their CFC-producers whose output and world trade were growing, responded by arguing for a different approach. They favoured a cap on production capacity arguing that only a limit to the manufacture of the pollutant could work in the long term. On this view, even if non-essential uses were eliminated the amounts of CFC dedicated to 'essential' uses might escalate. With this stalemate over strategies for controlling the pollutants, no immediate international limitations were going to be agreed. A convention was drawn up (the Vienna Convention for the Protection of the Ozone Layer) and adopted in March 1985, registering international concern over the issue, but specific protocols setting emission limits were to come later. Of itself, the Vienna Convention entailed 'no obligations to act' (Susskind, 1994: 168) though a commitment was made to start negotiations for a protocol agreement, to be prepared for 1987.

In the next two years continuing negotiations resulted in compromise positions. For example, a weighting system was devised allowing the ozone-depleting potential of various chemicals to be compared. Countries could then agree on reductions in total amounts of ozone-depleting chemicals while retaining discretion over which pollutants they cut most. Japanese industry, for example, was reluctant to cut CFC 113, a solvent ubiquitous in its electronics industry, but under the new system it could make disproportionate cuts in its use of other CFCs instead (Benedick, 1991: 79). According to the Montreal Protocol, signed in 1987, the 'basket' of CFCs was to be frozen at 1986 levels in 1990, cut by 20 per cent by 1993/4 and reduced to half 1986 levels by 1998/9. These targets applied both to production and to countries' consumption, defined as whatever they produced plus imports minus exports. These targets still faced several problems. For one thing, there was some dispute over the base year against which cuts should be measured. While European production was still on an upward trend (so that industries would benefit more the later the base year), the USA had already made large cuts and did not want to see its relative position further worsened. Second, there were problems of international trade. Relatively few countries were producers though there were many consumers. The technology for CFC production was comparatively simple and Third-World countries had a reasonable expectation that this was an area into which they could soon move. From the point of view of signatories there was clearly a danger that certain other countries would not sign up, but start to make CFCs for the developing-country market, effectively being given free rein in the market left open by signatory countries honouring the treaty. Such non-complying countries might also be able to use CFCs in making goods and export these to signatory countries, whose use of CFCs was now limited by international law. Two specific measures were accordingly included.

First, developing countries with an annual calculated consumption of below 0.3 kilograms per head were allowed a ten-year grace period before they had to introduce cuts and were allowed to increase consumption up to the 0.3 kilograms per head level during that period if they wished providing the consumption was to meet 'basic domestic needs' (Montreal Protocol cited in Benedick, 1991: 235). In this way they could somewhat increase CFC use without having to reject the international agreement. Second, trade restrictions were placed on countries that refused to sign up to the agreement. As Parson notes:

> The Protocol included several restrictions on trade with non-parties: bulk imports of restricted substances from non-parties were prohibited in 1990; bulk exports [from developing countries to non-parties] were prohibited from 1993; imports from non-parties of products containing controlled substances were banned [with certain exceptions] from 1992; and parties agreed to study the feasibility of banning imports of products made with controlled substances, even though not containing them. (1993: 44–5)

In these various ways, compliance with the treaty was being imposed on Third-World countries.

The Montreal Protocol had a further significant feature; it contained provision for a periodic review of the measures in case they proved too weak or excessively restrictive. New evidence on global ozone loss was published early in the following year (1988) and a corresponding attempt was made to advance the next review meeting. The parties met again in Helsinki in 1989, and a year later held a full conference in London to revise the treaty. The London Revisions to the Montreal Protocol stated that all 'fully halogenated' CFCs (that is, excluding the new substitutes – known as HCFCs and HFCs – which contained hydrogen in place of some or all of the chlorine) were to be phased out by 2000 and that other associated chemicals should also be withdrawn over similar time-scales (Parson, 1993: 49).

Given this background information to the ozone negotiations it is easy to come to (at least) moderately optimistic interpretations of this international process. The negotiations had generated a binding international agreement accepted by over seventy countries, including the producers and consumers of over 90 per cent of the world's ozone-depleting substances (Benedick, 1991: 265–9). Parson, for example, in an explicitly evaluative overview of the Montreal Protocol pronounces it the 'right measures enacted too late' (1993: 72). His reservations are not about what was agreed to, but about the length of time the agreement took. He is worried about the continued presence of ozone-destroying chemicals in the atmosphere which will peak in the early years of the twenty-first century and only return to the level of the mid-1980s two or three decades later. If these chemicals turn out to be any more effective at destroying ozone than is currently thought, the environmental consequences may still be very harmful.

Other commentators appear to approve the agreement also (for example Warr, 1991: 166). Indeed, it is common for authors to contrast ozone depletion with other pollution problems on the grounds that the ozone issue is one of the easier international threats to resolve since there is a small number of pollutants, alternatives are available or readily imaginable and the number of producers is relatively small. In other words, the Montreal Protocol is held up as a successful agreement, albeit in the context of warnings that other agreements may not be so easily achieved.

Benedick is even more enthusiastic, approvingly citing the claim by Mostafa Tolba (the Executive Director of UNEP) that the London Revisions meeting had amounted to 'a new chapter in the history of international relations' (1991: 196). Benedick proceeds to draw out some of the implications of this 'new chapter':

> Science became the driving force behind ozone policy. The formation of a commonly accepted body of data and analyses and the narrowing of ranges of uncertainty were prerequisites to a political solution among negotiating parties initially far apart. *In effect, a community of scientists from many nations, committed to scientific objectivity, developed through their research an interest in protecting the planet's ozone layer that transcended divergent national interests.* (1991: 204; my italics)

Here is an explicit claim that scientific objectivity allowed an impartial analysis of the planet's problems to be made, in a way that transcended national interest.

Given these claims that it was the 'right answer', that this was a relatively easy problem to solve, and that scientific objectivity won out in the international debate, one would be tempted to take the ozone-protection negotiations as an exemplary instance of the universality of scientific discourse. We now have to ask whether this interpretation holds up on closer inspection.

### Questioning the Universality of Science in the Ozone Negotiations

To begin this inspection we should turn first to a couple of practically important but conceptually undemanding issues which indicate that scientific discourse was not universally efficacious. First, there are persistent indications that the science was often uncertain and not persuasive. The event which is often associated with a scientific breakthrough in this area, the identification of the Antarctic ozone 'hole', is specifically discounted by Benedick as an influence on negotiations. At the time of the announcement of the dramatic hole (actually an area of extreme depletion rather than a literal hole) in the ozone layer it was unclear that the hole resulted from CFCs or that the existence of the hole was necessarily indicative of widespread ozone loss; the hole could just have been confined to the Antarctic (Benedick, 1991: 19–20).

Second, even when it was agreed that the scientific evidence did indicate the existence of a humanly-caused environmental problem, the evidence did not of itself reveal what kind of solution should be adopted. This was graphically shown by a twist in the US negotiating position in the run-up to the Montreal Protocol negotiations. The Reagan administration was in principle committed to 'rolling back' excessive regulation and the Republican Party was no enthusiast for centralized, 'progressive' environmental policies in the way the preceding Carter Administration had been. The initial large CFC reduction had been achieved under a Democratic president. In a sense therefore it was no surprise that in early 1987, when a second round of strong restrictions on ozone-depleting substances were again on the cards, a number of policy-makers and politicians, with an almost in-principle opposition to environmental regulation, spoke up against new restrictions. As Benedick notes, 'Characteristic of the libertarian attitude on this issue was the argument that skin cancer was a "self-inflicted disease" attributable to personal life-style preferences, and therefore protection against excessive radiation was the responsibility of the individual, not the government' (1991: 59–60). This was not the view of 'cranks' or outsiders, but was given support by officials in the Departments of the Interior, Commerce, and Agriculture, together with the Office of Management and Budget, the Office of Science and Technology Policy, and parts of the White House staff.

Although these libertarian opponents also tended to stress the amount of uncertainty surrounding scientific knowledge about ozone depletion and repeatedly counselled against over-hasty action, their main argument was not that ozone depletion was not happening. Rather, they proposed that even if it was, it was up to individuals to manage the risks. Apparently those who argued in this vein anticipated that their argument would prove popular with the US public who are stereotypically individualist and resentful of government interference. They thought that people would accept that wearing sun-hats, sunscreen and dark glasses was a reasonable price to pay for continued cheap air-conditioning and a minimum of disruption to industry through the need for new solvents and so on. Given that the US public repeatedly elects politicians who favour individualized solutions to societal problems (for instance politicians defend the right to bear arms as a personal defence against crime, rather than attempting to reduce gun ownership in the hope of reducing the threat from crime) this was not an unreasonable strategy. However, as Benedick reports, the libertarians opened themselves to satirical portrayal in the mainstream newspapers with, for examples, cartoons of wildlife applying sun-block. Environmental campaigners were then able to use this imagery as a new way of inducing public disquiet about the problem. Similarly, it was argued by public health officials that many at-risk people were not threatened because they foolishly stayed outdoors too long without taking precautionary measures. Instead, they were at risk because as agricultural workers, gardeners, or construction workers their jobs obliged them to do physical labour out of doors. The fact that the threat in this case concerned cancer, perhaps the greatest mass health fear in US society and the focus for policy interventions since at least the time of Nixon's presidency, meant that the libertarians had perhaps misjudged the case (see Studer and Chubin, 1980: 74ff.).

In other cases, 'self-help' answers to environmental problems have won more support. For example, in relation to global warming, where the principal source of pollution (the burning of fossil fuels) is so close to the core of modern industrial and industrializing societies, a very common argument has been that countries should look to ways of coping with sea-level rise since that is likely to be less disruptive than a move away from fossil fuels (see D. Pearce, 1991c: 15). It is not therefore only how certain and how grave the pollution threat is, but also how highly valued the alternative is. Politicians with car component manufacturers in their constituencies may see threats to raise the prices of air-conditioning units as critical, but this is likely to be a less sound basis for widespread interests than is the issue of fossil fuel burning. In any event, it is clear that the type of policy response adopted does not follow automatically from the scientific analysis.

But though there were at least these two kinds of doubt about the exact status of scientific information available to the negotiators and about the nature of the policy consequences which followed from the scientific advice, this lack of certainty did not inhibit the negotiating parties from deciding about Third-World countries' entitlements nor from agreeing about penalties to be imposed on non-complying Southern countries.

As we have already seen, in the negotiations for the Montreal Protocol it was agreed that developing countries could delay their compliance and in fact continue to increase consumption up to 0.3 kilograms per person per year. But this level was only around a quarter of the existing consumption in Europe and the USA, and only around half the anticipated per capita consumption in the First World after the Protocol-related cuts (Benedick, 1991: 93). International treaties were about to deny to the citizens of developing countries a level of resource use which had been enjoyed in the First World for two decades or more, and which was expected to continue in the North for the short to medium term.

Furthermore, as noted above, CFC production is relatively simple and inexpensive. Several Southern countries were just beginning to develop plans for plants (Benedick, 1991: 101). They were now about to be put in a

'Catch 22' situation. If they signed the treaty they were not allowed to export any CFCs they produced since the treaty specified that production was to meet basic domestic needs only. If they did not sign the treaty however they were to face sanctions. A ban was to come into place on importing products containing ozone-depleting substances (for example, air-conditioning equipment) from non-parties (1991: 92), and subsequently the parties were to consider how to deal with imports of products made with (but not containing) ozone-depleting substances (electronic equipment cleaned with CFCs for instance). After the Protocol negotiations some Southern-country spokespersons (notably the Malaysian negotiator) complained about the terms of the agreement, for example, relating to the low, binding limits set on Third-World consumption.

Among developing countries, China and India were in a significantly different position. Given their huge populations, they had no real need to develop international trade in CFCs in order to make production economically viable. It might have been worth their while to produce CFCs for the domestic market alone. As was also the case with carbon dioxide emissions (as shown by the calculations discussed in the last chapter), if Indians somehow managed to consume up to their allotted limit, that would place them among the highest emitters of ozone-eaters in the world, roughly equalling the pre-Treaty emissions of the USA.

The negotiators' hope was that it would prove unattractive to industrializing countries to move into CFC production, because the substances were harmful, because they were being phased out in any case and because there were limits on trading them. However, the new alternatives (HCFCs and HFCs) were both several times more expensive to manufacture than CFCs (Parson, 1993: 42). It turned out that withdrawing CFCs from aerosols had been reasonably straightforward and had even saved companies money (1993: 66), but in the remaining uses, for refrigeration (particularly for commercial food storage and preservation) and for temperature regulation, these savings were not available (Markandya, 1991: 67). Moreover, DuPont had spent many millions of dollars researching the alternatives (Parson, 1993: 42) and enjoyed commercial advantages in this market. There was accordingly a danger, at least from the point of view of India or China, that countries which were just developing their own capacity in an important chemicals sector were now to have to forgo that advantage, to pay more for replacement chemicals to do the same job, and to pay someone else to make the replacements (or pay royalties for the process) instead of making them themselves. They might even have to write off newly-constructed CFC plant. This had all the appearance of a multiply bad deal. The North's negotiators, correspondingly, worried that determined non-compliance by large sectors of the underdeveloped world could undo the emissions reductions work they had achieved.

These issues were raised explicitly at the London Revisions meeting, since the Montreal Protocol had only offered to 'facilitate access to environmentally safe alternative substances and technology' for Third-

World countries and to assist them in making expeditious use of those alternatives while undertaking to 'facilitate . . . the provision of subsidies, aid, credits . . . for the use of alternative technology and for substitute products' (Article 5, paragraphs 2 and 3 in Benedick, 1991: 236). Representatives of many Southern countries regarded these undertakings as insufficiently specific. It was, for instance, unclear exactly what was meant by 'facilitat[ing] access'. In any case, with the accelerated phasing out of pollutants which was to be agreed at the London meeting, there was much greater urgency for Third-World countries to adopt corrective measures. According to Benedick (1991: 188–9) the negotiations went right to the wire on this issue. Essentially, Southern countries wanted a guarantee of access to the new technologies on 'preferential and non-commercial terms' and they argued that they should not be obliged to comply with the terms of the revised treaty unless they received all the technological assistance they deemed necessary. In other words, they claimed that it was unfair to force them to meet the demands of the treaty unless they were given all the help they needed and that, since they already had access to CFC-technology, they should not have to pay extra to gain access to the successor technology.

By contrast, First-World negotiators emphasized above all the need for all parties to comply with the revised treaty. They did not want Southern countries to be able to plead inability to comply and therefore have an excuse for simply failing to reduce ozone-depleting pollution. Neither did they want to give an open-ended promise to pay for whatever upgrading of technologies Third-World countries deemed necessary. Similarly, Northern companies had invested large sums in research on replacements and they wanted to be able to recoup their investment, not give the results away on concessionary terms.

In the end, a compromise was reached on both aspects of this question. First, it was agreed that technology transfer would occur under 'fair and most favourable conditions' (Article 10A (b) in Benedick, 1991: 255). A developing country that felt that it was unable to meet the demands of the revised treaty because of shortcomings in the transfer of technology could have its objections heard and ruled on by the parties to the treaty at the next formal meeting. This left it to the treaty parties and the secretariat to judge the meaning of 'fair and most favourable' treatment.

The second contentious element was addressed by a revised treatment of the issue of financial aid to assist compliance. The Montreal Protocol had offered only the vaguest commitments about financial assistance for making the technological changes away from dependence on CFCs. By contrast, the London Revisions meeting gave rise to an elaborate structure aimed at covering 'the incremental costs of developing country parties in meeting their control obligations' (Parson, 1993: 49–50). A fund of $240 million was established with sums contributed by the industrial-country parties to the Treaty. A fourteen-person Executive Committee was set up to govern the fund; it is composed of seven members from the industrialized countries and seven from the Third World. Its constitutional structure demands that decisions are approved by a majority of both sets of members.

At the time of writing, the processes by which funding levels are agreed and by which budget allocations are made are still being finalized. The United Nations Development Programme, the UNEP and the World Bank are all eager to function as the channel through which the money is actually spent on such issues as studies of needs, training, and actual investment in new technologies. NGO representatives are to be permitted to attend most Executive Committee meetings (Parson, 1993: 51). It is proving difficult to arrive at agreement over the sums needed to meet the 'incremental costs' of compliance. For example, India's own estimates of the cost to the economy of switching away from CFCs and other ozone-depleting chemicals produce a total which is greater than all the money allocated to aiding Third-World countries. Domestically, there have been some calls for India to pull out of the agreement if more 'realistic' compensation is not made available. At the same time, politicians in the USA are under pressure to reduce government spending of all kinds and they have selected overseas aid as one of their targets for economizing. Accordingly, at the end of 1995 US officials proposed that Southern countries should be given longer to meet targets for phasing out ozone-depleting substances (see *Independent on Sunday*, 31 December 1995: 13). Changing the time-scale in this way would reduce the amount of financial assistance required, at least in the short term. The US proposal was overruled by other Treaty signatories, but serves as a warning that even this international agreement is still in many respects fragile.

### The Legitimacy of Scientific Representations of Global Needs

Though this has been a lengthy case study, a number of points central to the argument of this chapter can be quickly adduced from this story. On the face of it, ozone depletion is a leading candidate for an inherently global problem. Despite apparent misunderstandings early on by some governments that there was no damage to 'their country's' ozone layer (Parson, 1993: 37), the pollutants have a world-wide spread and so every country has to worry about its neighbours' conduct. In Benedick's view, the problem was objectively characterized by scientists; as we saw, he claimed that 'a community of scientists from many nations, committed to scientific objectivity, developed through their research an interest in protecting the planet's ozone layer that transcended divergent national interests' (1991: 204). Their objective knowledge of the problem was sufficient for them to convince politicians to drive through major restrictions on the use of industrially beneficial chemicals, and to justify imposing trade sanctions on Third-World countries which did not wish to cooperate.

On this view, the problem was clearly global, the discourse of science allowed that global problem to be analysed, quantified and expressed, and the objective language of science allowed the experts, largely appointed by the North, to speak in the interests of everyone. The issue of whether it was legitimate for such experts to be regarded as representatives of the globe appears never to have arisen, either for major negotiators (including Benedick) or for commentators such as Parson. Of course, underdeveloped country spokespersons occasionally challenged certain aspects of the unfolding agreement (the level of pollution they were permitted or the terms of aid for example), but neither account referred to in this chapter focuses on questions of legitimacy, as raised by parties in the South.

For present purposes, there are two major issues here. One starts out simply from concerns about 'rights' to representation. As the industrial countries came to form their best accounts of the nature of the ozone-thinning problem it appears to have been their objective to limit the damage as soon as possible. From what they took to be an authoritative depiction of the natural world, they moved quickly to an equally authoritative account of what action was needed. And in formulating responses in terms of which substances had to be phased out and how quickly, they did not take into account the historical pollution load-issue. They knew the globe had a problem and they knew what was needed; they did not involve the rest of the globe in coming up with an answer. Though Third-World countries were given the right to increase their CFC pollution, they were only allowed to do this in the course of meeting 'basic domestic needs'. The putative need to trade in order to achieve economic growth (a 'need' often seen as natural in other contexts, for example by the IMF) was not accepted. Using the privilege of its expert knowledge of the situation, the North effectively drew up the rules of the negotiation game.

The second point develops this a little further by raising questions about how these experts chose to frame the issue. To start by analogy with the $CO_2$ problem, was it right to speak of all ozone-depleting chemicals as being the same, or was it not possible to speak of more and less 'essential' uses? This is not a mere rhetorical question since, as we have seen, early on in the debate US policy-makers had made this kind of distinction when agreeing to phase out aerosols. They regulated against non-essential uses of CFCs. Moreover, some US officials returned to this point later on (prior to the Montreal Protocol talks) because they felt it was unfair that the USA, having already cut non-essential uses, should be agreeing to the same percentage cuts as other nations who had to date made no cuts at all. Similarly the French had apparently raised the matter in relation to the appropriate kinds of propellants for perfume sprays. They argued that the nature of the propellant may not matter much in most aerosol-spray uses, whereas for spraying perfume one has to take care not to upset the odour (Benedick, 1991: 43). In these terms, CFCs could be seen as 'essential' to perfumery. In these responses we can find the germ of an alternative policy idea which parallels the proposal of Agarwal and Narain: the response to the problem of ozone-depleting chemicals might not be to cut back on all uses but only on unnecessary uses. Different countries might have legitimate (though varying) 'needs' for those substances.

But this second question of how the overall issue was framed could be taken even further. For example, none of the international negotiators appeared to question the idea that the appropriate policy response was to switch from one set of chemicals to a set of (fundamentally similar) substitutes. The proposed solution allowed people to carry on with essentially the same technologies and was fully compatible with straightforward industrial expansion. One alternative route might have been through the introduction of different kinds of changes. Building design alteration, revisions in buildings management, and changing public expectations could have led to a reduction in the demand for air conditioning; other cultural and marketing changes could have led to a reduction in the use of spray cans. Admittedly, in the UK Friends of the Earth did press for options including 'banking' of certain ozone-depleting chemicals and for greater recycling (that is, ways of having less pollution from existing sources), but even they did not campaign against the use of spray cans per se. This move on the part of policy-makers is particularly interesting given the fact that the prime alternatives to CFCs (HCFCs) are also ozone depletors (although with a tenth to a fiftieth of the potency of most CFCs) with an atmospheric life up to twenty years. In other words, by embracing a 'business-as-usual' response with substitute substances, the international community was still faced with a continuing threat to the ozone layer.

### 'Scientification' and the Practical Weakness of the Universal Discourse of Science

In the late 1960s and early 1970s Habermas and other 'Critical Theory' authors outlined a critique of the role of scientific and technical decision-making procedures in Western states. In brief, their argument was that popular participation in politics was declining as more and more decisions were taken in line with the dictates of alleged scientific and technical rationality. By invoking the 'rationality' of certain courses of action, governments could free themselves from democratic accountability since, supposedly:

> The solution of technical problems is not dependent on public discussion. Rather, public discussion could render problematic the framework within which the tasks of government action present themselves as technical ones. Therefore the new politics of state interventionism requires a depoliticization of the mass of the population. (Habermas, 1971: 103–4)

Habermas referred to this process as the scientification of politics. In concrete terms, it raised the possibility of the usurpation of political power by technocrats, since 'The state seems forced to abandon the substance of power in favour of an efficient way of applying available techniques in the framework of strategies that are objectively called for. . . . It becomes . . . the organ of thoroughly rational administration' (1971: 64). Scientification is accordingly a threat to democratic control over politics and policy.

From the perspective of the close of the twentieth century, it is difficult to identify directly with Habermas' anxieties. He foresaw a growth in government intervention, legitimated by technocratic rationales, while the current trend is towards a shrinking of the state, this shrinking itself justified in terms of the 'logic' of the global economy. However, his point about the potential opposition between scientification and participatory or directly-accountable democracy is still useful and provides a way of talking about the practical weaknesses in the application of the universalizing discourse of science to global environmental problems. It seems that in this case what Habermas feared of the state has, in significant respects, become true of the international policy community.

Habermas was anxious about the growth of technocratic management because it allowed the state to get away without defending its policies to its citizens. It gave the state the chance to say that a policy had been decided on because the relevant experts had deemed it technically necessary. In the case of the negotiations leading up to the international treaty on ozone depletion we saw a similar process operating. Politicians, scientists and lobbyists in the North believed that ozone depletion was becoming a global problem. Since it was a technical problem, it was assumed that scientists from any country would have agreed about the problem, though in fact virtually all the concerned scientists, all the detection equipment and all the major negotiators were from the North. Scientists and environmentalists had few reservations about representing the interests of the globe because this was a technical problem to which there were rationally calculable, technical solutions. Given that they were operating in the interests of the globe on the advice of scientific experts, Northern policy-makers were happy to impose their solution on Third-World nations, employing trade sanctions to win compliance. However, there were assumptions made in the technical framing of the problem which Third-World technical delegates – had the Third World been more broadly represented – might have questioned. These could, for example, have included the small range of policy alternatives considered (building design was not an issue), the unwillingness to distinguish between core and unnecessary uses of ozone-depleting substances, and the issue of intellectual property rights over the new CFC-substitutes. *The conviction that science speaks objectively and disinterestedly means that one need have no qualms about excluding other people from decision-making since they would, in any event, have arrived at the same conclusions as oneself.*

The case of ozone depletion, which initially appeared so well suited to analysis in terms of a universal discourse of science, turns out instead to indicate the hazards of scientification, essentially because scientific depiction of practical problems, on the one hand, and evaluation or political assessment, on the other, are not completely separable. On this point, it is as important to clarify what I am not claiming as it is to specify what I am. My point here is not the important but well known question of the relationship between scientific description and moral prescription. For example, supposing everyone had agreed about the nature of ozone depletion and about the new chemicals needed to replace the ozone-eaters. It would still be possible for some people to argue that the costs of remedying the problem by changing the chemicals used in industry outweighed the benefits of resolving the problem, and that the problem should be allowed to continue while personal precautionary measures are adopted. This is a highly significant issue which occurs wherever factual information is used to inform policy-making. It arises in disputes over the advisability of medical treatments, over the levels of safety equipment to fit on trains and planes and so on. It is commonly discussed in terms of a trade-off between costs and benefits. One could draw attention to this point without ever questioning the universal applicability of the discourse of science. On this view the scientific, factual matters are sorted out first and only then are questions of morals and values assessed.

The point I am highlighting is that values and value-laden assumptions enter into the formulation of the issue before the 'facts' are even established. This can be seen several times over in the instances discussed already. First, it applies very clearly to the dispute between the WRI and CSE over the basis for generating 'facts' about various nations' greenhouse gas emissions. It is also relevant to the disagreement between the European and the US delegates over the appropriate facts about ozone-depleting substances: should one take production or the consumption figures as the relevant variable? In these cases, and in many other aspects of both the global warming and ozone protection debates, the 'facts' and the values/politics are in practice established at the same time.

The same kind of difficulty arises over the classification of certain pollutants as being different or as 'of the same kind'. A decision about whether to treat all molecules of $CO_2$ as the same, or whether to introduce the idea of luxury and survival uses, changes the 'objective' facts from which bargaining and agreement start out. Exactly the same consideration arose in relation to the alleged necessary and optional uses of CFCs and other ozone-depleting chemicals. Some halons, for example, are regarded as extremely effective fire extinguishers. The argument could easily be made that they should not be assessed according to the same rules as other ozone depletors whose use is more frivolous.

At this stage it may be tempting to suggest that I am splitting hairs. For instance, one might try to reassert the global validity of the scientific approach by suggesting that all molecules of $CO_2$ are 'naturally' alike and that any attempt to separate necessary from luxury emissions is an artificial division. Despite the apparent simplicity of this remedy it does not work; it does not let us arrive at basic 'facts' which everyone *has to* accept. For one thing, as already discussed, the whole approach to carbon dioxide 'accounts' is already based on drawing a distinction between the 'natural' and the 'human'. When there is a huge volcanic eruption which causes a cloud of pollution, obscures the sun's rays and thus gives rise to atmospheric cooling, the country which 'contributed' the volcano does not get a credit permitting it to lessen its contribution to global warming abatement. Yet if one considers it natural for people to breathe, to cultivate food and so on, then certain human contributions to climate change appear as inevitable as any other 'natural' source of atmospheric pollution. The very categories of 'natural' and 'human' are themselves based on conventions.

Alternatively, someone opposing my argument might argue that we could bypass all the problems of carbon dioxide 'accounts' by finding a 'rock-bottom' scientific basis upon which to build international agreements. The trouble with this move is that even the apparently most basic aspects of pollution monitoring are built on the backs of conventional agreements. Though the typical carbon atom stays in the atmosphere for around six years (Silvertown, 1990: 78–82), this is just an averaged figure. The cumulative amount of warming produced by any particular molecule of $CO_2$ will accordingly vary with its 'residence time' in the atmosphere. Depending on the location of the source, its proximity to the oceans, its aridity and so on, the carbon will tend to be washed out of the atmosphere or incorporated in plantlife comparatively quickly or slowly. Thus, the global warming potential of emissions from one city will not necessarily be the same as those from another even *if one treats all molecules of the gas as physically identical.* Cities or even whole countries which are favourably located could, in principle, make an argument for their carbon dioxide emissions being treated as less environmentally burdensome than those of other regions. It is a practical scientific impossibility to reach rock bottom in this matter.

Without at all intending this as a critique of science or as a defence of 'irrational alternatives' to science, the point is that the universalistic ambitions of science seem at first sight to equip it to be the ideal plain, politically neutral language for addressing global environmental problems. However, scientific accounts of global-level phenomena have to employ certain conventions. No practising scientist would be likely to deny this. There is no ultimate bedrock for describing global-level phenomena. Or – at least – if there were, it would be at a level of analysis so detailed as to be of no practical value in reaching transnational agreements.

The practical upshot of this point is that no one way of drawing up carbon dioxide accounts is, logically speaking, the 'last word'. A way can always be found to question or disagree with the conventions on which the science is based. Since the supposedly objective outcome will in all probability be more favourable to certain parties than to others, there will be scope for those who feel disadvantaged to generate criticisms. They can argue that the allegedly objective, universalistic scientific approach is, in practice, partisan. The CSE authors make precisely this move. They dispute the WRI's assumptions, and then end up criticizing the WRI against an implicit standard of neutrality: 'Just what kind of politics or morality is this which masquerades in the name of "one worldism" and "high minded internationalism"?' (Agarwal and Narain, 1991: 5).

Convinced that the WRI's figures are injurious to the interests of the Third World, Agarwal and Narain sense a malevolent force at work, as indicated by their decision to subtitle their study 'a case of environmental colonialism'. Instead of seeing the WRI's work as an attempt at objectivity, they interpret it as part of a history of arrogance on behalf of the North's experts. Directly analogous accusations of environmental colonialism were also made during the ozone negotiations (see Benedick, 1991: 189).

Two conclusions follow from these points. First, while the discourse of science is supposed to offer objectivity and disinterested authority, in practice the application of this discourse to global environmental problems does not resolve the issues once and for all; it can itself even give rise to accusations of partisanship. Second, international agreements, when they are reached (and even when they deal with matters, such as ozone depletion, apparently amenable to scientific analysis), will not arise from the absence of conceivable scientific alternatives, but from the parties' willingness to suspend argument – perhaps because there are political or economic incentives to strike a bargain or because a country lacks resources with which to continue to make the argument.

## Counting Nature's Diversity

So far in this chapter I have used examples dealing with attempts to regulate pollution; it is now time to see whether my arguments about the discourse of science apply to other environmental issues. Biodiversity has been mentioned already in this book as an example of the kind of universalizing approach to global environmental issues facilitated by science. Where previously people worried in a qualitative way about the loss of species, the language of biodiversity allows these concerns to be expressed in a systematic and quantitative fashion. According to Mazur and Lee:

> During the 1970s and early 1980s . . . biological scientists and wildlife ecologists articulated the loss of biodiversity as a new and catastrophic problem. Pleas by the World Wildlife Fund [now World Wide Fund for Nature] and other organizations in support of endangered species were no longer limited to attractive animals but now stressed the sheer quantity of species at risk, including insects. Wilderness, especially tropical rain forest, was defended not just for its beauty, but also for its value as habitat. These problems were energetically publicized by a network of influential biologists with foundation support and good contacts to the national news organs [in the USA]. (1993: 709)

It was in the context of this rising concern that the term biodiversity was coined in 1986 on the occasion of a conference in Washington to raise official consciousness of these issues (1993: 703; see also Hannigan, 1995).

As most authors now note (see UK Government, 1994: 10), biodiversity is held to consist of biological diversity at three levels: diversity between and within ecosystems and habitats; the diversity of species; and genetic variation within species. Biodiversity is highest where there are many types of habitat, large numbers of species (since not all habitats support many species) and a good deal of variation within each species. Following the 1992 Earth Summit at which the Biodiversity Convention was signed by over 150 nations, the protection of biodiversity has come to be accepted as one major objective of environmental policy across the globe (see Rojas and Thomas, 1992: 152–9; Swanson, 1991).

On the face of it, the fact that the protection of biodiversity – a term first developed by biological scientists and closely related to well established work in ecology – has come to be accepted internationally as a goal of environmental policy might lead us to expect that in this instance environmental objectives would be precisely stated and strictly agreed. However, this is not the case. For one thing, there is a difficulty caused by the three-fold nature of biodiversity. One cannot produce a single measure of biodiversity that works for all situations. Generally speaking, more biological diversity is better than less but, since some habitats are naturally species-poor (bogs support fewer species than most forests for example), there is no single scale for measuring the wealth of biodiversity. Additionally, the mere fact that biodiversity is high does not mean that the area in question is particularly natural. Botanical gardens such as Kew have very high levels of biological richness, so too can domestic gardens, but this does not make them valuable environments in themselves. Lastly, in most cases the biological richness of countries' wildlife has not been anything like comprehensively charted. One cannot make definitive calculations about the best way to boost global biodiversity in the absence of comprehensive surveys, and such surveys could cost up to $200 million according to figures from the US National Science Board (1989: 14).

In the light of this third point, without figures on current biological diversity, the scientific community cannot even hope to make the definitive policy recommendations it would wish. Accordingly, one major commitment by Northern governments has been to support biological research and the development of systematic databases in order that recommendations can be made (see, for example, UK Government, 1994: 142–50). The US National Science Board envisaged a global programme of information gathering, and ideally this would be based on a common, world-wide methodology.

The consequences of this trend towards the systematic collection of biological data can be examined by looking at a recent European initiative known as Corine (Coordination of Information on the Environment). Since 1985 this information-gathering programme has compiled data on habitats and nature conservation, on air pollution and on natural resources for Directorate General XI of the European Commission. Because, as noted in Chapter 3, the European Union has extended its competence in the environmental field, it has appeared sensible to collate comparable data for all member states so that environmental, planning and other associated policies can be undertaken in a uniform way. In this case a universalizing approach has been adopted, on the assumption that the diversity of habitats can be recorded on a common basis throughout the EU.

The practicalities of the operation of Corine, particularly in relation to measures of biological diversity, have recently been investigated by Waterton et al. (1995). Briefly expressed, their argument is that the pursuit of uniformity has ironically had a number of detrimental effects on the operation of this database. Starting with very straightforward issues, they note that the apparent uniformity of Europe-wide collection of data about ecological units (referred to in the Corine study as 'biotopes') is actually vitiated by the processes by which data are gathered. For example, they reproduce information from the database which shows that returns from the Netherlands indicate the presence of many raised bogs (a type of bog sometimes found in lowland areas) while few are shown for Britain, even though naturalists would agree that the Dutch bogs are generally smaller and more degraded than British examples (1995: 26). Conflicting local judgements about what data are worth recording can undermine the Europe-wide validity of the database.

Similarly, the authors note that there tends to be considerable variation from one country to another in terms of how systematically the returns were made. Since it appears that no returns were made for otters in the UK, the Corine database simply shows them as absent. The same is true for the biotope 'wet heath': 'the result is a misleading representation of available data, with no way of knowing this is the case except by way of "inside knowledge" which is available to only a few expert people in each Member State' (1995: 24). If this database is to be used for planning decisions or for advice on investment in nature conservation, then non-expert users will be misled if they assume that the database is – as intended – systematic. Though the motivating ideal of the database is universalistic, it is radically dependent on local data-gathering and validation 'cultures'.

More significantly Waterton et al. suggest that the Corine methodology was based on procedures established in the northern countries of the EU, whereas 'other Member States such as Greece and Spain simply have not had the conservation culture that engendered such systems in the first place' (1995: 53). Waterton et al. claim that this northern-European influence on the designation of the biotopes has meant 'an underestimation of the amount and variety of habitat sites and sheer numbers of species (many endemic) that merit inclusion' from southern Europe (1995: 54).

In this case, once again one might be tempted to argue that the solution is to make the database more or 'properly' universal, to include the Spanish species, the British otter figures and so on. However, Waterton et al. take the point the other way. In effect they argue that, since we can never be sure that the cultural variability has been completely removed from cross-cultural databases, it is better to acknowledge cultural diversity. They detected a 'notable absence of sensitivity to the effects on data of local and cultural contexts and prior institutional commitment within the Commission. This tendency is allied to a further tendency to emphasize the universal, standard and the technical at the expense of the social, cultural and local dimensions of information' (1995: 67).

Waterton et al. tentatively make the argument that political commitment to European harmonization, characteristic of the late 1980s and early 1990s, encouraged a view of scientific information as the kind of uniform commodity which could be handled at the European level. There was, accordingly, a possible ulterior reason for wanting to see information handled in a uniform way and for overlooking the practical shortcomings of this approach. In the case of biodiversity, too, it therefore appears that a scientification of the policy issue does not result in uncontested, impartial guidance on policies for nature conservation. The adoption of the universalizing discourse of science does not 'screen out' all political and cultural influences.

Although I have concentrated on Corine, this is not to imply that there are not many other contests over issues surrounding biodiversity. For example, the rights over valuable genetic material from Third-World countries are disputed. Negotiations are continuing over whether the rights should reside with the scientists (usually from the North) who identify the material or with the people in the South on whose land the genetic material was found and who might be said to have cultivated or, at least, conserved it (see Goodman and Redclift, 1991: 180–3; Yearley, 1992a: 169–70). Similarly, there is widespread public debate over the desirability of the genetic engineering of organisms (see Chapter 2; and Goodman and Redclift, 1991: 169–80). However, in both these cases biodiversity tends to be taken for granted as the measure of biological richness. The example of Corine shows that, in practice, universalistic discourses may not hold the key to agreements over the biological 'facts of the matter' and that more 'local' approaches, recognizing the culturally diverse reasons for biological classifications, may have certain advantages in negotiating workable policies (see Laurence and Wynne, 1989). Similarly, we can expect the official discourse of biodiversity to attract growing political criticism, especially since biodiversity protection has lately been identified as a 'global' objective, to be supported by the Global Environmental Facility.

### Economics and the World-wide 'Logic' of Action

Up to this point I have considered the role of scientific discourse in arriving at international agreements over environmental policy. Though, at first sight, science might be thought to be clearly universal and thus incontestably applicable to global problems, in practice its universality can be deconstructed and undermined. But science was only one of the universal discourses reviewed in Chapter 1. In the context of global environmental issues a second key discourse is that of logic and rationality. This comes into play most conspicuously in relation to the logic of economic action.

In the final two decades of the twentieth century, economic thinking has come to be applied to more and more aspects of policy-making, particularly in relation to aspects of public policy including medicine; according to Mulkay et al. (1987) it has 'colonized' much of policy discourse. In justifying their growing influence economists often argue that economics is not necessarily about money; rather it is the scientific study of choice (1987: 236). Rigorous economic analyses allow decision-making in other aspects of life to proceed just as logically as prices allow market decisions to be made. Economics helps people make correct choices and thus behave rationally. Since human societies are perpetually making choices about environmental matters (how much provision to make for nature conservation, how much pollution abatement to require of industry and so on), the application of economics to environmental issues helps societies make these choices rationally too. On this view, economics functions as a universalizing discourse because the making of the optimum choice is a rational question, not a matter of local contingencies.

Particularly since the mid-1980s, environmental economics has grown from a minor and rather 'academic' component of economics into an influential approach whose language and assumptions have been adopted by various governments – notably the pro-market conservative administration in the UK – and also by the World Bank itself. Indeed, the infamous memo authored by Summers which was discussed in the last chapter was expressed in the language of environmental economics.

The key starting point for the work of environmental economists, touched on near the beginning of the last chapter, is that although environmental goods are actually central to virtually all our economic practices there has generally been no basis for assigning prices or costs to them and there has been no market for them. They are accordingly used, and used up, by our commercial and other everyday practices in wasteful and irrational ways. As the example given in Chapter 3 indicated, until recently even in the First World, many forms of pollution by industry, from agriculture and from the activities of official agencies, were allowed to continue free of any cost to the polluter. Firms were permitted to discharge their wastes into the environment without paying the costs of the resulting environmental harm, in part because the environment was not considered to be of sufficient importance and partly because there were no mechanisms for putting a price on the amount of environmental harm done.

In certain cases the 'costs' of environmental despoliation can readily be seen, even if it is harder to attach a precise monetary value to them. As a result of factory discharges, for example, fish might be poisoned and thus a fishing resource wrecked, or the value of the amenity to visitors might be lessened and thus the receipts from tourism reduced. In such cases, the environmental damage has a financial cost which, at least in principle, could be calculated. But in some instances, where the monetary environmental costs are not so clear or where there is no mechanism for imposing them on the offending company or plant, individuals and firms actually have an economic incentive to pollute. Indeed, there are financial obstacles in the way of those who want to protect the environment. In principle, a company which incurred costs in order to reduce its pollution when it did not have to (even if pollution control was very cheap) would put itself in an unfavourable competitive situation compared with other firms and, in the extreme situation, might go out of business.

The argument of environmental economists is that they are able to remedy this situation by assigning prices to various environmental goods. This has two supposed advantages. The first claim made in favour of this procedure is that it allows environmental goods to be assigned a value when, in the past, they had often been simply ignored. Since considerations of costs are typically so central to decision-making, putting a properly calculated cost on environmental goods means that they can be taken fully into account by businesses or officials. Environmental economists would tend to say that while people claim to value the environment, unless they put an economic value on it, this 'value' will often be overlooked when people consider 'the bottom line'. For instance, people might agree that a landscape or a tract of rainforest is in many senses valuable. But unless one can put a monetary figure to that value there is a danger that this vague sense of value will be overridden by the material value of the houses that could be built on the landscape or the timber that could be logged from the forest. By introducing procedures which allow a price to be assigned to the landscape, it can be shown what the 'cost' of erecting the houses will be and the cost can be imposed on the developer and/or the purchasers of the homes. If the landscape has a high value its worth will be greater than that of the real estate and there will be no economic incentive to build the houses. As D. Pearce puts it: 'Very simply, if the "true" value of the environment were known, we would not degrade it as much' (1991b: 2).

The second claim is that, if the economic valuations are done properly, the market can lead people to make the environmentally correct decisions without the need for regulation or other forms of coercion. For example, the market typically prices oil in relation to how costly it is to extract and how great the demand for oil is. There is no recognition given to the fact that supplies of oil are necessarily limited and that we are running down the 'natural capital' represented by oil reserves. In the energy market, therefore, renewable energy (say, from wind power) is compared with energy from fossil fuels solely on the basis of the cost of producing it. The prices take no account of the fact that energy from one source can in principle continue indefinitely while the other is exhausting a unique resource. Environmental-economists argue that by assigning values to stocks of natural resources (as with any other assets) the relative prices of the two forms of energy generation will be changed since the cost of petrol will now include the extraction price plus a charge for the diminution of the reserve. Accordingly, market prices will encourage people to switch to renewables, thus conserving natural resources. Pearce et al. illustrate this point through another example:

At present, if an entire [tropical] forest is logged and the resulting revenues invested in a cement factory, national income shows a rise because of the investment in the cement factory *and* it would show a rise because of the logging activities. This . . . fails to allow for the decline in one productive asset (forests) while allowing for the increase in another asset (factories). (1989: 111)

Starting off from this kind of reasoning, environmental economists present themselves as the authentic spokespersons for the environment. As Jacobs explains:

Economists see that the environment is frequently undervalued: because it can often be used free of charge it tends to get over-used, and therefore degraded. If only the environment were given its proper value in economic decision-making, the economist reasons, it would be much more highly protected. So far from being the materialist philistines of the Greens' accusation, environmental economists regard themselves as the Earth's true friends, providing arguments for its protection which (unlike those of the emotional Greens) will carry weight in the real world of financial decision-making. (1994: 69)

Although environmental economics has often been applied within the economies of First-World countries, in *Blueprint 2: Greening the World Economy* (D. Pearce, 1991a) the argument is made that the discipline can be applied to such questions as the regulation of global warming, the control of biodiversity loss, the problem of ozone depletion and the analysis of world population problems. Early in the book a 'back-of-the-envelope' calculation is provided for the economics of preserving the rainforests (1991c: 26). From figures indicating the value that North Americans appear to place on their wildlife, Pearce estimates that the citizens of most of the developed North value the protection of the Brazilian rainforest at around eight dollars per year each. In other words, one might guess that 400 million people (Pearce's rough figure for the adult population of North America, Western Europe and Australasia) would between them stump up a little over three billion dollars annually to conserve the Amazonian rainforest. Since other statistics suggest that Amazonia contributes around 6.4 per cent of Brazil's Gross National Product, the exploitation of the rainforest appears to be worth about fifteen billion dollars to Brazil. On this very rough calculation, present levels of concern in the West are sufficient to compensate Brazil for leaving alone about one-fifth of the remaining rainforest. As Pearce points out, this rough calculation overlooks the economic benefits which could still be derived from conserved rainforest (nuts, rattan and so on). It is only intended to show how environmental economics can operate transnationally by resolving environmental options into a single currency: monetary valuations.

As presented by Jacobs (1994: 71ff.), this kind of exercise faces both practical and conceptual problems, although the two are far from distinct. At the practical level, environmental economists clearly have to produce prices for goods for which there is no established market. For instance, there is no actual market in clean air, in the sense that one cannot purchase this commodity from a shop. However, economists get around this problem in two ways. First, they maintain that the value of certain environmental goods *is* reflected in some actual prices. For example, houses with a good view or in a noise-free area tend to be worth more than those without a view or which suffer from loud disturbance. One can try to derive the worth of environmental goods from such price differentials. But in other cases the methodological problems are more severe. Some environmental goods appear to be valued not for the individual benefits they confer (such as the pleasure of a fine view) but because people treat the sheer existence of certain things as having value. People frequently appear to think about majestic wild animals and remote landscapes in this kind of way. Since the people who value these goods do not value them for their usefulness, economists tend to refer to the worth of these goods as their 'existence value'. Other environmental goods appear to be prized because of the value they may hold for other people, particularly future generations.

In these kinds of cases, 'existence value' and the other kinds of indirect values are hard to put a price on. The commonest method is to use a form of questionnaire to ask people what value they would place on such things. This method (known as contingent valuation) is regarded as a second-best since it does not reveal how people do behave in the market but indicates how they say they think they would behave. As Jacobs points out there are several difficulties here. People are often inexperienced in making such estimations. In modern capitalist societies there are not many contexts in which people are asked to come up with a price for goods. Most goods we buy come ready-priced. Accordingly, people's answers may be inconsistent or they may be influenced by the questioner since the exercise is so unfamiliar. Second, there appear to be persistent differences in the values that people offer depending on the question they are set. The value of a good can be established either by asking what people would pay to keep it or what they would need to compensate them for losing it. For rainforests, whales and so on, people commonly give a much higher figure for compensation against loss than for the sum they would be willing to pay. It is hard to know which is the 'true' value. Finally, large numbers of people appear to refuse to go along with the exercise at all. Jacobs notes that the people who conduct the surveys have devised a category of 'protest', where respondents explicitly object to the assumptions of the exercise. 'In several cases, particularly in valuation exercises for environmental goods such as famous landscapes and endangered species, up to 50 per cent of respondents have simply refused to participate, arguing that the exercises are an inappropriate method of expressing their environmental values' (1994: 79).

These methodological difficulties indicate that there are considerable problems in using environmental economics in practice. Economists must assume that there is a correct value for human preferences for each environmental good (see D. Pearce, 1991b: 5). But it is clear that, even in their own terms, economists' recommendations about the rational policies to follow can only be as good as the empirical data on which they are built.

There is a clear danger that apparently universal, 'rational' policies will be advanced on the basis of very contestable empirical findings.

Although this clearly indicates an immense practical problem for the validity of some calculations in environmental economics, there is another key issue at stake here. Environmental economists tend to argue that we are constantly making implicit economic judgements about the value of environmental goods. For instance, since it costs money to keep up nature reserves, the balance of public expenditure between environmental protection and, say, education or health indicates that economic choices have been made. Pearce makes this point sharply: 'We "trade off" either explicitly . . . or implicitly, since all decisions imply valuations' (1991b: 2). Economists maintain that people actually have underlying preferences and, if these can be made explicit, that will allow us to spend the correct amounts on environmental protection. Jacobs argues against this in the following way. He doubts that people really do have underlying individual preferences for the whole range of environmental goods, regarding people's refusal to participate in contingent valuation exercises as evidence that they do not in fact attribute values in the ways environmental economists suppose. Jacobs believes that environmental economics falls down as an accurate empirical account of how people reason about the 'value' of the environment because its methods 'strait-jacket' people into behaving as the theory predicts: 'the methods [of environmental economics] are specifically constructed to ensure that people can only participate if they take [the stance ascribed by the theory]' (1994: 78).

This critique immediately leads us on to another issue, this one raised most forcibly by O'Neill (1993: 68ff.). His critique of environmental economics is based on its willing embrace of the notion of preferences. Economics holds itself to be deliberately and self-consciously value-neutral. That is, it does not specify what people should want or value, it simply reports and analyses what they value and how much they value it. If people consume more of one chocolate bar than another or buy an expensive one rather than a cheap one, that indicates their preferences. Contingent valuation procedures invite us to treat the natural world similarly. If North Americans value the blue whale a lot more than the whooping crane and the crane only about a third as much as the visual amenity of the Grand Canyon, then so much worse for the crane. It will be rational to spend less money on crane conservation than on whale protection since people value the latter more. O'Neill doubts whether this is the way that people should, or indeed do, value certain classes of beings and things. His critique runs as follows:

> The grounds for complaint [about environmental economics and cost–benefit analysis in environmental management] are not that the procedure might produce 'bad' results *per se*. Even if it produced 'good' results it would be wrong. The complaint is that . . . the procedure itself is misconceived. It treats all preferences as identical save in the 'intensity' with which they are held. It is blind to the reasons and arguments that individuals have for or against different proposals.

Standardly, environmentalists appeal to features of the site on which a development is to take place . . . to its value as a habitat [etc.]. Cost-benefit analysis is blind to such reasons. The strength or weakness of the *intensity* of a preference count, but the strength or weakness of the *reasons* for a preference do not. Preferences grounded in aesthetic, scientific or historical judgements about the site are treated as on a par with preferences for a particular flavour of ice-cream. (1993: 78; original italics)

This argument is different from Jacobs'; it questions not the empirical but the conceptual adequacy of treating people's preferences as the 'value' to be captured by environmental economics. Value-neutral economics reduces all preferences to one dimension whereas O'Neill wishes to recognize a hierarchy of preferences. Preferences based on good reasons are better than ill-informed preferences. O'Neill argues that in certain areas we should value expert opinion rather more than people's preferences, preferences which are known to be open to change and possibly manipulation through advertising, lobbying and so on.

To draw this section to a close, the key argument is that environmental economics offers itself as a neutral and universal medium for talking about the value the environment holds for people. It proffers a globally convertible currency for expressing this value. However, environmental economics faces grave difficulties of principle and practice. In the first place, it turns out to be very difficult to assign unambiguous values to environmental goods. Worse still, there are conceptual grounds for resisting the idea that environmental values should be equated with 'individual human preferences for (or against) the flow of services from the environment' (D. Pearce, 1991b: 4). While environmental economics has recorded considerable successes in colonizing environmental policy discourse, its pretensions to represent a truly universalizing discourse are very suspect. Its claims to constitute a neutral medium for assessing the value of the environment the world over will continue to face resistance.[4]

### Sustainable Development as a Global Goal

Though the term 'sustainable development' and the associated notion of sustainability have a lengthy history, they have risen to international prominence following the publication of the Brundtland Report (World Commission on Environment and Development, 1987) and in the wake of the Earth Summit of 1992 (Bartelmus, 1994: 144–8). As mentioned in Chapter 3, at that summit, political leaders signed up to the idea that the world's societies should move towards sustainability. In the years since the Brundtland Report there has been a great deal of analysis of the concept of sustainable development from academics, journalists and environmental campaigners. These analyses have given rise to the apparently contradictory view that the concept is readily understood and yet that it defies simple definition. Thus, as I proposed in the last chapter, sustainable development refers to a form of socioeconomic advancement which can continue indefinitely without exhausting the world's resources or overburdening the ability of natural systems to cope with pollution. The key point is often expressed through analogy, by saying that sustainable development means living off the interest of the Earth's natural productivity, without gnawing away at the capital. Development of that sort could, in principle, continue indefinitely; it would face no natural limits.

Straightforward though this appears, there are many people who argue that it is hard to determine the exact meaning of the term. D. Pearce et al. give a droll 12-page list of definitions (1989: 173–85). Lafferty points to the contested nature of the concept (1995: 223). This ambiguity emerges only when one tries to formulate a definition. Let us take, for instance, the everywhere-quoted Brundtland definition:

> Sustainable development is development that meets the needs of the present without compromising the ability of future generations to meet their own needs. It contains within it two key concepts:
>
> - the concept of 'needs', in particular the essential needs of the world's poor, to which overriding priority should be given; and
> - the idea of limitations imposed by the state of technology and social organization on the environment's ability to meet present and future needs. (1987: 43)

Though apparently clear, this definition has attracted most criticism for its dependence on the contentious idea of 'needs', although many questions have also been raised about the meaning of 'development'.

Of course, one might argue that definitions do not matter very much providing that the term is widely understood. However, precision does count when one is trying to use the concept of sustainable development as a criterion for judging policies. For example, since coal has formed only extremely slowly, no use of coal can continue indefinitely. Does a commitment to sustainable development accordingly imply that one stops using all non-renewable materials immediately? Similarly, a commitment to sustainable development does not of itself give a clear indication of exactly how much rainforest, scrub, or grassland the world should contain.

But, before pursuing the issue of clarity further, it should be noted that the concept has attracted criticisms on other grounds too. For some authors, such as Middleton et al. (1993), the concept is flawed because it represents only the juxtaposition of the North's demand for environmental protection and the South's need for economic and social development; it puts the two terms together without reconciling them. On this view, the term merely represents an aspiration; simply giving something a name does not indicate that it can actually exist viably. Others, as Lafferty notes (1995: 224), see the definition as having an anthropocentric bias. In most versions, it refers only to human needs, not to those of animals, ecosystems or the global environment as a whole. Though the Brundtland definition may give us human-centred reasons for wishing to conserve species diversity or maintain large areas of forest, it ignores reasons arising from the needs of the wildlife itself.

The issue of the adequacy of the concept is further complicated because questions of development and improvement in economic circumstances cannot be disentangled from concerns about equity. Though the Brundtland Report itself acknowledges that sustainability 'in a physical sense' could be pursued under more or less any political and social system (1987: 43), the development component of the term refers to improvements in people's quality of life. Most would agree that those in poverty can be helped by becoming wealthier. To take the extreme cases, this could be achieved either by a redistribution of wealth or by everyone becoming wealthier, even while present inequalities persist. The leading question then becomes, do the requirements of sustainable development favour one option over the other? The Brundtland Report offers a practical argument for preferring the former route. Some redistribution of wealth actually lifts people out of poverty more quickly, allowing development to reach more people sooner, and with a lower impact on the environment (1987: 50–1). Other commentators believe that a much stronger commitment to equity follows from the principle of sustainability. Like Middleton et al., they suggest that people have equal rights to the natural resources of the planet. The point here is identical to Agarwal and Narain's (1991) assumption (in the context of 'shares' in atmospheric pollution) that rights to development ought to be democratic and that, therefore, people all have equal entitlement to the use of resources and to cause 'their share' of whatever pollution the environment can tolerate.

While all these points will be critical to the shaping of future policy, for present purposes the principal issue is that sustainable development too offers a universalizing discourse for assessing the globe's environmental problems (see Bartelmus, 1994). Thus the Brundtland Report, even in its very title *Our Common Future*, offered sustainable development as the *shared goal* of humankind. As with global warming or ozone depletion, the only apparently sensible level for carrying out policies for sustainable development is that of the globe because non-sustainability by even a minority will undermine sustainable development for all. Previously, economic growth was a development objective that could be pursued by all nations individually. For the first time, (sustainable) development is not something that everyone can do separately but a joint global project; as the Brundtland Report expresses it, 'the goals of economic and social development must be defined in terms of sustainability in all countries' (1987: 43).

The discourse of sustainable development is accordingly a powerful one precisely because it suggests that no reasonable policy-maker would want to do anything else. Just as economic rationality 'colonizes' the mind of actors by implying that, since we all make choices, we *must* want to make them as rationally as possible, so sustainable development colonizes environmental policy by offering an objective from which one apparently *could not wish* to diverge.

Lafferty (1995: 223) suggests that there is an analogy between sustainable development and democracy, in that both are held to be universally desirable but liable to different and contested interpretations. At one level this is a reasonable enough point, though its force is diminished somewhat by the observation that the same difficulties attach to a range of other concepts: justice, human rights, accountability and so on. But what Lafferty's claim misses is the special sense of physical (to borrow Brundtland's term) penalty attached to non-compliance with the demands of sustainability. The argument is not just that 'we' ought to live sustainably, but that in the long run we cannot live any other way. It is, so the argument runs, objectively necessary to become sustainable. It is an inescapable, global imperative. Such a claim is not available to advocates of democracy.

The sense of a common, objectively obligatory goal is consolidated by the role economists have played in spelling out the meaning of sustainable development (see D. Pearce, 1993). As Pearce et al. note (1989: 48), economists tend to hold one or other of two views about sustainable development. They regard it either as equivalent to passing on to the next generation at least the same capital as the present generation inherited, or as passing on the same 'natural capital'. The latter view implies that 'the stock of environmental assets as a whole should not decrease' while the former allows humanly-made capital to be traded for natural capital (improvements in health-care provision or increases in the stock of fine buildings might be exchanged for declining areas of forest for example). While there are significant differences between these interpretations, the crucial point is that both depend on attaching economic values to environmental goods. Otherwise there is no way of telling whether the capital stock (natural or natural-plus-human) is declining.[5]

Though environmental economics offers to be the neutral medium for assessing sustainability, it is precisely in the context of these assessments that the problems become acute. For example, if there are no agreed environmental prices then non-declining capital cannot be determined impersonally. Under these circumstances, economists cannot serve as adjudicators when there are rival claims about what the correct 'sustainable path' is. Second, the problems mentioned in the last section about 'existence value' arise again. Arguably, whales and pelicans, cranes and osprey are not needed for the sustaining of human societies. Except in the case of those species that can be proven to contribute to sustainable development, a commitment to sustainability does not determine how much attention one should give to the protection of the natural world itself. Third, the economist's definition of sustainability as non-declining capital does not address distributional issues in the present, and thus does little to resolve transnational disputes about 'rights' of access to environmental resources. Finally, though economists appear to have an internally consistent microeconomics of the sustainable economy (dealing with the theory of the trade in environmental goods and so on), it does not follow from this that the system can function at a macroeconomic level. Environmental microeconomics does not guarantee that a sustainable market economy is viable in the long term.

The discourse of sustainable development has become influential very quickly. It is a powerful discourse, from which it is hard to disaffiliate since it appears that no one could reasonably disagree with the objective of sustainable development. Yet, for all its appeal, the meaning of the term is neither as transparent nor as technical and objective as appears at first sight. Like the other universalizing discourses, it turns out to be less incontestable in practice than its proponents routinely imply.

## NGOs, Authenticity and Universalizing Discourse

Though NGOs were considered at the start of this chapter (in relation to the WRI and CSE) it is appropriate at this stage to consider once again the relationship of environmental movement organizations such as Greenpeace and the World Wide Fund for Nature (WWF) to the universalizing discourses. This is so for two reasons. First, it is of interest because (as seen in Chapter 3) NGOs are, increasingly, an influential social force. Such organizations impact in at least three ways on societies' response to the world's environmental problems. They play a big role in stimulating public awareness of and interest in environmental issues, in both the First and Third Worlds. They have frequently acted as 'watch dogs', aiming to hold governments and commercial organizations to their espoused standards, and seeking publicity to shame those governments and companies which are perceived to be 'bad performers'. Lastly, and this is a rapidly developing trend, NGOs are moving from a primarily critical stance to one in which they offer policy proposals and aim to join with governments and commerce in the formulation of policies which affect the environment.[6]

The second major reason is that in each of these roles they use the skills and the rhetoric of science and other universalizing discourses such as rights (see Weiss, 1992: 199ff.). They face the familiar problem of maintaining scientific authority, but at the same time must be seen by their supporters to be arguing 'authentically'. They generally have members whose interests they have to be seen to represent and from whose support they draw much of their political muscle. Besides having to meet demands for technical correctness, they must secure legitimacy within the movement. It is for this reason that WWF, FoE and Greenpeace and other membership organizations are in a different situation from predominantly trust- and corporate-financed WRI (see Dowie, 1995: 119).

In the twenty years following the end of the 1960s nearly all environmental organizations increased their use of scientific, technical and other universalistic methods. They recruited scientific staffs and even submitted their work to outside referees. In the celebratory publication to mark its twenty-first anniversary, UK Friends of the Earth cites as the very first item a quote from Geoffrey Lean, then Environment Correspondent of the authoritative weekly newspaper *The Observer*, who, in 1992, wrote that:

> About fifteen years ago, someone told me that Friends of the Earth's campaigners were likely to know more about their subjects than the relevant Government Minister. I didn't believe it. Since then I have found that this has usually been the case. Friends of the Earth has maintained its reputation as a reliable and indispensable source of information. (Friends of the Earth, 1992b: 2)

This quote is followed by a further testimony, this time from the head of the UK's official pollution-monitoring body, Her Majesty's Inspectorate of Pollution, praising the organization's 'technical dialogue'. The fact that the group plays up the quality of its information and gives pride of place in its anniversary publication to boasts about its technical expertise presents a very different 'institutional body language' to early publicity from the movement organizations. This difference is demonstrated by the findings of Greenberg's work, carried out at the start of the 1980s, on FoE's contemporary media image. According to his analysis, the stunts and other attention-grabbing devices used at the time were interpreted by policymakers as evidence of the unscientific and emotive character of FoE's arguments (1985: 347–60; see also F. Pearce, 1991: 48–57). Care is taken to present a different image today.

And this dependence on science affects not only the ethos of the movement organizations but some of the practicalities of their actions. Scientific information-gathering places heavy demands on resources of time and finance. Once the organization's reputation is linked to the quality of the information it puts out, it cannot give instantaneous responses in the way that a less fastidious body might. Similarly, this commitment leads to a loss of flexibility as campaigning expertise has to be marshalled around a set number of themes and, therefore, new issues – for example, biotechnology or a sudden environmental incident such as an oil-tanker wreck – cannot straight away be taken on board, however urgent or demanding they may seem to the media, the public or one's supporters. While F. Pearce seems to accept Greenpeace's own assessment that 'scientists remain on tap rather than on top' (1991: 40), there is an important sense in which the growth of expertise and of facilities leads to an inertial influence over policy. Expertise is a more dominant factor than is normally acknowledged.

This shift has many consequences. Thus, the pursuit of scientific campaigning tends to develop staff with very specific expertise who, in part because of their respect for expertise, are reluctant to respond to issues about which they are not maximally informed. This point should not be exaggerated. It is clear that NGOs take an opportunistic approach to mounting arguments, just as governments and industries do; they are not strait-jacketed by their commitment to expertise. Still, they are reluctant to publicize arguments which they cannot stand over in detail and, the more expert they grow, the higher their standards of acceptability become. Furthermore, expert campaign staff may also become distant from the lay membership whose environmental interests they are supposed to represent and on whose (financial and personal) support they depend. The possibility exists that the importance of scientific expertise has added to the distance between the professional cadres in leading social movement organizations and the casual movement supporter. While campaign professionals learn more and more about acid pollution or radioisotopes, 'ordinary' members are encouraged to deal chiefly in terms of general principles such as the 'polluter pays' or 'precautionary' principles. Of course, many 'ordinary' greens are very knowledgeable about ecological issues. None the less scientific specialization tends to inhibit rather than assist democratization in green campaigning.

Indeed, in Britain the groups which are both radical and effective tend to be centralized. Greenpeace is famously so, leading Allen, a campaigning journalist working on waste incineration, to complain that:

> in Britain Greenpeace is very definitely bureaucratic and was seduced by the establishment fairly quickly. From a small grouping at the beginning of the eighties, Greenpeace displays all the trappings of a multinational company or a civil service department. (1992: 223)

Though in fact Greenpeace does continue to engage in direct actions and even occasional law breaking, Allen's apparent resentment stems from the alienation sometimes felt by community campaigners in the face of professionalized and wealthy campaign organizations. McCormick notes that through the 1980s Greenpeace became 'less confrontational, and more inclined to use the same tactics of lobbying and discreet political influence once reserved by the more conservative groups' (1991: 158; see Yearley, 1994a: 155–8).

Friends of the Earth has self-consciously sought to develop an alternative model, institutionalizing an arrangement for cooperation between a centralized London-based staff and its regional local groups. The latter can select their own campaign targets but are bound by a licence agreement with FoE which prevents them acting in FoE's own name. Local groups have a form of shareholders' meeting at the annual conference but cannot require (only recommend) the board to change its policies. The headquarters staff have a highly professionalized ethos. The structure lessens but does not remove tensions between the core and the regionally active members. Even FoE which has tried to build in a mechanism for sustained member participation cannot be viewed as the *expression* of the movement or, for that matter, as its vanguard.

It is these twin issues of the authority of science and of the influence of scientification on campaigning and – therefore – on representativeness that we need to bear in mind as we turn to look at NGOs' actions in the context of international campaigns. As described at the end of Chapter 3 there are some institutional reasons for NGOs to be hopeful about the prospects of international action. Some transnational agencies have shown themselves more receptive to NGOs than have the majority of national governments, and there is scope for NGOs to occupy the moral high ground. However there are problems too.

At the level of scientific authority there are difficulties because ecological problems which are so big as to be global tend to be technically complex. Being international, they also give rise to conflicting interests. And these two factors interact since there will be many parties to any technical dispute. Consequently, the evidence is likely to be contested and charges of tendentious interpretation are likely to fly. The complexity of global climate modelling, for example, means that while NGOs are well motivated to become involved, it is hard for them to identify (and therefore occupy) the technical high ground. Worse still, the science involved is usually so costly and time-consuming that the campaign groups could not expect to take it on themselves to any great extent. Admittedly, with issues such as global warming, the synthesis and review of existing information is itself an important scientific task and one in which Greenpeace, for example, has sought to involve itself. All the same, NGOs are bound to be dependent on science produced for other people's agendas.

If these are the problems arising from attempting to deploy scientific authority in an international context, allied difficulties arise from the issue of the scientification of campaign issues. In their move to 'global thinking', Northern NGOs have often assumed that environmental 'goods' to be sought after in the First World are presumably good for the rest of the world too. But groups have run into controversy by generalizing about the presumed interests of other peoples. And scientific expertise – and counter-expertise – have come to be central to these disputes. This is illustrated in the well publicized and much discussed case of the seal cull around northern Canada. In the 1970s and through into the next decade, Greenpeace and the International Fund for Animal Welfare (IFAW) campaigned to halt the killing of seals. Indigenous hunters argued that they should be exempted from any proposed ban since they had 'traditionally' hunted these animals which were essential for their customary lifestyle. Controversy subsequently centred on the extent to which seal culling was truly a traditional activity among indigenous peoples. These people now used modern technology for seal hunting and many campaigners chose to interpret the use of motorized transport and guns as evidence of commercial hunting, particularly since such activity was, by definition, non-sustainable without entering the cash nexus – in order to buy fuel, ammunition and snowmobiles. By contrast, community campaigners and sympathetic anthropologists claimed that this was just a minor adaptation of traditional practices. Given the changing population structure of the Canadian Arctic it was only by the use of these modern technologies that a traditional way of life could be maintained at all (Wenzel, 1991: 165–6). In this case appeal was made to 'scientific' approaches to settle the apparently factual question of the 'traditional-ness' of hunting techniques. But, rather than resolve the problem these appeals merely fuelled the disagreement.

A further example of difficulties with the adequacy of technical expertise for campaigning on international themes comes from rainforest campaigns. Such campaigns indicate how technical expertise can be confounded by moral complexity. Rainforest protection has proved a great popular success in the North. Indeed, so much public interest has been excited by rainforest conservation that groups which previously had more or less nothing to do with the rainforests have begun to find distinctive ways into this publicity hot-spot. Among the cleverest such links is that made by Britain's largest wildlife organization, the Royal Society for the Protection of Birds, which has identified an endangered rainforest bird on whose behalf it can campaign (Yearley, 1993a: 65ff.). Given the recognized publicity benefits of such campaigning, it becomes important to justify this preoccupation on the part of Northern NGOs, who have often been rather less concerned to preserve northern forests or peatbogs, even though these too are major carbon reservoirs. And the exact rationale for campaigns focused on the South is open to being contested. Thus, if the claim is that rainforest destruction contributes to the anthropogenic greenhouse gas it has not been demonstrated that other campaign strategies (say, in favour of enhanced energy conservation) could not be more efficacious in limiting $CO_2$ accumulation. And Northern groups' eagerness to conserve rainforests has also excited local mistrust and opposition because of the implicit threat to sovereignty and to people's rights to control over their own countries' resources.

However the final and perhaps starkest example of the way in which Northern NGOs' concerns with the supposed technical needs of the natural world can conflict with moral values comes from the World Wide Fund for Nature's (WWF's) approach to wildlife conservation in Africa. At the end of the 1980s WWF was found to be assisting the Zimbabwean authorities with the purchase of a helicopter to assist in the protection of the black rhino, despite the authorities' known shoot-to-kill policy towards poachers (*The Guardian*, 4 September 1990: 1). The Fund also aided Kenya's wildlife rangers in purchasing assault weapons and helicopter gunships for hunting down elephant poachers (F. Pearce, 1991: 74–6). Even leaving aside suggestions that national rivalries (offensives against Somalis) were being disguised as wildlife protection, this case demonstrates that very different standards are proposed in the Third World to those which would be accepted in the NGOs' Northern homes. Again, when technical considerations are allowed to displace moral ones, some very contentious policies arise. WWF's actions, once publicized, generated an outcry in Britain.

So far I have examined the difficulties arising when Northern NGOs seek to move to a global level of campaigning by extension from their existing concerns. But an alternative approach employed by some is to work back from future limits rather than forwards from current campaigns. This procedure is helpfully exemplified in a recent discussion document from Netherlands FoE (Milieu Defensie, 1992) called *Action Plan: Sustainable Netherlands*. The basis for this document is the notion of 'environmental space' – that is, access to the environmental resources needed to sustain a standard of welfare. Calculations of environmental space requirements were made under five headings: energy, water, non-renewable resources (such as minerals), agricultural commodities and timber/paper. These calculations were aimed at introducing sustainable exploitation by, in most cases, 2010 although it was accepted that the turnaround to energy sustainability would take twenty years longer.

In very many respects this piece of futurology is stimulating and original. It fully acknowledges the global nature of the environmental 'problematique', emphasizing that 'Until now, the northern environmental movement has not really developed strategies towards a redistribution of the world's natural resources' (1992: 2). Equally it departs from much environmental writing in taking very seriously the question of how the transition from the present state to the desired future state (sustainable and reasonably equitable demands on environmental resources) is to be accomplished. As the authors express it, their question is: 'What will the consumption level be when we take into account the needs of all world citizens, and does this provide an attractive [prospect] for the average citizen in our affluent country?' (1992: 5).

None the less, at a fundamental level the document is still surprisingly technocratic. It does not deal with the kinds of government or participation which will allow for adherence to these agreements nor does it talk about the kinds of notions of worth and desert which will legitimize the distribution of resources within future society. There is no notion of the moral or the financial economy which will sustain the anticipated society. The only explicit recognition of a political dimension comes during discussion of the distribution of environmental space, and the authors' response is to invite input from trades unions and other social movement actors.

The overall approach seeks to attend in a sensitive way to the physical limits within which a global future must be planned. But without consideration of the socioeconomic features of that future these calculations fall far short of a blueprint. Moreover, any projections of physical limits are themselves highly unlikely to be accepted consensually. Drawing on our experience of other estimation exercises (projected fuel reserves, climate modelling) we know both that there will be scope for legitimate differences of opinion and that people will have a tendentious interest in over- or under-emphasizing the particular commodities in which they have a commercial or political interest. The Milieu Defensie authors do not confront this difficulty.

In summary, environmental NGOs of virtually all complexions are becoming more technically sophisticated. But despite this sophistication they face two sorts of problem: they are handicapped in attempts to 'cash-in' on the authority of science and they face difficulties in avoiding the creeping domination of expertise and a technocratic outlook over their campaign style and strategy.

This indicates, I suggest, that issues of equity and social justice cannot be omitted from their campaigning by the kind of 'division of labour' apparently practised by many NGOs and seemingly encouraged in Milieu Defensie's publication. There is some evidence that NGOs are examining organizational mechanisms for combating aspects of this problem. For example, in the run-up to the Earth Summit, Greenpeace representatives from the North went to some lengths to discuss their policy positions with representatives of Southern NGOs in an effort to overcome ethnocentrism. Subsequently, attempts have been made to institutionalize these links in the Global Forum conferences for NGOs. But so long as Northern NGOs formulate their policies towards international issues within boards composed exclusively of Northern representatives answerable to a Northern membership, they will be unable to claim a 'global' democratic legitimacy. Since, as we have seen, technical expertise will not suffice to make good this democratic deficit, we can anticipate that this issue of ethnocentrism and representativeness will be at the heart of international environmental campaigning in the coming years.

## Conclusions

Universalistic discourses offer many attractions to those analysing or dealing with global environmental problems. They appear to offer a way of speaking with world-wide authority. Scientific analysis has been central to the identification of global environmental problems, such as ozone depletion and loss of biodiversity; it now appears equally central to the formation of policy responses.

However, some commentators have argued that the assumptions associated with scientific analysis (for example that one molecule of carbon dioxide is the same as another) or with the rational logic of economics, are not always appropriate for the just interpretation of international environmental problems. Not only have some spokespersons from the South argued that the North's identification of 'global' environmental problems is very selective, like Agarwal and Narain they have claimed that the use of universalistic discourses to represent these problems can actually *conceal political assumptions and mask self-interest*. On this view, the North has given priority to its concerns (for example over air pollution) by implying that these problems are the most urgent for the globe as a whole; 'impartial' science has then been used to render this view incontestable. It is precisely because they are difficult to disaffiliate from that universalistic discourses have such strength. But scientification and a loss of participation are dangers frequently associated with such discourses. This issue is taken up again in the concluding chapter.

## Notes

1 It is perhaps more accurate to say 'established within the Western analytical tradition'.

2 Two points should be made here. First, these figures are 'greenhouse equivalents' as produced by the WRI method; they do not correspond to the figures given in Chapter 3 since they aggregate together all greenhouse gases; those in the last chapter simply indicated $CO_2$ emissions. Also, the point at issue here is different from the critique of greenhouse contributions made in the last chapter *where the figures themselves were taken for granted*. In Chapter 3 the issue was about the correct principles for allocating shares; in this case it is about the politics of arriving at the figures before negotiations over shares can commence.

3 This whole section on the ozone negotiations draws on Benedick (1991), Parson (1993), Susskind (1994), and particularly on Jasanoff (1996) as well as on extensive discussions with her.

4 By the end of 1995 public controversy had already arisen over the application of environmental economics to the issue of climate change. Environmental economists had written a technical report for the Intergovernmental Panel on Climate Change (IPCC) examining the extent to which steps should be taken to halt climate change and the extent to which societies should simply adapt to it. In making their calculations for this report the economists had put a price on the various sorts of loss likely to arise from climate change and sea-level rise, including the loss of human life. These values, together with the cost of preventative policies, could then be used in a cost-benefit analysis to compute the optimal course of action. They calculated the 'value' of human lives by reference to such things as how much people would be willing and able to pay to avoid environmental hazards. Accordingly Northern lives appeared far more valuable than those of citizens in the South. This apparently technical valuation was opposed by a small London-based NGO, the Global Commons Institute (GCI), which succeeded in attracting international publicity for its arguments and won the support of Cuban and Brazilian delegates to the IPCC (*The Guardian*, 1 November 1995: 6–7). At the time of writing, the GCI is continuing its campaign against this use of environmental economics within the work of the IPCC.

5 Of course, constant natural capital in a world of rising population still leads to declining natural wealth per person.

6 This section draws heavily on Yearley (1996), see also Yearley (1993a, 1994a).

# 5

# Rethinking the Global

## The Sociology of Globalization and the Study of the Global Environment

There are several discrete issues to attend to in this concluding chapter. I will turn first to the question of the connection between sociological analyses of globalization and the study of global environmental problems. Though, as mentioned in Chapter 1, nearly all sociological authors dealing with globalization mention environmental issues or the Earth Summit, there has generally been little systematic attention to what environmental phenomena and environmentalism can tell us about globalization. In some cases, environmental issues appear to slip through the net of globalization analysis altogether. For example, while Appadurai offers five dimensions for analysing global cultural flows (1990: 296), environmentalism does not sit easily in any of them. At the same time – and reinforced by this lack of attention – there has been equally little consideration of the appropriate sociological approach to the analysis of the global environment (though see Redclift and Benton, 1994). Much writing on global environmental issues makes little room for sociology and finds no space at all for the sociology of globalization (as noted by Robertson, 1992: 187). Since these two approaches have often passed each other by, an initial – though rather obvious – conclusion from this study is that the rise of environmental problems and of environmental 'consciousness' constitute strong evidence in support of the significance of processes of globalization. As the preceding chapters have demonstrated, there are world-wide environmental problems, some of which are receiving transnational policy responses. There is growing awareness of 'the Earth' (or, as the yoghurt-pot example of the Preface reminded us, 'the planet') as a cultural reference point with widely accepted connotations. Furthermore, specialized discourses, such as that of sustainable development, are emerging in relation to the putative policy requirements of the globe.

But the present analysis of global environmental problems allows us to conclude more than merely that environmentalism is a globalized cultural phenomenon. The analyses presented in this book offer evidence relevant to the continuing debate over the nature of globalization. As described in Chapter 1, there are, loosely speaking, a group of approaches which ascribes globalization to one principal cause (for example, the logic of capitalist development or the cultural logic of modernity). These are opposed to accounts such as Robertson's which stress the multiplicity of causes and the heterogeneous nature of the influences on globalization (see 1992: 60, and McGrew, 1992: 66–7). Indeed, Robertson and Lechner had proposed:

> that cultural pluralism is itself a constitutive feature of the modern world system and that conceptions of the world system, symbolic responses to globalization, are themselves important factors in determining the trajectories of that very process. (1985: 103)

The arguments presented in this book lend weight to the latter position: there are multiple, interacting spurs to the globalization of environmental awareness and environmentalism. And this holds true, even though – as argued in Chapter 3 – we can see that economic factors are at the heart of the causation of many environmental problems.

The spurs to globalization are multiple in at least two senses. First, at the level of the *root of environmental problems*, it is evident that economic considerations are not the sole cause even though they do predominate. Some environmental problems are only loosely related to economic considerations. Thus, states' preference for nuclear power was often more attributable to political than to economic rationales, as the subsequent lack of commercial justification for nuclear power commonly showed (Yearley, 1992a: 43–4; for the case of France see Bunyard, 1988). As was seen in Chapter 2, the issue of population growth is even further from being directly economic. The problems surrounding population increase relate to cultural variables and, in particular, to women's educational opportunities, as well as to global income distribution and to families' prospects for economic development. Even the question of environmental accounting (about how 'natural capital' is to be priced and so on) depends as much on the professional practices of accountants and civil servants as on directly economic matters. Lastly, there are some widespread environmental problems which are barely economic at all, as with the genetic pollution caused by introduced species described in Chapter 2. In any case, the specific local impact of world-wide environmental problems can be affected by the details of geology and geography, as well as by cultural and by socio-economic factors.

But as well as the issue of how environmental problems are caused, there is the question of the *promotion of environmentalist concern for and awareness of the planet* as a cultural symbol. As Robertson expresses this, a crucial factor:

> is the scope and depth of consciousness of the world as a single place. . . . Globalization does not simply refer to the objectiveness of increasing interconnectedness. It also refers to cultural and subjective matters. In very simple terms, we are thus talking about issues surrounding the idea of the world being 'for-itself'. (1992: 183)

The argument of this book is that 'global environmental problems' are *global problems* because people and organizations have worked at making 'the environment' a world-wide phenomenon. We have seen this operating in very many ways. It has been shown in the names and images selected by environmental groups, in their choice of campaigning targets and in their developing cross-national organization. It is equally evident in the operation of self-consciously international bodies such as UNEP, and in the development of an interest in the global environment by the World Bank. At first sight it might be tempting to suppose that environmental issues are inherently global and that UNEP, NGOs, the World Bank and all the rest are only pursuing the 'logic' of the globalization of environmental problems. In fact, however, this 'logic' has been cashed in very differently by various actors. The Global Environmental Facility has lighted on just four areas, while Greenpeace or Friends of the Earth or CSE in Delhi have selected others. This conclusion mirrors closely the outcome of Robertson's attempt to 'map' the global condition (1990: 27–8). He calls for further empirical studies of the promotion of 'consciousness of the world' and:

> In more theoretical vein, much more needs to be done so as to demonstrate the ways in which the selective responses of relevant collective actors – most particularly societies – to globalization play a crucial part in the making of the world-as-a-whole. (1990: 27)

Chapters 3 and 4 are offered as empirical and theoretical analyses which advance our understanding of the making of the world-as-a-whole.

If the case of environmentalism shows globalization to be taking place, and helps identify the nature and relative significance of the mechanisms by which it is proceeding, there remains the separate question about how much the sociological literature on globalization advances the understanding of the world-wide environment and of global environmentalism. The answer here is again two-fold. There are first of all insights which a sociological or social-science perspective brings to the analysis of the global environment. The question of how global environmental issues get their 'globality' or questions about the practicalities of the operation of universalizing discourses are standardly sociological. Though they are important and have been a central component of my argument, they do not specifically draw on the globalization literature. From this literature itself comes the important reminder that environmental issues are not alone in being globalized. Given the way that environmentalists and the media have tended to align talk of the globe with a concern for environmental protection – so that 'Earth Day' is immediately recognized as a day supposedly committed to care for the environment and so that the yoghurt-buying public knows what it means to contribute a share of the company's profits to 'the planet' – it is easy for greens to assume that only their concerns are global. As was noted in Chapter 3, there is a utopian element in much green writing. Greens cannot consider themselves deserving of exceptional support just on the grounds that they are concerned with the 'global', since credible claims to globality can be made in most socioeconomic and cultural spheres. The globalization literature reminds those with environmental sensibilities that many other elements of present-day culture are globalized too, in the same ways as the environment and often for similar reasons.

Robertson emphasizes that the term globalization is itself contested (1992: 182). This should be no surprise as we have already noted Robertson and Lechner's observation that 'symbolic responses' – people's own conceptualizations – regarding globalization are constitutive of the phenomenon (1985: 103). Against the utopian assumptions of some greens and even some policy-makers, what we have seen in this book is the extent to which global 'common' interests, the identification of the globe's environmental problems, and the specification of facts about the global condition are themselves *all contested*. And this contestation is more significant than Robertson appears to recognize. The supposed capacity of global environmental discourses to speak on behalf of the world as a whole gives such discourses a heightened value. The pursuit of this value means that claims about 'global needs' and 'common interests' are prone to exceptional contestation and dispute.

A final conclusion about the globalizing of environmental issues appears contrary to one of the assumptions behind the last quote from Robertson. In that passage from his 'mapping' of globalization he implied that, among all possible 'collective actors', 'societies' have a particular role to play in processes of globalization. Though ultimately it is nations which strike agreements on many transnational environmental issues, a great many other collective actors play major roles. For example, in Chapter 3 I reviewed the contributory parts played by firms and financial organizations, by NGOs, by supranational bodies and even by local authorities and small-scale, local groups. As McGrew notes (1992: 74–5) in a globalized society one anticipates an increased diversity of actors in the shaping, negotiation and implementation of policy. This expectation is especially strong in the case of environmental issues since, as argued in Chapter 3, these issues themselves overlap with so many other aspects of economic and cultural life. There can be no policy towards $CO_2$ abatement which does not take energy generation into account, nor any transport campaign which does not impact on the interests of the motor-manufacturing industry and the 'great car economy'. A globalized world contains a complex and changing constellation of collective actors.

## Globalization, Universal Discourses and the Sociology of Expert Knowledge

While Chapter 3 displayed the contests over the 'globality' of global issues and highlighted the diversity of collective actors involved in creating global identities and agreements about global environmental issues, Chapter 4 focused on discourses which purported to transcend the local and the global through their universal applicability (see also Ancarani, 1995). The first major point here concerns the potential for deconstructing the global/ universal authority of claims from science or microeconomics. While many authors, including otherwise sceptical ones, advocate acceptance of scientific authority in environmental matters (O'Neill, 1993: 144), the cases discussed in Chapter 4 indicated that scientific and other universalizing approaches to environmental problems have been routinely and successfully questioned. The central claim here was that it is always potentially possible to question a scientific viewpoint or finding. 'Facts' (whether about responsibilities for greenhouse-warming emissions, the value of blue whales or whatever) do not compel agreement, though they may facilitate it.

This is not an abstract point nor a 'merely' philosophical one. The history of attempts at environmental regulation in the USA indicates just how controversial the use of scientific expertise can be (see Jasanoff, 1990a; Yearley, 1995a: 465–7). Essentially there are two reasons why these issues came to particular prominence in the United States. First, major regulatory bodies such as the Environmental Protection Agency (EPA) were established relatively early and took steps which were seen as radical at the time, including pressing for the adoption of scrubbers in coal-fired power-station chimneys and for the fitting of catalytic converters to cars.

Second, the separation of political powers meant that there were various judicial remedies which could be used to challenge these bodies' rulings. Accordingly, when industrial interests and environmental groups wished to question the agencies' views they were able, on the one hand, to employ lobbying and various forms of political manoeuvre and, on the other, could pursue their regulatory interests through the courts, marshalling counter-expertise to combat the judgements and technical opinions of the EPA and other bodies.

Given the resources which industry could devote to challenging environmental regulations and the high stakes involved in these challenges – for example, a ruling that formaldehyde promotes cancer in humans would have affected a billion-dollar industry in the early 1980s (Jasanoff, 1990a: 195) – it is no surprise that disputes over scientific evidence were fought tenaciously and with great inventiveness. Since these challenges were channelled through the courts, technical disputes over safety and environmental hazards were all opened to judicial – and hence public – scrutiny.

From the point of view of the sociology of science (see Yearley, 1988: 16–43 and 1994b), these courtroom arguments ran a familiar course. As Yearley notes:

> Studies of controversy, both within academic science and in the public arena, have alerted analysts to ways in which scientific knowledge claims can face deconstruction. For example, if toxicity tests are repeated, leading to new and different results, we enter the domain of the 'experimenters' regress' (Collins, 1985: 2). The 'correct' results are, by definition, the ones produced by the better test, but there are no independent means of determining which test is better unless the 'correct' outcome is known in advance. There is no separate touchstone of credibility. This problem is bad enough in 'pure' science, where the reasons for distrusting others' results are disciplinary or occasionally personal. In

disputes over environmental safety, huge commercial and political motivations may also be involved, creating further incentives for discrediting the opposing side's claims to scientific knowledge. (1995a: 465–6)

There are of course some peculiar features to the scientific issues which the EPA and other environmental agencies often have to decide. They deal with quantities which are hard to measure, physical phenomena which are highly interactive, and diseases which occur over the course of a lifetime and for which there may be many plausible causes. The science involved in such issues lends itself to controversy (see Collingridge and Reeve, 1986). But the fundamental insight which science studies brings to the analysis of environmentalism and environmental policy concerns the disputability of scientific knowledge per se, not the special disputability of the science of cancer or of pesticide toxicity.

The intractability of these issues is further indicated by the subsequent experience of the EPA. Following setbacks and embarrassments, the EPA repeatedly had to take stock of its position. Internal reviews commonly proposed that the EPA improve its science and recommended that it separate issues of science from those of policy or political judgement (see Jasanoff, 1990a: 84; 1992: 15–23). However this was not possible in practice since key aspects of its scientific practice depended on methodological assumptions which could not be justified in exclusively scientific terms. For instance, evidence of environmental risk to humans comes – in part at least – from animal toxicity studies; yet the question whether evidence about deceased rats should be taken as relevant proof at all is both a policy matter and an issue of methodology.

In the case of the EPA Jasanoff concludes:

one of the bitter lessons of its first twenty years was that transparency alone is worth little in the public political arena unless it is accompanied by factual claims that can resist deconstruction. . . . In its earlier years the agency sought to defend its claims against skeptical assault primarily by asserting its specialized expertise, but although this approach won initial support from the courts, it failed to protect the agency from the more concerted opposition that it confronted after the 'Reagan revolution' of 1980. Rhetorical boundary drawing proved to be an inadequate instrument for certifying as 'science' decisions that fell on the murky boundary between science and policy. . . . The period of environmental decision making that began in the mid 1980s can rightly be seen as a return to fact making, but to fact making with a difference. . . . EPA recognized that it could no longer serve as the exclusive, or even the primary, forum for the construction (or reconstruction) of policy-relevant facts. The basis for making expert claims was renegotiated as the agency increasingly relied on satellite scientific bodies [special consultative bodies and ad hoc expert panels] . . . to originate or certify *claims that would stand up to political testing.* On the other hand, these institutions were themselves required to be sufficiently sensitive to the norms of politics to maintain scientific credibility. Their impartiality too, had to be secured through administrative and political controls. . . . *It is a final irony of environmental decision making that, in the effort to keep politics distinct from science, the processes of scientific fact making so freely accommodated themselves to the demands of politics.* (1992: 23; my italics)

On this view, the EPA's relative success in winning credibility in the 1980s arose not from its ability to produce incontestable science but from its skill in devising ways of producing knowledge that already took account of likely opposition.

If universalizing discourses (and this includes legal principles as well as scientific ones – see the discussion of MacKinnon's work in Chapter 1) cannot take hold and direct policy within the relatively homogeneous culture of the USA, it is all the more unlikely that they will be able to do so internationally. The significance of these sociological studies for the analysis of relations between states has hardly been noticed (except by Jasanoff herself, 1996), which bears out the point Roberston makes about the distance between the various social science disciplines concerned with global phenomena. Where sociology 'came to deal often *comparatively* with societies . . . international relations (and portions of political science) dealt with them *interactively*, with relations between nations' (1992: 16; original italics). Sociologists of science and international relations scholars interested in science are relative strangers.

Writers from the international relations tradition – particularly those who talk of epistemic communities – tend to focus on the potential for scientific analysis to offer a common currency in which greenhouse-warming potential or the loss of biological riches in any part of the world can be assessed. As noted in Chapter 4 the universalizing discourse of science implies several things: that there is a common currency; that this common currency is not arbitrary but is founded in well established scientific theory; and that any properly trained scientist can use this common currency to make assessments which will be recognized as objectively valid by other scientists and policy-makers the world over. Though this remains the ideal of science, the case studies in Chapter 4 indicate that there is no practical reason to expect that epistemic communities will be able to end disagreements transnationally any more effectively than they did in the case of the US EPA – rather worse in fact given the greater diversity of interests on the global stage and the entrenched history of North–South distrust.

Without the benefit of detailed sociological work on the scientific community or on scientists as policy advisers, even those globalization writers who have recognized the problems with universalizing discourses have few ideas about their solution. Thus, Wallerstein ends his consideration of cultural universalism in the world system with the hope that:

> Beyond scientism, I suspect there lies a more broadly defined science, one which will be able to reconcile itself dramatically with the humanities. . . . This will make possible a new rendezvous of world civilizations. Will some 'universals' emerge out of this rendezvous? Who knows? Who even knows what a 'universal' is? . . . If we go back to metaphysical beginnings, and reopen the question of the nature of science, I believe that it is probable, or at least possible, that we can reconcile our understanding of the origins and legitimacies of group particularisms with our sense of the social, psychological, and biological meanings of

humanity and humaneness. I think that perhaps we can come up with a concept of culture that sublates [existing] usages. (1990b: 54)

This passage appears to me both unattractively vague and an exercise in wishful thinking. Instead of hoping for a new, transcendent culture (or railing against relativism as Archer (1990) does) we need instead institutions which face up to the practical shortcomings of universalizing discourses. We need to invent institutions which are flexible and self-aware, which are in that sense reflexive. They need, as Jasanoff says, to be 'sufficiently sensitive to the norms of politics to maintain scientific credibility' (1992: 23).

The issues of participation in technical decision-making and of scientification are clearly central ingredients of this need for reflexiveness. As we saw with the ozone negotiations, there is a danger that the conviction that science speaks objectively and disinterestedly means that one need have no qualms about excluding other people from decision-making since they would, in any event, have arrived at the same conclusions as oneself. This beguiling line of reasoning may seem correct in principle. But, as is indicated by the experience of the US EPA, by the Corine database, by the WRI greenhouse figures, by Summers' economic logic and by the history of ozone diplomacy, such reasoning is practically inadequate. The difficulties encountered in the practical application of the universalizing discourse of science lead one to a sceptical view of any idea that the recognition of global 'oneness' prepares the way for authoritative 'master' discourses.

## The Global Specificity of Environmentalism

This book has dealt with globalization in an area of social concern and social action which coincides with the interests of a leading social movement, environmentalism. The argument has been that, while many globalization authors have overlooked this topic in favour of the globalization of production, of media or of popular culture, the environment lends itself to analysis in these terms. Given the close links between the concerns of the environmentalist movement and globalization, the question of the implications of this study for the interpretation of other social movements naturally arises also.

As was noted in Chapter 3, proponents of many sorts of social movements and ideologies wish to claim that their view is somehow in everyone's or the world-wide interest. I have argued elsewhere that the environmental movement stands out from other movements in three ways: with regard to 'its intimate relationship to science, its practical claims to international solidarity and its ability to offer a concerted critique of, and alternative to, capitalist industrialism' (1994a: 167). In this final section I want to comment briefly on these differences in the light of globalization.

The relationship to science is the special feature most comprehensively considered in this book. The connection is complex. For one thing, as the experience of the 'progressive' EPA described above (see also Yearley, 1992c: 515–25) indicates, science has been no straightforward friend to the environmental movement, even though the urgency of environmental problems such as ozone depletion has often been attested to by scientific evidence. Scientific expertise and counter-expertise are crucial to the making of environmental arguments, even if epistemic communities are far less straightforward than the international relations literature tends to imply. Moreover, as the Brundtland Report acknowledged in a different context, questions about sustainability are anchored in physical, chemical and biological systems.

This physical basis is commonly also transboundary. As noted in Chapters 2 and 3, polluted rivers cross state boundaries, air pollution disperses internationally and marine pollution spreads from the rim of one continent to another. Though the environmental movement has an internationalist *ideology*, the issues to which it attends are also treated as transnational policy matters by states themselves and by other political agencies. Environmental pressure groups have become adept at international campaigning; on average, ecological groups cooperate across borders rather better than nations do, and supranational bodies such as UNEP and the EU have often facilitated environmental organizations' attempts to internationalize their cause. As noted in Chapter 3, some practical features militate against this internationalism. Environmental NGOs develop a deep familiarity with their own countries' laws, politicians, civil servants and media. The green movement has not, despite some advocates' claims, transcended national barriers. But in this book I have outlined sociological and political reasons for believing that it stands a better chance of doing so than other putatively universal social movements.

Lastly, let us turn to the idea that 'greens offer a critique of capitalism, an alternative value system and a view of the alternative society which they would wish to see ushered in' (Yearley, 1994a: 160). More than other contemporary social movements, environmentalists offer a comprehensive alternative. In terms of the useful phrase which came into brief currency on the disintegration of the Eastern bloc, only the environmental movement offers a distinctive challenge to the idea that we have arrived at the 'end to history'. Particularly through the concept of sustainable development they have a vocabulary for describing a coherent future which departs from 'business-as-usual' liberal capitalism. Greens have, as Dobson recently argued (1990), a coherent green political philosophy; they have distinctive views on the economy. They of all social movements have founded political parties in many countries, North and South, and experienced some electoral success. As asserted by Lowe and Rüdig, 'Only the ecological movement represents a totally new political cleavage' (1986: 537).

But it is all too easy to exaggerate the potential for international environmental solidarity. For one thing, however wrong Marxists were about the dynamics of capitalist societies, it was clear which social group was supposed to have the political interest and the potential for self-identification necessary to drive through fundamental social change. Environmentalists may feel they are on firmer ground than Marxists in identifying the problems with industrial capitalism, but environmentalism is much less clear about which social groups are supposed to be the agents for change (Dobson, 1990: 15). Moreover, though in principle there may be grounds for supposing that there is literally a global interest in environmental reforms, as we have seen in Chapters 3 and 4, the prospects for transnational unity on environmental matters are not favourable. Too often policies in the 'global interest' have been formulated without participation and consent. The special conditions shaping social movement formation in the Third World are still little researched as are relationships between Third-World environmentalists and development and environmental NGOs in the North.

Environmentalism surely counts as one of the best candidates we have for a global ideology and globalizing movement. Further study of its strengths and weaknesses can only advance the understanding of globalization and of the development of global awareness and planet-wide identities. A decisive element in improving our ability to deal with global environmental issues will be the shaking off of modernist assumptions about the ability of expertise to stand impartially for all. Such change will need to be accompanied by the transformation of major transnational institutions into far more reflexive bodies. Accordingly, a clear practical consequence of this book's argument is that environmentalists need to pay greater attention to the character of knowledge-making institutions and may in future need to grant demands for the re-design of such institutions a prominent place in their list of campaign objectives.

# References

Agarwal, Anil and Narain, Sunita (1991) *Global Warming in an Unequal World: a Case of Environmental Colonialism*. Delhi: Centre for Science and Environment.

Aguilar-Fernández, Susana (1994) 'Spanish pollution control policy and the challenge of the European Union', in S. Baker, K. Milton and S. Yearley (eds), *Protecting the Periphery: Environmental Policy in Peripheral Regions of the European Union*. London: Frank Cass. pp. 102–17.

Ahuja, Dilip R. (1992) 'Estimating national contributions of greenhouse gas emissions: the CSE–WRI controversy', *Global Environmental Change*, 2 (2): 83–7.

Allen, Robert (1992) *Waste Not, Want Not*, London: Earthscan.

Ancarani, Vittorio (1995) 'Globalizing the world: science and technology in international relations', in Sheila Jasanoff, Gerald E. Markle, James C. Petersen and Trevor Pinch (eds), *Handbook of Science and Technology Studies*. London: Sage. pp. 652–70.

Anderson, Benedict (1991) *Imagined Communities: Reflections on the Origin and Spread of Nationalism*. London: Verso.

Appadurai, Arjun (1990) 'Disjuncture and difference in the global cultural economy', in Mike Featherstone (ed.), *Global Culture: Nationalism, Globalization and Modernity*. London: Sage. pp. 295–310.

Archer, Margaret S. (1990) 'Resisting the revival of relativism', in Martin Albrow and Elizabeth King (eds), *Globalization, Knowledge and Society*. London: Sage. pp. 19–33.

Archer, Margaret S. (1991) 'Sociology for one world: unity and diversity', *International Sociology*, 6 (2): 131–47.

Bartelmus, Peter (1994) *Environment, Growth and Development: the Concepts and Strategies of Sustainability*. London: Routledge.

Benedick, Richard E. (1991) *Ozone Diplomacy: New Directions in Safeguarding the Planet*. London: Harvard University Press.

Benton, Ted (1991) 'Biology and social science: why the return of the repressed should be given a (cautious) welcome', *Sociology*, 25 (1): 1–29.

Benton, Ted (1994) 'Biology and social theory in the environmental debate', in Michael Redclift and Ted Benton (eds), *Social Theory and Global Environmental Change*. London: Routledge. pp. 28–50.

Berger, Peter J. (1987) *The Capitalist Revolution*. Aldershot: Wildwood House.

Birnie, Patricia and Boyle, Alan E. (1992) *International Law and the Environment*, Oxford: Oxford University Press.

Blowers, Andrew and Lowry, David (1991) 'The politics of radioactive waste disposal', in John Blunden and Alan Reddish (eds), *Energy, Resources and Environment*. London: Hodder and Stoughton. pp. 292–330.

Blunden, John (1991a) 'Mineral resources', in John Blunden and Alan Reddish (eds), *Energy, Resources and Environment*. London: Hodder and Stoughton. pp. 43–78.

Blunden, John (1991b) 'The environmental impact of mining and mineral processing', in John Blunden and Alan Reddish (eds), *Energy, Resources and Environment*. London: Hodder and Stoughton. pp. 79–131.

Bramble, Barbara J. and Porter, Gareth (1992) 'Non-governmental organizations and the making of US international environmental policy', in Andrew Hurrell and Benedict Kingsbury (eds), *The International Politics of the Environment*. Oxford: Clarendon Press. pp. 313–53.

Bunyard, Peter (1988) 'The myth of France's cheap nuclear electricity', *The Ecologist*, 18 (1): 4–8.

Collingridge, David and Reeve, Colin (1986) *Science Speaks to Power: the Role of Experts in Policy Making*. New York: St Martin's Press.

Collins, H.M. (1985) *Changing Order: Replication and Induction in Scientific Practice*. London: Sage.

Connett, Paul and Connett, Ellen (1994) 'Municipal waste incineration: wrong question, wrong answer', *The Ecologist*, 24 (1): 14–20.

Deal, Carl (1993) *The Greenpeace Guide to Anti-Environmental Organizations*. Berkeley, CA: Odonian Press.

Dobson, Andrew (1990) *Green Political Thought: an Introduction*. London: Unwin Hyman.

Dowie, Mark (1995) *Losing Ground: American Environmentalism at the Close of the Twentieth Century*. London: MIT Press.

*The Economist* (1992) *The Atlas of the New Europe*. New York: Henry Holt.

Edwards, Rob (1995) 'Danes defend ban on toxic trade', *New Scientist*, 145 (issue 1970), 25 March: 5.

Elsworth, Steve (1990) *A Dictionary of the Environment*. London: Paladin.

Featherstone, Mike (ed.) (1990) *Global Culture: Nationalism, Globalization and Modernity*. London: Sage.

Friends of the Earth (1989) *The Aerosol Connection*. London: Friends of the Earth.

Friends of the Earth (1990) *How Green is Britain?* London: Hutchinson.

Friends of the Earth (1992a) *A Survey of Gassing Landfill Sites in England and Wales*. London: Friends of the Earth.

Friends of the Earth (1992b) *Twenty-One Years of Friends of the Earth*. London: Friends of the Earth.

Friends of the Earth (1994) *The Climate Resolution: a Guide to Local Authority Action to Take the Heat off the Planet*. London: Friends of the Earth.

Gellner, Ernest (1983) *Nations and Nationalism*. Oxford: Blackwell.

George, Susan (1988) *A Fate Worse than Debt*. Harmondsworth: Penguin.

George, Susan (1992) *The Debt Boomerang: How Third World Debt Harms Us All*. London: Pluto.

Giddens, Anthony (1981) *A Contemporary Critique of Historical Materialism*. London: Macmillan.

Giddens, Anthony (1985) *The Nation-State and Violence*. Cambridge: Polity.

Giddens, Anthony (1990) *The Consequences of Modernity*. Cambridge: Polity.

Goodman, David and Redclift, Michael (1991) *Refashioning Nature: Food, Ecology and Culture*. London: Routledge.

Grant, Wyn (1993) 'Transnational companies and environmental policy making: the trend of globalisation', in J.D. Liefferink, P.D. Lowe and A.P.J. Mol (eds), *European Integration and Environmental Policy*. London: Belhaven. pp. 59–74.

Greenberg, Donald W. (1985) 'Staging media events to achieve legitimacy: a case study of Britain's Friends of the Earth', *Political Communication and Persuasion*, 2 (4): 347–62.

Haas, Peter M. (1989) 'Do regimes matter? Epistemic communities and Mediterranean pollution control', *International Organization*, 43 (3): 377–403.

Haas, Peter M. (1990) *Saving the Mediterranean: the Politics of International Environmental Cooperation*. New York: Columbia University Press.

Haas, Peter M. (1992) 'Introduction: epistemic communities and international policy coordination', *International Organization*, 46 (1): 1–35.

Haas, Peter M., Keohane, Robert O. and Levy, Marc A. (eds) (1993) *Institutions for the Earth: Sources of Effective International Environmental Protection*. London: MIT Press.

Habermas, Jürgen (1971) *Toward a Rational Society*. London: Heinemann.

Hammond, A.L., Rodenburg, E. and Moomaw, W.R. (1991) 'Calculating national accountability for climate change', *Environment*, 33 (1): 11–35.

Hannigan, John (1995) *Environmental Sociology: a Social Constructionist Perspective*. London: Routledge.

Harrison, Paul (1992) 'Battle of the bulge', *The Guardian*, 1 May: 25.

Ives, Jane H. (ed.) (1985) *The Export of Hazard*. London: Routledge and Kegan Paul.

Jacobs, Michael (1991) *The Green Economy*. London: Pluto.

Jacobs, Michael (1994) 'The limits to neoclassicism: towards an institutional environmental economics', in Michael Redclift and Ted Benton (eds), *Social Theory and Global Environmental Change*. London: Routledge. pp. 67–91.

Jasanoff, Sheila (1990a) *The Fifth Branch: Science Advisers as Policymakers*. London: Harvard University Press.

Jasanoff, Sheila (1990b) 'American exceptionalism and the political acknowledgment of risk', *Daedalus*, 119 (4): 61–81.

Jasanoff, Sheila (1992) 'Science, politics, and the renegotiation of expertise at EPA', *Osiris*, 7: 1–23.

Jasanoff, Sheila (1993) 'India at the crossroads in global environmental policy', *Global Environmental Change*, 3 (1): 32–52.

Jasanoff, Sheila (1996) 'The normative structure of scientific agreements about the global environment', in Fen O. Hampson and Judith Reppy (eds), *Global Environmental Change and Social Justice*. Ithaca, NY: Cornell University Press. forthcoming.

Jordan, Andrew (1994) 'The Global Environmental Facility (GEF)', *Global Environmental Change*, 4 (3): 265–7.

Kripke, Saul A. (1980) *Naming and Necessity*. 2nd edn. Oxford: Blackwell.

Lafferty, William M. (1995) 'The implementation of sustainable development in the European Union', in Joni Lovenduski and Jeffrey Stanyer (eds), *Contemporary Political Studies 1995*. Vol. 1. Belfast: Political Studies Association of the UK. pp. 223–32.

Laurence, Duncan and Wynne, Brian (1989) 'Transporting waste in the European Community: a free market', *Environment*, 31 (6): 12–17.

Lean, Geoffrey (1993) 'Troubled waters', *The Observer Magazine*, 4 July: 16–25.

Leonard, H. Jeffrey (1988) *Pollution and the Struggle for the World Product*. Cambridge: Cambridge University Press.

Lever, Harold and Huhne, Christopher (1985) *Debt and Danger: the World Financial Crisis*. Harmondsworth: Penguin.

Levy, Marc A. (1993) 'European acid rain: the power of tote-board diplomacy', in Peter M. Haas, Robert O. Keohane and Marc A. Levy (eds), *Institutions for the Earth: Sources of Effective International Environmental Protection*. London: MIT Press. pp. 75–132.

Lindborg, Nancy (1992) 'Nongovernmental organizations: their past, present and future role in international environmental negotiations', in Lawrence E. Susskind, Eric J. Dolin and J. William Breslin (eds), *International Environmental Treaty Making*. Cambridge, MA: Program on Negotiation Books. pp. 1–25.

Lovelock, James (1988) *The Ages of Gaia*. Oxford: Oxford University Press.

Lowe, Philip D. and Rüdig, Wolfgang (1986) 'Review article: political ecology and the social sciences – the state of the art', *British Journal of Political Science*, 16 (4): 513–50.

McCormick, John (1991) *British Politics and the Environment*. London: Earthscan.

McCully, Patrick (1991a) 'How WRI is attempting to shift the blame for global warming', *The Ecologist*, 21 (4): 157–65.

McCully, Patrick (1991b) 'The case against climate aid', *The Ecologist*, 21 (6): 244–51.

McGrew, Anthony (1992) 'A global society?', in Stuart Hall, David Held and Anthony McGrew (eds), *Modernity and Its Futures*. Cambridge: Polity Press. pp. 61–116.

MacIntyre, Alasdair (1981) *After Virtue: a Study in Moral Theory*. London: Duckworth.

MacKinnon, Catharine A. (1987) *Feminism Unmodified, Discourses on Life and Law*. London: Harvard University Press.

MacKinnon, Catharine A. (1989) *Toward a Feminist Theory of the State*. London: Harvard University Press.

Markandya, Anil (1991) 'Economics and the ozone layer', in David Pearce (ed.), *Blueprint 2: Greening the World Economy*. London: Earthscan. pp. 63–74.

Mazey, Sonia and Richardson, Jeremy J. (1992) 'Environmental groups and the EC: challenges and opportunities', *Environmental Politics*, 4 (1): 110–28.

Mazur, Allan and Lee, Jinling (1993) 'Sounding the global alarm: environmental issues in the US national news', *Social Studies of Science*, 23 (4): 681–720.

Mendelssohn, Kurt (1976) *Science and Western Domination*. London: Thames and Hudson.

Michalowski, R.J. and Kramer, R.C. (1987) 'The space between laws: the problem of corporate crime in a transnational context', *Social Problems*, 34 (1): 34–53.

Middleton, Neil, O'Keefe, Phil and Moyo, Sam (1993) *Tears of the Crocodile: from Rio to Reality in the Developing World*. London: Pluto.

Milieu Defensie (1992) *Action Plan: Sustainable Netherlands*. Amsterdam: Milieu Defensie.

Mitchell, Ronald (1993) 'Intentional oil pollution of the oceans', in Peter M. Haas, Robert O. Keohane and Marc A. Levy (eds), *Institutions for the Earth: Sources of Effective International Environmental Protection*. London: MIT Press. pp. 183–247.

Mulkay, Michael, Pinch, Trevor and Ashmore, Malcolm (1987) 'Colonizing the mind: dilemmas in the application of social science', *Social Studies of Science*, 17 (2): 231–56.

National Science Board (US) (1989) *Loss of Biological Diversity: a Global Crisis Requiring International Solutions*. Washington: National Science Foundation.

Newton-Smith, William H. (1981) *The Rationality of Science*. London: Routledge and Kegan Paul.

Offe, Claus (1985) 'New social movements: challenging the boundaries of institutional politics', *Social Research*, 52 (4): 817–68.

O'Neill, John (1993) *Ecology, Policy and Politics: Human Well-Being and the Natural World*. London: Routledge.

Parson, Edward A. (1993) 'Protecting the ozone layer', in Peter M. Haas, Robert O. Keohane and Marc A. Levy (eds), *Institutions for the Earth: Sources of Effective International Environmental Protection*. London: MIT Press. pp. 27–73.

Patterson, Walter C. (1976) *Nuclear Power*. Harmondsworth: Penguin.

Peace, Adrian (1993) 'Environmental protest, bureaucratic closure: the politics of discourse in rural Ireland', in Kay Milton (ed.), *Environmentalism: the View from Anthropology*. London: Routledge. pp. 189–204.

Peace, Adrian (1994) 'Chemicals, conflicts and the Irish Environmental Protection Agency', *CEA (Cork Environmental Alliance) News*, 9: 17–22.

Pearce, David (ed.) (1991a) *Blueprint 2: Greening the World Economy*. London: Earthscan.

Pearce, David (1991b) 'Introduction', in David Pearce (ed.), *Blueprint 2: Greening the World Economy*. London: Earthscan. pp. 1–10.

Pearce, David (1991c) 'The global commons', in David Pearce (ed.), *Blueprint 2: Greening the World Economy*. London: Earthscan. pp. 11–30.

Pearce, David (ed.) (1993) *Blueprint 3: Measuring Sustainable Development*. London: Earthscan.

Pearce, David, Markandya, Anil and Barbier, Edward B. (1989) *Blueprint for a Green Economy*. London: Earthscan.

Pearce, Fred (1991) *Green Warriors: the People and the Politics Behind the Environmental Revolution*. London: Bodley Head.

Pepper, David (1984) *The Roots of Modern Environmentalism*. London: Croom Helm.

Peterson, M.J. (1993) 'International fisheries management', in Peter M. Haas, Robert O. Keohane and Marc A. Levy (eds), *Institutions for the Earth: Sources of Effective International Environmental Protection*. London: MIT Press. pp. 249–305.

Pickering, Kevin T. and Owen, Lewis A. (1994) *An Introduction to Global Environmental Issues*. London: Routledge.

Piddington, Ken (1992) 'The role of the World Bank', in Andrew Hurrell and Benedict Kingsbury (eds), *The International Politics of the Environment*. Oxford: Clarendon Press. pp. 212–27.

Pimentel, David, Harman, Rebecca, Pacenza, Matthew, Pecarsky, Jason and Pimental, Marcia (1994) 'Natural resources and an optimum human population', *Population and Environment*, 15 (5): 347–69.

Porritt, Jonathon (1986) *Seeing Green*. Oxford: Blackwell.

Porritt, Jonathon (1994) 'Birth of a new world order', *The Guardian*, 2 September: 8–9.

Porritt, Jonathon and Winner, D. (1988) *The Coming of the Greens*. London: Fontana.

Porter, Gareth and Brown, Janet W. (1991) *Global Environmental Politics*. Boulder, CO: Westview Press.

Rawls, John (1972) *A Theory of Justice*. Oxford: Oxford University Press.

Redclift, Michael and Benton, Ted (eds) (1994) *Social Theory and Global Environmental Change*. London: Routledge.

Reddish, Alan (1991) 'Energy resources', in John Blunden and Alan Reddish (eds), *Energy, Resources and Environment*. London: Hodder and Stoughton. pp. 3–42.

Rich, Bruce (1994) *Mortgaging the Earth: the World Bank, Environmental Impoverishment, and the Crisis of Development*. Boston, MA: Beacon Press.

Robertson, Roland (1990) 'Mapping the global condition: globalization as the central concept', in Mike Featherstone (ed.), *Global Culture: Nationalism, Globalization and Modernity*. London: Sage. pp. 15–30.

Robertson, Roland (1992) *Globalization: Social Theory and Global Culture*. London: Sage.

Robertson, Roland and Lechner, Frank (1985) 'Modernization, globalization and the problem of culture in world-systems theory', *Theory, Culture and Society*, 2 (3): 103–17.

Rojas, Martha and Thomas, Chris (1992) 'The convention on biological diversity: negotiating a global regime', in Lawrence E. Susskind, Eric J. Dolin and J. William Breslin (eds), *International Environmental Treaty Making*. Cambridge, MA: Program on Negotiation Books. pp. 143–62.

Rose, Chris (1990) *The Dirty Man of Europe: the Great British Pollution Scandal*. London: Simon and Schuster.

Ross, Shelagh (1991) 'Atmospheres and climatic change', in Paul M. Smith and Kiki Warr (eds), *Global Environmental Issues*. London: Hodder and Stoughton. pp. 72–120.

Rucht, Dieter (1993) '"Think globally, act locally"? Needs, forms and problems of cross-national cooperation among environmental groups', in J.D. Liefferink, P.D. Lowe and A.P.J. Mol (eds), *European Integration and Environmental Policy*. London: Belhaven. pp. 75–95.

Russell, Bertrand (1945) *A History of Western Philosophy*. New York: Simon and Schuster.

Sachs, Wolfgang (1994) 'The blue planet: an ambiguous modern icon', *The Ecologist*, 24 (5): 170–5.

Seager, Joni (1995) *The New State of the Earth Atlas*. New York: Simon and Schuster.

Silvertown, Jonathan (1990) 'Earth as an environment for life', in Jonathan Silvertown and Philip Sarre (eds), *Environment and Society*. London: Hodder and Stoughton. pp. 48–87.

Sklair, Leslie (1991) *Sociology of the Global System*. Hemel Hempstead: Harvester Wheatsheaf.

Sklair, Leslie (1994) 'Global sociology and global environmental change', in Michael Redclift and Ted Benton (eds), *Social Theory and Global Environmental Change*. London: Routledge. pp. 205–27.

Stairs, Kevin and Taylor, Peter (1992) 'Non-Governmental organizations and the legal protection of the oceans: a case study', in Andrew Hurrell and Benedict Kingsbury (eds), *The International Politics of the Environment*. Oxford: Clarendon Press. pp. 110–41.

Stott, Martin (1984) 'Industrial pollution in the Third World', *Links*, 19: 28–30.

Studer, Kenneth E. and Chubin, Daryl E. (1980) *The Cancer Mission: Social Contexts of Biomedical Research*. London: Sage.

Susskind, Lawrence E. (1994) *Environmental Diplomacy: Negotiating More Effective Global Agreements*. Oxford: Oxford University Press.

Susskind, Lawrence E. and Ozawa, Connie (1992) 'Negotiating more effective international environmental agreements', in Andrew Hurrell and Benedict Kingsbury (eds), *The International Politics of the Environment*. Oxford: Clarendon Press. pp. 142–65.

Swanson, Tim (1991) 'Conserving biological diversity', in David Pearce (ed.), *Blueprint 2: Greening the World Economy*. London: Earthscan. pp. 181–208.

Taylor, Peter J. and Buttel, Frederick H. (1992) 'How do we know we have global environmental problems? Science and the globalization of environmental discourse', *Geoforum*, 23 (3): 405–16.

Taylor, Ronnie (1992) *Poverty, Population and the Planet*. London: Friends of the Earth.

Thacher, Peter (1992) 'The role of the United Nations', in Andrew Hurrell and Benedict Kingsbury (eds), *The International Politics of the Environment*. Oxford: Clarendon Press. pp. 183–211.

Tickell, Oliver and Hildyard, Nicholas (1992) 'Green dollars, green menace', *The Ecologist*, 25 (3): 82–3.

Tierney, John (1990) 'Betting the planet', *The Guardian*, 28 December: 25.

Turner, Bryan S. (1990) 'The two faces of sociology: global or national?', in Mike Featherstone (ed.), *Global Culture: Nationalism, Globalization and Modernity*. London: Sage. pp. 343–58.

UK Government (1994) *Biodiversity: the UK Action Plan*. London: HMSO Cm 2428.

United Nations (1992) *Agenda 21: Programme of Action for Sustainable Development*. Geneva: United Nations.

Wallerstein, Immanuel (1990a) 'Societal development, or development of the world-system?', in Martin Albrow and Elizabeth King (eds), *Globalization, Knowledge and Society*. London: Sage. pp. 157–71.

Wallerstein, Immanuel (1990b) 'Culture as the ideological battleground of the modern world-system', in Mike Featherstone (ed.), *Global Culture: Nationalism, Globalization and Modernity*. London: Sage. pp. 31–55.

Warr, Kiki (1991) 'The ozone layer', in P.M. Smith and K. Warr (eds), *Global Environmental Issues*. London: Hodder and Stoughton. pp. 121–71.

Waterton, Claire, Grove-White, Robin, Rodwell, John and Wynne, Brian (1995) *Corine: Databases and Nature Conservation – the New Politics of Information in the European Union*. Lancaster: Centre for the Study of Environmental Change and Unit of Vegetation Science, Lancaster University.

Watson, Alan (1993) 'Britain's toxic legacy: the silence over contaminated land', *The Ecologist*, 23 (5): 174–8.

Weale, Albert (1992) *The New Politics of Pollution*. Manchester: Manchester University Press.

Weiss, Edith Brown (ed.) (1992) *Environmental Change and International Law, New Challenges and Dimensions*. Tokyo: United Nations University Press.

Wenzel, George (1991) *Animal Rights, Human Rights: Ecology, Economy and Ideology in the Canadian Arctic*. Toronto: University of Toronto Press.

World Commission on Environment and Development (1987) *Our Common Future*. (The Brundtland Report). Oxford: Oxford University Press.

World Resources Institute (1990) *World Resources 1990–91*. New York: Oxford University Press.

Yearley, Steven (1988) *Science, Technology and Social Change*. London: Unwin Hyman.

Yearley, Steven (1992a) *The Green Case*. London: Routledge.

Yearley, Steven (1992b) 'Environmental challenges', in Stuart Hall, David Held and Anthony McGrew (eds), *Modernity and its Futures*. Cambridge: Polity. pp. 117–67.

Yearley, Steven (1992c) 'Green ambivalence about science: legal-rational authority and the scientific legitimation of a social movement', *British Journal of Sociology*, 43 (4): 511–32.

Yearley, Steven (1993a) 'Standing in for nature: the practicalities of environmental organisations' use of science', in Kay Milton (ed.), *Environmentalism: the View from Anthropology*. London: Routledge. pp. 59–72.

Yearley, Steven (1993b) 'Industrial relations and environmentalism', *Review of Employment Topics*, 1: 103–13.

Yearley, Steven (1994a) 'Social movements and environmental change', in Michael Redclift and Ted Benton (eds), *Social Theory and Global Environmental Change*. London: Routledge. pp. 150–68.

Yearley, Steven (1994b) 'Understanding science from the perspective of the sociology of scientific knowledge: an overview', *Public Understanding of Science*, 3 (2): 245–58.

Yearley, Steven (1995a) 'The environmental challenge to science studies', in Sheila Jasanoff, Gerald E. Markle, James C. Petersen and Trevor Pinch (eds), *Handbook of Science and Technology Studies*. London: Sage. pp. 457–79.

Yearley, Steven (1995b) 'Dirty connections: transnational pollution', in John Allen and Chris Hamnett (eds), *A Shrinking World? Global Unevenness and Inequality*. Oxford: Oxford University Press. pp. 143–81.

Yearley, Steven (1995c) 'The local and the global: the transnational politics of the environment', in James Anderson, Chris Brook and Allan Cochrane (eds), *A Global World? Re-ordering Political Space*. Oxford: Oxford University Press. pp. 209–47.

Yearley, Steven (1995d) 'The social shaping of the environmental movement in Ireland', in Patrick Clancy, Sheelagh Drudy, Kathleen Lynch and Liam O'Dowd (eds), *Irish Society: Sociological Perspectives*. Dublin: Institute of Public Administration. pp. 652–74.

Yearley, Steven (1996) 'Science, campaigning and critique: public interests groups and arguments for global environmental change', in Fen O. Hampson and Judith Reppy (eds), *Global Environmental Change and Social Justice*. Ithaca, NY: Cornell University Press. forthcoming.

# Index